# The Ultimate Flavorful

# Ninja

# Air Fryer

## Cookbook

**2000+** Days of Mouthwatering and Easy Air Fryer Recipes for Beginners to Enjoy a Stress-free Gourmet Life, Incl. Tips & Tricks

*Jose C. Fisher*

# Table of Contents

## Chapter 4 Poultry                    30

## Chapter 5 Beef, Pork, and Lamb          41

## Chapter 6 Vegetables and Sides                52

## Chapter 7 Vegetarian Mains                61

## Chapter 8 Snacks and Appetizers                66

## Chapter 9 Fast and Easy Everyday Favorites

76

## Chapter 10 Family Favorites

82

## Appendix Air Fryer Cooking Chart

87

# INTRODUCTION

Welcome to the world of Ninja Air Fryer cooking! If you're looking for a way to cook healthier, more delicious meals without sacrificing taste or convenience, then you've come to the right place. With the Ninja Air Fryer, you can enjoy all your favorite foods with less oil and fewer calories, making it the perfect kitchen appliance for anyone who wants to live a healthier lifestyle.

But the Ninja Air Fryer is much more than just a healthier way to cook. It's a versatile and powerful tool that can help you create a wide range of dishes, from classic comfort foods to more exotic and adventurous recipes. And with this cookbook, you'll discover a whole new world of possibilities for your Ninja Air Fryer.

From amazing desserts to healthy snacks, this cookbook has something for everyone. And with easy-to-follow recipes and step-by-step instructions, even novice cooks can create delicious meals that will impress their friends and family.

So why wait? Start exploring the endless possibilities of Ninja Air Fryer cooking today and take your culinary skills to the next level with the help of this cookbook. Whether you're a seasoned chef or a beginner in the kitchen, the Ninja Air Fryer Cookbook has everything you need to create healthy, delicious meals that your whole family will love.

## Tips for Using

Using the Ninja air fryer is easy and straightforward. Here are the basic steps to get you started:

**1. Preheat the air fryer:** Preheat your Ninja air fryer by setting the temperature and timer according to the recipe or food you're cooking. This will ensure that the air fryer is heated up and ready to go when you add your food.

**2. Prepare your food:** While the air fryer is preheating, prepare your food by washing, cutting, and seasoning it as desired. You can use a variety of ingredients, from fresh vegetables and meats to frozen foods like french fries or chicken wings.

**3. Place the food in the air fryer basket:** Once the air fryer is preheated, open the basket and place your food inside. Be sure not to overcrowd the basket, as this can prevent proper air circulation and affect the cooking process.

**4. Set the timer and temperature:** Set the timer and temperature according to the recipe or food you're cooking. Recipes in this cookbook will provide specific instructions on cooking time and temperature.

**5. Check and flip the food:** Check your food periodically during the cooking process to ensure it's cooking evenly. You may need to flip or shake the basket to ensure even cooking on all sides.

**6. Enjoy your delicious meal:** Once your food is cooked to perfection, remove it from the air fryer basket and serve immediately. You can enjoy crispy, delicious meals without the added calories and unhealthy oils.

With these simple steps, you can easily use your Ninja air fryer to create healthy, delicious meals for you and your family.

# Chapter 1

## Breakfasts

## Chimichanga Breakfast Burrito

### Prep time: 10 minutes | Cook time: 10 minutes | Serves 2

- 2 large (10- to 12-inch) flour tortillas
- ½ cup canned refried beans (pinto or black work equally well)
- 4 large eggs, cooked scrambled
- 4 corn tortilla chips, crushed
- ½ cup grated Pepper Jack cheese
- 12 pickled jalapeño slices
- 1 tablespoon vegetable oil
- Guacamole, salsa, and sour cream, for serving (optional)

1. Place the tortillas on a work surface and divide the refried beans between them, spreading them in a rough rectangle in the center of the tortillas. Top the beans with the scrambled eggs, crushed chips, pepper jack, and jalapeños. Fold one side over the fillings, then fold in each short side and roll up the rest of the way like a burrito. 2. Brush the outside of the burritos with the oil, then transfer to the air fryer, seam-side down. Air fry at 350°F (177°C) until the tortillas are browned and crisp and the filling is warm throughout, about 10 minutes. 3. Transfer the chimichangas to plates and serve warm with guacamole, salsa, and sour cream, if you like.

## Bacon-and-Eggs Avocado

### Prep time: 5 minutes | Cook time: 17 minutes | Serves 1

- 1 large egg
- 1 avocado, halved, peeled, and pitted
- 2 slices bacon
- Fresh parsley, for serving (optional)
- Sea salt flakes, for garnish (optional)

1. Spray the air fryer basket with avocado oil. Preheat the air fryer to 320°F (160°C). Fill a small bowl with cool water. 2. Soft-boil the egg: Place the egg in the air fryer basket. Air fry for 6 minutes for a soft yolk or 7 minutes for a cooked yolk. Transfer the egg to the bowl of cool water and let sit for 2 minutes. Peel and set aside. 3. Use a spoon to carve out extra space in the center of the avocado halves until the cavities are big enough to fit the soft-boiled egg. Place the soft-boiled egg in the center of one half of the avocado and replace the other half of the avocado on top, so the avocado appears whole on the outside. 4. Starting at one end of the avocado, wrap the bacon around the avocado to completely cover it. Use toothpicks to hold the bacon in place. 5. Place the bacon-wrapped avocado in the air fryer basket and air fry for 5 minutes. Flip the avocado over and air fry for another 5 minutes, or until the bacon is cooked to your liking. Serve on a bed of fresh parsley, if desired, and sprinkle with salt flakes, if desired. 6. Best served fresh. Store extras in an airtight container in the fridge for up to 4 days. Reheat in a preheated 320°F (160°C) air fryer for 4 minutes, or until heated through.

## Keto Quiche

### Prep time: 10 minutes | Cook time: 1 hour | Makes 1 (6-inch) quiche

Crust:
- 1¼ cups blanched almond flour
- 1¼ cups grated Parmesan or

Filling:
- ½ cup chicken or beef broth (or vegetable broth for vegetarian)
- 1 cup shredded Swiss cheese (about 4 ounces / 113 g)
- 4 ounces (113 g) cream cheese (½ cup)
- 1 tablespoon unsalted butter,

- Gouda cheese
- ¼ teaspoon fine sea salt
- 1 large egg, beaten

- melted
- 4 large eggs, beaten
- ⅓ cup minced leeks or sliced green onions
- ¾ teaspoon fine sea salt
- ⅛ teaspoon cayenne pepper
- Chopped green onions, for garnish

1. Preheat the air fryer to 325°F (163°C). Grease a pie pan. Spray two large pieces of parchment paper with avocado oil and set them on the countertop. 2. Make the crust: In a medium-sized bowl, combine the flour, cheese, and salt and mix well. Add the egg and mix until the dough is well combined and stiff. 3. Place the dough in the center of one of the greased pieces of parchment. Top with the other piece of parchment. Using a rolling pin, roll out the dough into a circle about 1/16 inch thick. 4. Press the pie crust into the prepared pie pan. Place it in the air fryer and Air Fry for 12 minutes, or until it starts to lightly brown. 5. While the crust Air Frys, make the filling: In a large bowl, combine the broth, Swiss cheese, cream cheese, and butter. Stir in the eggs, leeks, salt, and cayenne pepper. When the crust is ready, pour the mixture into the crust. 6. Place the quiche in the air fryer and Air Fry for 15 minutes. Turn the heat down to 300°F (149°C) and Air Fry for an additional 30 minutes, or until a knife inserted 1 inch from the edge comes out clean. You may have to cover the edges of the crust with foil to prevent burning. 7. Allow the quiche to cool for 10 minutes before garnishing it with chopped green onions and cutting it into wedges. 8. Store leftovers in an airtight container in the refrigerator for up to 4 days or in the freezer for up to a month. Reheat in a preheated 350°F (177°C) air fryer for a few minutes, until warmed through.

## Simple Cinnamon Toasts

**Prep time: 5 minutes | Cook time: 4 minutes | Serves 4**

- 1 tablespoon salted butter
- 2 teaspoons ground cinnamon
- 4 tablespoons sugar
- ½ teaspoon vanilla extract
- 10 bread slices

1. Preheat the air fryer to 380ºF (193ºC). 2. In a bowl, combine the butter, cinnamon, sugar, and vanilla extract. Spread onto the slices of bread. 3. Put the bread inside the air fryer and Air Fry for 4 minutes or until golden brown. 4. Serve warm.

## Fried Cheese Grits

**Prep time: 10 minutes | Cook time: 10 to 12 minutes | Serves 4**

- ⅔ cup instant grits
- 1 teaspoon salt
- 1 teaspoon freshly ground black pepper
- ¾ cup whole or 2% milk
- 3 ounces (85 g) cream
- cheese, at room temperature
- 1 large egg, beaten
- 1 tablespoon butter, melted
- 1 cup shredded mild Cheddar cheese
- Cooking spray

1. Mix the grits, salt, and black pepper in a large bowl. Add the milk, cream cheese, beaten egg, and melted butter and whisk to combine. Fold in the Cheddar cheese and stir well. 2. Preheat the air fryer to 400ºF (204ºC). Spray a baking pan with cooking spray. 3. Spread the grits mixture into the baking pan and place in the air fryer basket. 4. Air fry for 1o to 12 minutes, or until the grits are cooked and a knife inserted in the center comes out clean. Stir the mixture once halfway through the cooking time. 5. Rest for 5 minutes and serve warm.

## Smoky Sausage Patties

**Prep time: 30 minutes | Cook time: 9 minutes | Serves 8**

- 1 pound (454 g) ground pork
- 1 tablespoon coconut aminos
- 2 teaspoons liquid smoke
- 1 teaspoon dried sage
- 1 teaspoon sea salt
- ½ teaspoon fennel seeds
- ½ teaspoon dried thyme
- ½ teaspoon freshly ground black pepper
- ¼ teaspoon cayenne pepper

1. In a large bowl, combine the pork, coconut aminos, liquid smoke, sage, salt, fennel seeds, thyme, black pepper, and cayenne pepper. Work the meat with your hands until the seasonings are fully incorporated. 2. Shape the mixture into 8 equal-size patties. Using your thumb, make a dent in the center of each patty. Place the patties on a plate and cover with plastic wrap. Refrigerate the patties for at least 30 minutes. 3. Working in batches if necessary, place the patties in a single layer in the air fryer, being careful not to overcrowd them. 4. Set the air fryer to 400ºF (204ºC) and air fry for 5 minutes. Flip and cook for about 4 minutes more.

## Mushroom-and-Tomato Stuffed Hash Browns

**Prep time: 10 minutes | Cook time: 20 minutes | Serves 4**

- Olive oil cooking spray
- 1 tablespoon plus 2 teaspoons olive oil, divided
- 4 ounces (113 g) baby bella mushrooms, diced
- 1 scallion, white parts and green parts, diced
- 1 garlic clove, minced
- 2 cups shredded potatoes
- ½ teaspoon salt
- ¼ teaspoon black pepper
- 1 Roma tomato, diced
- ½ cup shredded mozzarella

1. Preheat the air fryer to 380°F(193ºC). Lightly coat the inside of a 6-inch cake pan with olive oil cooking spray. 2. In a small skillet, heat 2 teaspoons olive oil over medium heat. Add the mushrooms, scallion, and garlic, and cook for 4 to 5 minutes, or until they have softened and are beginning to show some color. Remove from heat. 3. Meanwhile, in a large bowl, combine the potatoes, salt, pepper, and the remaining tablespoon olive oil. Toss until all potatoes are well coated. 4. Pour half of the potatoes into the bottom of the cake pan. Top with the mushroom mixture, tomato, and mozzarella. Spread the remaining potatoes over the top. 5. Air Fry in the air fryer for 12 to 15 minutes, or until the top is golden brown. 6. Remove from the air fryer and allow to cool for 5 minutes before slicing and serving.

## Breakfast Pita

**Prep time: 5 minutes | Cook time: 6 minutes | Serves 2**

- 1 whole wheat pita
- 2 teaspoons olive oil
- ½ shallot, diced
- ¼ teaspoon garlic, minced
- 1 large egg
- ¼ teaspoon dried oregano
- ¼ teaspoon dried thyme
- ⅛ teaspoon salt
- 2 tablespoons shredded Parmesan cheese

1. Preheat the air fryer to 380°F(193ºC). 2. Brush the top of the pita with olive oil, then spread the diced shallot and minced garlic over the pita. 3. Crack the egg into a small bowl or ramekin, and season it with oregano, thyme, and salt. 4. Place the pita into the air fryer basket, and gently pour the egg onto the top of the pita. Sprinkle with cheese over the top. 5. Air Fry for 6 minutes. 6. Allow to cool for 5 minutes before cutting into pieces for serving.

# Spinach and Mushroom Mini Quiche

## Prep time: 10 minutes | Cook time: 15 minutes | Serves 4

- 1 teaspoon olive oil, plus more for spraying
- 1 cup coarsely chopped mushrooms
- 1 cup fresh baby spinach, shredded
- 4 eggs, beaten
- ½ cup shredded Cheddar cheese
- ½ cup shredded Mozzarella cheese
- ¼ teaspoon salt
- ¼ teaspoon black pepper

1. Spray 4 silicone baking cups with olive oil and set aside. 2. In a medium sauté pan over medium heat, warm 1 teaspoon of olive oil. Add the mushrooms and sauté until soft, 3 to 4 minutes. 3. Add the spinach and cook until wilted, 1 to 2 minutes. Set aside. 4. In a medium bowl, whisk together the eggs, Cheddar cheese, Mozzarella cheese, salt, and pepper. 5. Gently fold the mushrooms and spinach into the egg mixture. 6. Pour ¼ of the mixture into each silicone baking cup. 7. Place the baking cups into the air fryer basket and air fry at 350ºF (177ºC) for 5 minutes. Stir the mixture in each ramekin slightly and air fry until the egg has set, an additional 3 to 5 minutes.

# Gyro Breakfast Patties with Tzatziki

## Prep time: 10 minutes | Cook time: 20 minutes per batch | Makes 16 patties

Patties:
- 2 pounds (907 g) ground lamb or beef
- ½ cup diced red onions
- ¼ cup sliced black olives
- 2 tablespoons tomato sauce
Tzatziki:
- 1 cup full-fat sour cream
- 1 small cucumber, chopped
- ½ teaspoon fine sea salt
- ½ teaspoon garlic powder, or
For Garnish/Serving:
- ½ cup crumbled feta cheese (about 2 ounces / 57 g)
- Diced red onions

- 1 teaspoon dried oregano leaves
- 1 teaspoon Greek seasoning
- 2 cloves garlic, minced
- 1 teaspoon fine sea salt

  1 clove garlic, minced
- ¼ teaspoon dried dill weed, or 1 teaspoon finely chopped fresh dill

- Sliced black olives
- Sliced cucumbers

1. Preheat the air fryer to 350ºF (177ºC). 2. Place the ground lamb, onions, olives, tomato sauce, oregano, Greek seasoning, garlic, and salt in a large bowl. Mix well to combine the ingredients. 3. Using your hands, form the mixture into sixteen 3-inch patties. Place about 5 of the patties in the air fryer and air fry for 20 minutes, flipping halfway through. Remove the patties and place them on a serving platter. Repeat with the remaining patties. 4. While the patties cook, make the tzatziki: Place all the ingredients in a small bowl and stir well. Cover and store in the fridge until ready to serve. Garnish with ground black pepper before serving. 5. Serve the patties with a dollop of tzatziki, a sprinkle of crumbled feta cheese, diced red onions, sliced black olives, and sliced cucumbers. 6. Store leftovers in an airtight container in the refrigerator for up to 5 days or in the freezer for up to a month. Reheat the patties in a preheated 390ºF (199ºC) air fryer for a few minutes, until warmed through.

# Poached Eggs on Whole Grain Avocado Toast

## Prep time: 5 minutes | Cook time: 7 minutes | Serves 4

- Olive oil cooking spray
- 4 large eggs
- Salt
- Black pepper
- 4 pieces whole grain bread
- 1 avocado
- Red pepper flakes (optional)

1. Preheat the air fryer to 320°F(160°C). Lightly coat the inside of four small oven-safe ramekins with olive oil cooking spray. 2. Crack one egg into each ramekin, and season with salt and black pepper. 3. Place the ramekins into the air fryer basket. Close and set the timer to 7 minutes. 4. While the eggs are cooking, toast the bread in a toaster. 5. Slice the avocado in half lengthwise, remove the pit, and scoop the flesh into a small bowl. Season with salt, black pepper, and red pepper flakes, if desired. Using a fork, smash the avocado lightly. 6. Spread a quarter of the smashed avocado evenly over each slice of toast. 7. Remove the eggs from the air fryer, and gently spoon one onto each slice of avocado toast before serving.

# Onion Omelet

## Prep time: 10 minutes | Cook time: 12 minutes | Serves 2

- 3 eggs
- Salt and ground black pepper, to taste
- ½ teaspoons soy sauce
- 1 large onion, chopped
- 2 tablespoons grated Cheddar cheese
- Cooking spray

1. Preheat the air fryer to 355ºF (179ºC). 2. In a bowl, whisk together the eggs, salt, pepper, and soy sauce. 3. Spritz a small pan with cooking spray. Spread the chopped onion across the bottom of the pan, then transfer the pan to the air fryer. 4. Air Fry in the preheated air fryer for 6 minutes or until the onion is translucent. 5. Add the egg mixture on top of the onions to coat well. Add the cheese on top, then continue baking for another 6 minutes. 6. Allow to cool before serving.

# Canadian Bacon Muffin Sandwiches

**Prep time: 5 minutes | Cook time: 8 minutes | Serves 4**

- ◄ 4 English muffins, split
- ◄ 8 slices Canadian bacon
- ◄ 4 slices cheese
- ◄ Cooking spray

1. Preheat the air fryer to 370°F (188°C). 2. Make the sandwiches: Top each of 4 muffin halves with 2 slices of Canadian bacon, 1 slice of cheese, and finish with the remaining muffin half. 3. Put the sandwiches in the air fryer basket and spritz the tops with cooking spray. 4. Air Fry for 4 minutes. Flip the sandwiches and Air Fry for another 4 minutes. 5. Divide the sandwiches among four plates and serve warm.

# Breakfast Sammies

**Prep time: 15 minutes | Cook time: 20 minutes | Serves 5**

Biscuits:
- ◄ 6 large egg whites
- ◄ 2 cups blanched almond flour, plus more if needed
- ◄ 1½ teaspoons baking powder
- ◄ ½ teaspoon fine sea salt

Eggs:
- ◄ 5 large eggs
- ◄ ½ teaspoon fine sea salt
- ◄ ¼ teaspoon ground black pepper
- ◄ ¼ cup (½ stick) very cold unsalted butter (or lard for dairy-free), cut into ¼-inch pieces
- ◄ 5 (1 ounce / 28 g) slices Cheddar cheese (omit for dairy-free)
- ◄ 10 thin slices ham

1. Spray the air fryer basket with avocado oil. Preheat the air fryer to 350°F (177°C). Grease two pie pans or two baking pans that will fit inside your air fryer. 2. Make the biscuits: In a medium-sized bowl, whip the egg whites with a hand mixer until very stiff. Set aside. 3. In a separate medium-sized bowl, stir together the almond flour, baking powder, and salt until well combined. Cut in the butter. Gently fold the flour mixture into the egg whites with a rubber spatula. If the dough is too wet to form into mounds, add a few tablespoons of almond flour until the dough holds together well. 4. Using a large spoon, divide the dough into 5 equal portions and drop them about 1 inch apart on one of the greased pie pans. (If you're using a smaller air fryer, work in batches if necessary.) Place the pan in the air fryer and Air Fry for 11 to 14 minutes, until the biscuits are golden brown. Remove from the air fryer and set aside to cool. 5. Make the eggs: Set the air fryer to 375°F (191°C). Crack the eggs into the remaining greased pie pan and sprinkle with the salt and pepper. Place the eggs in the air fryer to Air Fry for 5 minutes, or until they are cooked to your liking. 6. Open the air fryer and top each egg yolk with a slice of cheese (if using). Air Fry for another minute, or until the cheese is melted. 7. Once the biscuits are cool, slice them in half lengthwise. Place 1 cooked egg topped with cheese and 2 slices of ham in each biscuit. 8. Store leftover biscuits, eggs, and ham in separate airtight containers in the fridge for up to 3 days. Reheat the biscuits and eggs on a baking sheet in a preheated 350°F (177°C) air fryer for 5 minutes, or until warmed through.

# Not-So-English Muffins

**Prep time: 5 minutes | Cook time: 10 minutes | Serves 4**

- ◄ 2 strips turkey bacon, cut in half crosswise
- ◄ 2 whole-grain English muffins, split
- ◄ 1 cup fresh baby spinach,
- long stems removed
- ◄ ¼ ripe pear, peeled and thinly sliced
- ◄ 4 slices Provolone cheese

1. Place bacon strips in air fryer basket and air fry at 390°F (199°C) for 2 minutes. Check and separate strips if necessary so they cook evenly. Cook for 3 to 4 more minutes, until crispy. Remove and drain on paper towels. 2. Place split muffin halves in air fryer basket and cook for 2 minutes, just until lightly browned. 3. Open air fryer and top each muffin with a quarter of the baby spinach, several pear slices, a strip of bacon, and a slice of cheese. 4. Air fry at 360°F (182°C) for 1 to 2 minutes, until cheese completely melts.

# Western Frittata

**Prep time: 10 minutes | Cook time: 19 minutes | Serves 1 to 2**

- ◄ ½ red or green bell pepper, cut into ½-inch chunks
- ◄ 1 teaspoon olive oil
- ◄ 3 eggs, beaten
- ◄ ¼ cup grated Cheddar cheese
- ◄ ¼ cup diced cooked ham
- ◄ Salt and freshly ground black pepper, to taste
- ◄ 1 teaspoon butter
- ◄ 1 teaspoon chopped fresh parsley

1. Preheat the air fryer to 400°F (204°C). 2. Toss the peppers with the olive oil and air fry for 6 minutes, shaking the basket once or twice during the cooking process to redistribute the ingredients. 3. While the vegetables are cooking, beat the eggs well in a bowl, stir in the Cheddar cheese and ham, and season with salt and freshly ground black pepper. Add the air-fried peppers to this bowl when they have finished cooking. 4. Place a cake pan into the air fryer basket with the butter using an aluminum sling to lower the pan into the basket. Air fry for 1 minute at 380°F (193°C) to melt the butter. Remove the cake pan and rotate the pan to distribute the butter and grease the pan. Pour the egg mixture into the cake pan and return the pan to the air fryer, using the aluminum sling. 5. Air fry at 380°F (193°C) for 12 minutes, or until the frittata has puffed up and is lightly browned. Let the frittata sit in the air fryer for 5 minutes to cool to an edible temperature and set up. Remove the cake pan from the air fryer, sprinkle with parsley and serve immediately.

## Strawberry Toast

### Prep time: 10 minutes | Cook time: 8 minutes | Makes 4 toasts

- ◄ 4 slices bread, ½-inch thick
- ◄ Butter-flavored cooking spray
- ◄ 1 cup sliced strawberries
- ◄ 1 teaspoon sugar

1. Spray one side of each bread slice with butter-flavored cooking spray. Lay slices sprayed side down. 2. Divide the strawberries among the bread slices. 3. Sprinkle evenly with the sugar and place in the air fryer basket in a single layer. 4. Air fry at 390ºF (199ºC) for 8 minutes. The bottom should look brown and crisp and the top should look glazed.

## Golden Avocado Tempura

### Prep time: 5 minutes | Cook time: 10 minutes | Serves 4

- ◄ ½ cup bread crumbs
- ◄ ½ teaspoons salt
- ◄ 1 Haas avocado, pitted,
- peeled and sliced
- ◄ Liquid from 1 can white beans

1. Preheat the air fryer to 350ºF (177ºC). 2. Mix the bread crumbs and salt in a shallow bowl until well-incorporated. 3. Dip the avocado slices in the bean liquid, then into the bread crumbs. 4. Put the avocados in the air fryer, taking care not to overlap any slices, and air fry for 10 minutes, giving the basket a good shake at the halfway point. 5. Serve immediately.

## Apple Cider Doughnut Holes

### Prep time: 10 minutes | Cook time: 6 minutes | Makes 10 mini doughnuts

Doughnut Holes:
- ◄ 1½ cups all-purpose flour
- ◄ 2 tablespoons granulated sugar
- ◄ 2 teaspoons baking powder
- ◄ 1 teaspoon baking soda
- ◄ ½ teaspoon kosher salt
- ◄ Pinch of freshly grated nutmeg

- ◄ ¼ cup plus 2 tablespoons buttermilk, chilled
- ◄ 2 tablespoons apple cider (hard or nonalcoholic), chilled
- ◄ 1 large egg, lightly beaten
- ◄ Vegetable oil, for brushing

Glaze:
- ◄ ½ cup powdered sugar
- ◄ 2 tablespoons unsweetened applesauce

- ◄ ¼ teaspoon vanilla extract
- ◄ Pinch of kosher salt

1. Make the doughnut holes: In a bowl, whisk together the flour, granulated sugar, baking powder, baking soda, salt, and nutmeg until smooth. Add the buttermilk, cider, and egg and stir with a small rubber spatula or spoon until the dough just comes together. 2. Using a 1 ounce (28 g) ice cream scoop or 2 tablespoons, scoop and drop 10 balls of dough into the air fryer basket, spaced evenly apart, and brush the tops lightly with oil. Air fry at 350ºF (177ºC) until the doughnut holes are golden brown and fluffy, about 6 minutes. Transfer the doughnut holes to a wire rack to cool completely. 3. Make the glaze: In a small bowl, stir together the powdered sugar, applesauce, vanilla, and salt until smooth. 4. Dip the tops of the doughnuts holes in the glaze, then let stand until the glaze sets before serving. If you're impatient and want warm doughnuts, have the glaze ready to go while the doughnuts cook, then use the glaze as a dipping sauce for the warm doughnuts, fresh out of the air fryer.

## Vanilla Granola

### Prep time: 5 minutes | Cook time: 40 minutes | Serves 4

- ◄ 1 cup rolled oats
- ◄ 3 tablespoons maple syrup
- ◄ 1 tablespoon sunflower oil
- ◄ 1 tablespoon coconut sugar
- ◄ ¼ teaspoon vanilla
- ◄ ¼ teaspoon cinnamon
- ◄ ¼ teaspoon sea salt

1. Preheat the air fryer to 248ºF (120ºC). 2. Mix together the oats, maple syrup, sunflower oil, coconut sugar, vanilla, cinnamon, and sea salt in a medium bowl and stir to combine. Transfer the mixture to a baking pan. 3. Place the pan in the air fryer basket and Air Fry for 40 minutes, or until the granola is mostly dry and lightly browned. Stir the granola four times during cooking. 4. Let the granola stand for 5 to 10 minutes before serving.

## Mini Shrimp Frittata

### Prep time: 15 minutes | Cook time: 20 minutes | Serves 4

- ◄ 1 teaspoon olive oil, plus more for spraying
- ◄ ½ small red bell pepper, finely diced
- ◄ 1 teaspoon minced garlic
- ◄ 1 (4 ounces / 113 g) can of
- tiny shrimp, drained
- ◄ Salt and freshly ground black pepper, to taste
- ◄ 4 eggs, beaten
- ◄ 4 teaspoons ricotta cheese

1. Spray four ramekins with olive oil. 2. In a medium skillet over medium-low heat, heat 1 teaspoon of olive oil. Add the bell pepper and garlic and sauté until the pepper is soft, about 5 minutes 3. Add the shrimp, season with salt and pepper, and cook until warm, 1 to 2 minutes. Remove from the heat. 4. Add the eggs and stir to combine. 5. Pour one quarter of the mixture into each ramekin. 6. Place 2 ramekins in the air fryer basket and Air Fry at 350ºF (177ºC) for 6 minutes. 7. Remove the air fryer basket from the air fryer and stir the mixture in each ramekin. Top each frittata with 1 teaspoon of ricotta cheese. Return the air fryer basket to the air fryer and cook until eggs are set and the top is lightly browned, 4 to 5 minutes. 8. Repeat with the remaining two ramekins.

## Scotch Eggs

**Prep time: 10 minutes | Cook time: 20 to 25 minutes | Serves 4**

- 2 tablespoons flour, plus extra for coating
- 1 pound (454 g) ground breakfast sausage
- 4 hard-boiled eggs, peeled
- 1 raw egg
- 1 tablespoon water
- Oil for misting or cooking spray
- Crumb Coating:
- ¾ cup panko bread crumbs
- ¾ cup flour

1. Combine flour with ground sausage and mix thoroughly. 2. Divide into 4 equal portions and mold each around a hard-boiled egg so the sausage completely covers the egg. 3. In a small bowl, beat together the raw egg and water. 4. Dip sausage-covered eggs in the remaining flour, then the egg mixture, then roll in the crumb coating. 5. Air fry at 360ºF (182ºC) for 10 minutes. Spray eggs, turn, and spray other side. 6. Continue cooking for another 10 to 15 minutes or until sausage is well done.

## Hearty Cheddar Biscuits

**Prep time: 10 minutes | Cook time: 22 minutes | Makes 8 biscuits**

- 2⅓ cups self-rising flour
- 2 tablespoons sugar
- ½ cup butter (1 stick), frozen for 15 minutes
- ½ cup grated Cheddar cheese, plus more to melt on top
- 1⅓ cups buttermilk
- 1 cup all-purpose flour, for shaping
- 1 tablespoon butter, melted

1. Line a buttered 7-inch metal cake pan with parchment paper or a silicone liner. 2. Combine the flour and sugar in a large mixing bowl. Grate the butter into the flour. Add the grated cheese and stir to coat the cheese and butter with flour. Then add the buttermilk and stir just until you can no longer see streaks of flour. The dough should be quite wet. 3. Spread the all-purpose (not self-rising) flour out on a small cookie sheet. With a spoon, scoop 8 evenly sized balls of dough into the flour, making sure they don't touch each other. With floured hands, coat each dough ball with flour and toss them gently from hand to hand to shake off any excess flour. Put each floured dough ball into the prepared pan, right up next to the other. This will help the biscuits rise, rather than spreading out. 4. Preheat the air fryer to 380ºF (193ºC). 5. Transfer the cake pan to the basket of the air fryer. Let the ends of the aluminum foil sling hang across the cake pan before returning the basket to the air fryer. 6. Air fry for 20 minutes. Check the biscuits twice to make sure they are not getting too brown on top. If they are, re-arrange the aluminum foil strips to cover any brown parts. After 20 minutes, check the biscuits by inserting a toothpick into the center of the biscuits. It should come out clean. If it needs a little more time, continue to air fry for two extra minutes. Brush the tops of the biscuits with some melted butter and sprinkle a little more grated cheese on top if desired. Pop the basket back into the air fryer for another 2 minutes. 7. Remove the cake pan from the air fryer. Let the biscuits cool for just a minute or two and then turn them out onto a plate and pull apart. Serve immediately.

## Air Fryd Peach Oatmeal

**Prep time: 5 minutes | Cook time: 30 minutes | Serves 6**

- Olive oil cooking spray
- 2 cups certified gluten-free rolled oats
- 2 cups unsweetened almond milk
- ¼ cup raw honey, plus more for drizzling (optional)
- ½ cup nonfat plain Greek yogurt
- 1 teaspoon vanilla extract
- ½ teaspoon ground cinnamon
- ¼ teaspoon salt
- 1½ cups diced peaches, divided, plus more for serving (optional)

1. Preheat the air fryer to 380°F(193ºC). Lightly coat the inside of a 6-inch cake pan with olive oil cooking spray. 2. In a large bowl, mix together the oats, almond milk, honey, yogurt, vanilla, cinnamon, and salt until well combined. 3. Fold in ¾ cup of the peaches and then pour the mixture into the prepared cake pan. 4. Sprinkle the remaining peaches across the top of the oatmeal mixture. Air Fry in the air fryer for 30 minutes. 5. Allow to set and cool for 5 minutes before serving with additional fresh fruit and honey for drizzling, if desired.

## Quesadillas

**Prep time: 10 minutes | Cook time: 15 minutes | Serves 4**

- 4 eggs
- 2 tablespoons skim milk
- Salt and pepper, to taste
- Oil for misting or cooking spray
- 4 flour tortillas
- 4 tablespoons salsa
- 2 ounces (57 g) Cheddar cheese, grated
- ½ small avocado, peeled and thinly sliced

1. Preheat the air fryer to 270ºF (132ºC). 2. Beat together eggs, milk, salt, and pepper. 3. Spray a baking pan lightly with cooking spray and add egg mixture. 4. Air Fry for 8 to 9 minutes, stirring every 1 to 2 minutes, until eggs are scrambled to your liking. Remove and set aside. 5. Spray one side of each tortilla with oil or cooking spray. Flip over. 6. Divide eggs, salsa, cheese, and avocado among the tortillas, covering only half of each tortilla. 7. Fold each tortilla in half and press down lightly. 8. Place 2 tortillas in air fryer basket and air fry at 390ºF (199ºC) for 3 minutes or until cheese melts and outside feels slightly crispy. Repeat with remaining two tortillas. 9. Cut each cooked tortilla into halves or thirds.

## Cajun Breakfast Sausage

### Prep time: 10 minutes | Cook time: 15 to 20 minutes | Serves 8

- 1½ pounds (680 g) 85% lean ground turkey
- 3 cloves garlic, finely chopped
- ¼ onion, grated
- 1 teaspoon Tabasco sauce
- 1 teaspoon Creole seasoning
- 1 teaspoon dried thyme
- ½ teaspoon paprika
- ½ teaspoon cayenne

1. Preheat the air fryer to 370ºF (188ºC). 2. In a large bowl, combine the turkey, garlic, onion, Tabasco, Creole seasoning, thyme, paprika, and cayenne. Mix with clean hands until thoroughly combined. Shape into 16 patties, about ½ inch thick. (Wet your hands slightly if you find the sausage too sticky to handle.) 3. Working in batches if necessary, arrange the patties in a single layer in the air fryer basket. Pausing halfway through the cooking time to flip the patties, air fry for 15 to 20 minutes until a thermometer inserted into the thickest portion registers 165ºF (74ºC).

## Mexican Breakfast Pepper Rings

### Prep time: 5 minutes | Cook time: 10 minutes | Serves 4

- Olive oil
- 1 large red, yellow, or orange bell pepper, cut into four ¾-inch rings
- 4 eggs
- Salt and freshly ground black pepper, to taste
- 2 teaspoons salsa

1. Preheat the air fryer to 350ºF (177ºC). Lightly spray a baking pan with olive oil. 2. Place 2 bell pepper rings on the pan. Crack one egg into each bell pepper ring. Season with salt and black pepper. 3. Spoon ½ teaspoon of salsa on top of each egg. 4. Place the pan in the air fryer basket. Air fry until the yolk is slightly runny, 5 to 6 minutes or until the yolk is fully cooked, 8 to 10 minutes. 5. Repeat with the remaining 2 pepper rings. Serve hot.

## Asparagus and Bell Pepper Strata

### Prep time: 10 minutes | Cook time: 14 to 20 minutes | Serves 4

- 8 large asparagus spears, trimmed and cut into 2-inch pieces
- ⅓ cup shredded carrot
- ½ cup chopped red bell pepper
- 2 slices low-sodium whole-
- wheat bread, cut into ½-inch cubes
- 3 egg whites
- 1 egg
- 3 tablespoons 1% milk
- ½ teaspoon dried thyme

1. In a baking pan, combine the asparagus, carrot, red bell pepper, and 1 tablespoon of water. Air Fry in the air fryer at 330ºF (166ºC) for 3 to 5 minutes, or until crisp-tender. Drain well. 2. Add the bread cubes to the vegetables and gently toss. 3. In a medium bowl, whisk the egg whites, egg, milk, and thyme until frothy. 4. Pour the egg mixture into the pan. Air Fry for 11 to 15 minutes, or until the strata is slightly puffy and set and the top starts to brown. Serve.

## Pumpkin Donut Holes

### Prep time: 15 minutes | Cook time: 14 minutes | Makes 12 donut holes

- 1 cup whole-wheat pastry flour, plus more as needed
- 3 tablespoons packed brown sugar
- ½ teaspoon ground cinnamon
- 1 teaspoon low-sodium baking powder
- ⅓ cup canned no-salt-
- added pumpkin purée (not pumpkin pie filling)
- 3 tablespoons 2% milk, plus more as needed
- 2 tablespoons unsalted butter, melted
- 1 egg white
- Powdered sugar (optional)

1. In a medium bowl, mix the pastry flour, brown sugar, cinnamon, and baking powder. 2. In a small bowl, beat the pumpkin, milk, butter, and egg white until combined. Add the pumpkin mixture to the dry ingredients and mix until combined. You may need to add more flour or milk to form a soft dough. 3. Divide the dough into 12 pieces. With floured hands, form each piece into a ball. 4. Cut a piece of parchment paper or aluminum foil to fit inside the air fryer basket but about 1 inch smaller in diameter. Poke holes in the paper or foil and place it in the basket. 5. Put 6 donut holes into the basket, leaving some space around each. Air fry at 360ºF (182ºC) for 5 to 7 minutes, or until the donut holes reach an internal temperature of 200ºF (93ºC) and are firm and light golden brown. 6. Let cool for 5 minutes. Remove from the basket and roll in powdered sugar, if desired. Repeat with the remaining donut holes and serve.

## Pita and Pepperoni Pizza

### Prep time: 10 minutes | Cook time: 6 minutes | Serves 1

- 1 teaspoon olive oil
- 1 tablespoon pizza sauce
- 1 pita bread
- 6 pepperoni slices
- ¼ cup grated Mozzarella cheese
- ¼ teaspoon garlic powder
- ¼ teaspoon dried oregano

1. Preheat the air fryer to 350ºF (177ºC). Grease the air fryer basket with olive oil. 2. Spread the pizza sauce on top of the pita bread. Put the pepperoni slices over the sauce, followed by the Mozzarella cheese. 3. Season with garlic powder and oregano. 4. Put the pita pizza inside the air fryer and place a trivet on top. 5. Air Fry in the preheated air fryer for 6 minutes and serve.

# Bacon Cheese Egg with Avocado

**Prep time: 15 minutes | Cook time: 20 minutes | Serves 4**

- 6 large eggs
- ¼ cup heavy whipping cream
- 1½ cups chopped cauliflower
- 1 cup shredded medium Cheddar cheese
- 1 medium avocado, peeled

and pitted
- 8 tablespoons full-fat sour cream
- 2 scallions, sliced on the bias
- 12 slices sugar-free bacon, cooked and crumbled

1. In a medium bowl, whisk eggs and cream together. Pour into a round baking dish. 2. Add cauliflower and mix, then top with Cheddar. Place dish into the air fryer basket. 3. Adjust the temperature to 320ºF (160ºC) and set the timer for 20 minutes. 4. When completely cooked, eggs will be firm and cheese will be browned. Slice into four pieces. 5. Slice avocado and divide evenly among pieces. Top each piece with 2 tablespoons sour cream, sliced scallions, and crumbled bacon.

# Easy Sausage Pizza

**Prep time: 10 minutes | Cook time: 6 minutes | Serves 4**

- 2 tablespoons ketchup
- 1 pita bread
- ⅓ cup sausage
- ½ pound (227 g) Mozzarella

cheese
- 1 teaspoon garlic powder
- 1 tablespoon olive oil

1. Preheat the air fryer to 340ºF (171ºC). 2. Spread the ketchup over the pita bread. 3. Top with the sausage and cheese. Sprinkle with the garlic powder and olive oil. 4. Put the pizza in the air fryer basket and Air Fry for 6 minutes. 5. Serve warm.

# Oat Bran Muffins

**Prep time: 10 minutes | Cook time: 10 to 12 minutes per batch | Makes 8 muffins**

- ⅔ cup oat bran
- ½ cup flour
- ¼ cup brown sugar
- 1 teaspoon baking powder
- ½ teaspoon baking soda
- ⅛ teaspoon salt
- ½ cup buttermilk

- 1 egg
- 2 tablespoons canola oil
- ½ cup chopped dates, raisins, or dried cranberries
- 24 paper muffin cups
- Cooking spray

1. Preheat the air fryer to 330ºF (166ºC). 2. In a large bowl, combine the oat bran, flour, brown sugar, baking powder, baking soda, and salt. 3. In a small bowl, beat together the buttermilk, egg, and oil. 4. Pour buttermilk mixture into bowl with dry ingredients and stir just until moistened. Do not beat. 5. Gently stir in dried fruit. 6. Use triple baking cups to help muffins hold shape during baking. Spray them with cooking spray, place 4 sets of cups in air fryer basket at a time, and fill each one ¾ full of batter. 7. Cook for 10 to 12 minutes, until top springs back when lightly touched and toothpick inserted in center comes out clean. 8. Repeat for remaining muffins.

# Homemade Toaster Pastries

**Prep time: 10 minutes | Cook time: 11 minutes | Makes 6 pastries**

- Oil, for spraying
- 1 (15 ounces / 425 g) package refrigerated piecrust
- 6 tablespoons jam or

preserves of choice
- 2 cups confectioners' sugar
- 3 tablespoons milk
- 1 to 2 tablespoons sprinkles of choice

1. Preheat the air fryer to 350ºF (177ºC). Line the air fryer basket with parchment and spray lightly with oil. 2. Cut the piecrust into 12 rectangles, about 3 by 4 inches each. You will need to reroll the dough scraps to get 12 rectangles. 3. Spread 1 tablespoon of jam in the center of 6 rectangles, leaving ¼ inch around the edges. 4. Pour some water into a small bowl. Use your finger to moisten the edge of each rectangle. 5. Top each rectangle with another and use your fingers to press around the edges. Using the tines of a fork, seal the edges of the dough and poke a few holes in the top of each one. Place the pastries in the prepared basket. 6. Air fry for 11 minutes. Let cool completely. 7. In a medium bowl, whisk together the confectioners' sugar and milk. Spread the icing over the tops of the pastries and add sprinkles. Serve immediately

# Drop Biscuits

**Prep time: 10 minutes | Cook time: 9 to 10 minutes | Serves 5**

- 4 cups all-purpose flour
- 1 tablespoon baking powder
- 1 tablespoon sugar (optional)
- 1 teaspoon salt
- 6 tablespoons butter, plus

more for brushing on the biscuits (optional)
- ¾ cup buttermilk
- 1 to 2 tablespoons oil

1. In a large bowl, whisk the flour, baking powder, sugar (if using), and salt until blended. 2. Add the butter. Using a pastry cutter or 2 forks, work the dough until pea-size balls of the butter-flour mixture appear. Stir in the buttermilk until the mixture is sticky. 3. Preheat the air fryer to 330ºF (166ºC). Line the air fryer basket with parchment paper and spritz it with oil. 4. Drop the dough by the tablespoonful onto the prepared basket, leaving 1 inch between each, to form 10 biscuits. 5. Air Fry for 5 minutes. Flip the biscuits and cook for 4 minutes more for a light brown top, or 5 minutes more for a darker biscuit. Brush the tops with melted butter, if desired.

## Cheesy Bell Pepper Eggs

**Prep time: 10 minutes | Cook time: 15 minutes | Serves 4**

◄ 4 medium green bell peppers
◄ 3 ounces (85 g) cooked ham, chopped
◄ ¼ medium onion, peeled and
◄ chopped
◄ 8 large eggs
◄ 1 cup mild Cheddar cheese

1. Cut the tops off each bell pepper. Remove the seeds and the white membranes with a small knife. Place ham and onion into each pepper. 2. Crack 2 eggs into each pepper. Top with ¼ cup cheese per pepper. Place into the air fryer basket. 3. Adjust the temperature to 390ºF (199ºC) and air fry for 15 minutes. 4. When fully cooked, peppers will be tender and eggs will be firm. Serve immediately.

## Buffalo Egg Cups

**Prep time: 10 minutes | Cook time: 15 minutes | Serves 2**

◄ 4 large eggs
◄ 2 ounces (57 g) full-fat cream cheese
◄ 2 tablespoons buffalo sauce
◄ ½ cup shredded sharp Cheddar cheese

1. Crack eggs into two ramekins. 2. In a small microwave-safe bowl, mix cream cheese, buffalo sauce, and Cheddar. Microwave for 20 seconds and then stir. Place a spoonful into each ramekin on top of the eggs. 3. Place ramekins into the air fryer basket. 4. Adjust the temperature to 320ºF (160ºC) and Air Fry for 15 minutes. 5. Serve warm.

## BLT Breakfast Wrap

**Prep time: 5 minutes | Cook time: 10 minutes | Serves 4**

◄ 8 ounces (227 g) reduced-sodium bacon
◄ 8 tablespoons mayonnaise
◄ 8 large romaine lettuce
◄ leaves
◄ 4 Roma tomatoes, sliced
◄ Salt and freshly ground black pepper, to taste

1. Arrange the bacon in a single layer in the air fryer basket. (It's OK if the bacon sits a bit on the sides.) Set the air fryer to 350ºF (177ºC) and air fry for 10 minutes. Check for crispiness and air fry for 2 to 3 minutes longer if needed. Cook in batches, if necessary, and drain the grease in between batches. 2. Spread 1 tablespoon of mayonnaise on each of the lettuce leaves and top with the tomatoes and cooked bacon. Season to taste with salt and freshly ground black pepper. Roll the lettuce leaves as you would a burrito, securing with a toothpick if desired.

## Spinach and Bacon Roll-ups

**Prep time: 5 minutes | Cook time: 8 to 9 minutes | Serves 4**

◄ 4 flour tortillas (6- or 7-inch size)
◄ 4 slices Swiss cheese
◄ 1 cup baby spinach leaves
◄ 4 slices turkey bacon
◄ Special Equipment:
◄ 4 toothpicks, soak in water for at least 30 minutes

1. Preheat the air fryer to 390ºF (199ºC). 2. On a clean work surface, top each tortilla with one slice of cheese and ¼ cup of spinach, then tightly roll them up. 3. Wrap each tortilla with a strip of turkey bacon and secure with a toothpick. 4. Arrange the roll-ups in the air fryer basket, leaving space between each roll-up. 5. Air fry for 4 minutes. Flip the roll-ups with tongs and rearrange them for more even cooking. Air fry for another 4 to 5 minutes until the bacon is crisp. 6. Rest for 5 minutes and remove the toothpicks before serving.

## Bunless Breakfast Turkey Burgers

**Prep time: 5 minutes | Cook time: 15 minutes | Serves 4**

◄ 1 pound (454 g) ground turkey breakfast sausage
◄ ½ teaspoon salt
◄ ¼ teaspoon ground black pepper
◄ ¼ cup seeded and chopped green bell pepper
◄ 2 tablespoons mayonnaise
◄ 1 medium avocado, peeled, pitted, and sliced

1. In a large bowl, mix sausage with salt, black pepper, bell pepper, and mayonnaise. Form meat into four patties. 2. Place patties into ungreased air fryer basket. Adjust the temperature to 370ºF (188ºC) and air fry for 15 minutes, turning patties halfway through cooking. Burgers will be done when dark brown and they have an internal temperature of at least 165ºF (74ºC). 3. Serve burgers topped with avocado slices on four medium plates.

# Chapter 2

# Desserts

# Chapter 2 Desserts

## Chocolate Bread Pudding

**Prep time: 10 minutes | Cook time: 10 to 12 minutes | Serves 4**

- Nonstick flour-infused baking spray
- 1 egg
- 1 egg yolk
- ¾ cup chocolate milk
- 2 tablespoons cocoa powder
- 3 tablespoons light brown sugar
- 3 tablespoons peanut butter
- 1 teaspoon vanilla extract
- 5 slices firm white bread, cubed

1. Spray a 6-by-2-inch round baking pan with the baking spray. Set aside. 2. In a medium bowl, whisk the egg, egg yolk, chocolate milk, cocoa powder, brown sugar, peanut butter, and vanilla until thoroughly combined. Stir in the bread cubes and let soak for 10 minutes. Spoon this mixture into the prepared pan. 3. Insert the crisper plate into the basket and the basket into the unit. Preheat the unit by selecting Air Fry, setting the temperature to 325ºF (163ºC), and setting the time to 3 minutes. Select START/PAUSE to begin. 4. Once the unit is preheated, place the pan into the basket. Select Air Fry, set the temperature to 325ºF (163ºC), and set the time to 12 minutes. Select START/PAUSE to begin. 5. Check the pudding after about 10 minutes. It is done when it is firm to the touch. If not, resume cooking. 6. When the cooking is complete, let the pudding cool for 5 minutes. Serve warm.

## Peaches and Apple Crumble

**Prep time: 10 minutes | Cook time: 10 to 12 minutes | Serves 4**

- 2 peaches, peeled, pitted, and chopped
- 1 apple, peeled and chopped
- 2 tablespoons honey
- ½ cup quick-cooking oatmeal
- ⅓ cup whole-wheat pastry
- flour
- 2 tablespoons unsalted butter, at room temperature
- 3 tablespoons packed brown sugar
- ½ teaspoon ground cinnamon

1. Preheat the air fryer to 380ºF (193ºC). 2. Mix together the peaches, apple, and honey in a baking pan until well incorporated. 3. In a bowl, combine the oatmeal, pastry flour, butter, brown sugar, and cinnamon and stir to mix well. Spread this mixture evenly over the fruit. 4. Place the baking pan in the air fryer basket and Air Fry for 10 to 12 minutes, or until the fruit is bubbling around the edges and the topping is golden brown. 5. Remove from the basket and serve warm.

## Cream Cheese Shortbread Cookies

**Prep time: 30 minutes | Cook time: 20 minutes | Makes 12 cookies**

- ¼ cup coconut oil, melted
- 2 ounces (57 g) cream cheese, softened
- ½ cup granular erythritol
- 1 large egg, whisked
- 2 cups blanched finely ground almond flour
- 1 teaspoon almond extract

1. Combine all ingredients in a large bowl to form a firm ball. 2. Place dough on a sheet of plastic wrap and roll into a 12-inch-long log shape. Roll log in plastic wrap and place in refrigerator 30 minutes to chill. 3. Remove log from plastic and slice into twelve equal cookies. Cut two sheets of parchment paper to fit air fryer basket. Place six cookies on each ungreased sheet. Place one sheet with cookies into air fryer basket. Adjust the temperature to 320ºF (160ºC) and Air Fry for 10 minutes, turning cookies halfway through cooking. They will be lightly golden when done. Repeat with remaining cookies. 4. Let cool 15 minutes before serving to avoid crumbling.

## Bananas Foster

**Prep time: 5 minutes | Cook time: 7 minutes | Serves 2**

- 1 tablespoon unsalted butter
- 2 teaspoons dark brown sugar
- 1 banana, peeled and halved lengthwise and then crosswise
- 2 tablespoons chopped
- pecans
- ⅛ teaspoon ground cinnamon
- 2 tablespoons light rum
- Vanilla ice cream, for serving

1. In a baking pan, combine the butter and brown sugar. Place the pan in the air fryer basket. Set the air fryer to 350ºF (177ºC) for 2 minutes, or until the butter and sugar are melted. Swirl to combine. 2. Add the banana pieces and pecans, turning the bananas to coat. Set the air fryer to 350ºF (177ºC) for 5 minutes, turning the banana pieces halfway through the cooking time. Sprinkle with the cinnamon. 3. Remove the pan from the air fryer and place on an unlit stovetop for safety. Add the rum to the pan, swirling to combine it with the butter mixture. Carefully light the sauce with a long-reach lighter. Spoon the flaming sauce over the banana pieces until the flames die out. 4. Serve the warm bananas and sauce over vanilla ice cream.

## Sweet Potato Donut Holes

### Prep time: 10 minutes | Cook time: 4 to 5 minutes per batch | Makes 18 donut holes

- 1 cup flour
- ⅓ cup sugar
- ¼ teaspoon baking soda
- 1 teaspoon baking powder
- ⅛ teaspoon salt
- ½ cup cooked mashed purple sweet potatoes
- 1 egg, beaten
- 2 tablespoons butter, melted
- 1 teaspoon pure vanilla extract
- Oil for misting or cooking spray

1. Preheat the air fryer to 390ºF (199ºC). 2. In a large bowl, stir together the flour, sugar, baking soda, baking powder, and salt. 3. In a separate bowl, combine the potatoes, egg, butter, and vanilla and mix well. 4. Add potato mixture to dry ingredients and stir into a soft dough. 5. Shape dough into 1½-inch balls. Mist lightly with oil or cooking spray. 6. Place 9 donut holes in air fryer basket, leaving a little space in between. Cook for 4 to 5 minutes, until done in center and lightly browned outside. 7. Repeat step 6 to cook remaining donut holes.

## Maple-Pecan Tart with Sea Salt

### Prep time: 15 minutes | Cook time: 25 minutes | Serves 8

Tart Crust:
- Vegetable oil spray
- ⅓ cup (⅔ stick) butter, softened
- ¼ cup firmly packed brown

Filling:
- 4 tablespoons (½ stick) butter, diced
- ½ cup packed brown sugar
- ¼ cup pure maple syrup
- ¼ cup whole milk

- sugar
- 1 cup all-purpose flour
- ¼ teaspoon kosher salt

- ¼ teaspoon pure vanilla extract
- 1½ cups finely chopped pecans
- ¼ teaspoon flaked sea salt

1. For the crust: Line a baking pan with foil, leaving a couple of inches of overhang. Spray the foil with vegetable oil spray. 2. In a medium bowl, combine the butter and brown sugar. Beat with an electric mixer on medium-low speed until light and fluffy. Add the flour and kosher salt and beat until the ingredients are well blended. Transfer the mixture (it will be crumbly) to the prepared pan. Press it evenly into the bottom of the pan. 3. Place the pan in the air fryer basket. Set the air fryer to 350ºF (177ºC) for 13 minutes. When the crust has 5 minutes left to cook, start the filling. 4. For the filling: In a medium saucepan, combine the butter, brown sugar, maple syrup, and milk. Bring to a simmer, stirring occasionally. When it begins simmering, cook for 1 minute. Remove from the heat and stir in the vanilla and pecans. 5. Carefully pour the filling evenly over the crust, gently spreading with a rubber spatula so the nuts and liquid are evenly distributed. Set the air fryer to 350ºF (177ºC) for 12 minutes, or until mixture is bubbling. (The center should still be slightly jiggly, it will thicken as it cools.) 6. Remove the pan from the air fryer and sprinkle the tart with the sea salt. Cool completely on a wire rack until room temperature. 7. Transfer the pan to the refrigerator to chill. When cold (the tart will be easier to cut), use the foil overhang to remove the tart from the pan and cut into 8 wedges. Serve at room temperature.

## Apple Fries

### Prep time: 10 minutes | Cook time: 7 minutes | Serves 8

- Oil, for spraying
- 1 cup all-purpose flour
- 3 large eggs, beaten
- 1 cup graham cracker crumbs
- ¼ cup sugar
- 1 teaspoon ground cinnamon
- 3 large Gala apples, peeled, cored, and cut into wedges
- 1 cup caramel sauce, warmed

1. Preheat the air fryer to 380ºF (193ºC). Line the air fryer basket with parchment and spray lightly with oil. 2. Place the flour and beaten eggs in separate bowls and set aside. In another bowl, mix together the graham cracker crumbs, sugar, and cinnamon. 3. Working one at a time, coat the apple wedges in the flour, dip in the egg, and dredge in the graham cracker mix until evenly coated. 4. Place the apples in the prepared basket, taking care not to overlap, and spray lightly with oil. You may need to work in batches, depending on the size of your air fryer. 5. Cook for 5 minutes, flip, spray with oil, and cook for another 2 minutes, or until crunchy and golden brown. 6. Drizzle the caramel sauce over the top and serve.

## Pecan Clusters

### Prep time: 10 minutes | Cook time: 8 minutes | Serves 8

- 3 ounces (85 g) whole shelled pecans
- 1 tablespoon salted butter, melted
- 2 teaspoons confectioners'
- erythritol
- ½ teaspoon ground cinnamon
- ½ cup low-carb chocolate chips

1. In a medium bowl, toss pecans with butter, then sprinkle with erythritol and cinnamon. 2. Place pecans into ungreased air fryer basket. Adjust the temperature to 350ºF (177ºC) and air fry for 8 minutes, shaking the basket two times during cooking. They will feel soft initially but get crunchy as they cool. 3. Line a large baking sheet with parchment paper. 4. Place chocolate in a medium microwave-safe bowl. Microwave on high, heating in 20-second increments and stirring until melted. Place 1 teaspoon chocolate in a rounded mound on ungreased parchment-lined baking sheet, then press 1 pecan into top, repeating with remaining chocolate and pecans. 5. Place baking sheet into refrigerator to cool at least 30 minutes. Once cooled, store clusters in a large sealed container in refrigerator up to 5 days.

# Coconut-Custard Pie

**Prep time: 10 minutes | Cook time: 20 to 23 minutes | Serves 4**

- 1 cup milk
- ¼ cup plus 2 tablespoons sugar
- ¼ cup biscuit baking mix
- 1 teaspoon vanilla
- 2 eggs
- 2 tablespoons melted butter
- Cooking spray
- ½ cup shredded, sweetened coconut

1. Place all ingredients except coconut in a medium bowl. 2. Using a hand mixer, beat on high speed for 3 minutes. 3. Let sit for 5 minutes. 4. Preheat the air fryer to 330ºF (166ºC). 5. Spray a baking pan with cooking spray and place pan in air fryer basket. 6. Pour filling into pan and sprinkle coconut over top. 7. Cook pie at 330ºF (166ºC) for 20 to 23 minutes or until center sets.

# Pecan Bars

**Prep time: 5 minutes | Cook time: 40 minutes | Serves 12**

- 2 cups coconut flour
- 5 tablespoons erythritol
- 4 tablespoons coconut oil, softened
- ½ cup heavy cream
- 1 egg, beaten
- 4 pecans, chopped

1. Mix coconut flour, erythritol, coconut oil, heavy cream, and egg. 2. Pour the batter in the air fryer basket and flatten well. 3. Top the mixture with pecans and cook the meal at 350ºF (177ºC) for 40 minutes. 4. Cut the cooked meal into the bars.

# Dark Chocolate Lava Cake

**Prep time: 5 minutes | Cook time: 10 minutes | Serves 4**

- Olive oil cooking spray
- ¼ cup whole wheat flour
- 1 tablespoon unsweetened dark chocolate cocoa powder
- ⅛ teaspoon salt
- ½ teaspoon baking powder
- ¼ cup raw honey
- 1 egg
- 2 tablespoons olive oil

1. Preheat the air fryer to 380°F(193ºC). Lightly coat the insides of four ramekins with olive oil cooking spray. 2. In a medium bowl, combine the flour, cocoa powder, salt, baking powder, honey, egg, and olive oil. 3. Divide the batter evenly among the ramekins. 4. Place the filled ramekins inside the air fryer and Air Fry for 10 minutes. 5. Remove the lava cakes from the air fryer and slide a knife around the outside edge of each cake. Turn each ramekin upside down on a saucer and serve.

# Apple Dutch Baby

**Prep time: 30 minutes | Cook time: 16 minutes | Serves 2 to 3**

Batter:
- 2 large eggs
- ¼ cup all-purpose flour
- ¼ teaspoon baking powder
- 1½ teaspoons granulated sugar
- Pinch kosher salt
- ½ cup whole milk
- 1 tablespoon butter, melted
- ½ teaspoon pure vanilla extract
- ¼ teaspoon ground nutmeg

Apples:
- 2 tablespoon butter
- 4 tablespoons granulated sugar
- ¼ teaspoon ground cinnamon
- ¼ teaspoon ground nutmeg
- 1 small tart apple (such as Granny Smith), peeled, cored, and sliced
- Vanilla ice cream (optional), for serving

1. For the batter: In a medium bowl, combine the eggs, flour, baking powder, sugar, and salt. Whisk lightly. While whisking continuously, slowly pour in the milk. Whisk in the melted butter, vanilla, and nutmeg. Let the batter stand for 30 minutes. (You can also cover and refrigerate overnight.) 2. For the apples: Place the butter in a baking pan. Place the pan in the air fryer basket. Set the air fryer to 400ºF (204ºC) for 2 minutes. In a small bowl, combine 2 tablespoons of the sugar with the cinnamon and nutmeg and stir until well combined. 3. When the pan is hot and the butter is melted, brush some butter up the sides of the pan. Sprinkle the spiced sugar mixture over the butter. Arrange the apple slices in the pan in a single layer and sprinkle the remaining 2 tablespoons sugar over the apples. Set the air fryer to 400ºF (204ºC) to 2 minutes, or until the mixture bubbles. 4. Gently pour the batter over the apples. Set the air fryer to 350ºF (177ºC) for 12 minutes, or until the pancake is golden brown around the edges, the center is cooked through, and a toothpick emerges clean. 5. Serve immediately with ice cream, if desired.

# Air Fryd Apple

**Prep time: 10 minutes | Cook time: 20 minutes | Makes 6 apple halves**

- 3 small Honey Crisp or other baking apples
- 3 tablespoons maple syrup
- 3 tablespoons chopped
- pecans
- 1 tablespoon firm butter, cut into 6 pieces

1. Put ½ cup water in the drawer of the air fryer. 2. Wash apples well and dry them. 3. Split apples in half. Remove core and a little of the flesh to make a cavity for the pecans. 4. Place apple halves in air fryer basket, cut side up. 5. Spoon 1½ teaspoons pecans into each cavity. 6. Spoon ½ tablespoon maple syrup over pecans in each apple. 7. Top each apple with ½ teaspoon butter. 8. Air Fry at 360ºF (182ºC) for 20 minutes, until apples are tender.

## Cinnamon-Sugar Almonds

### Prep time: 5 minutes | Cook time: 8 minutes | Serves 4

◄ 1 cup whole almonds
◄ 2 tablespoons salted butter, melted
◄ 1 tablespoon sugar
◄ ½ teaspoon ground cinnamon

1. In a medium bowl, combine the almonds, butter, sugar, and cinnamon. Mix well to ensure all the almonds are coated with the spiced butter. 2. Transfer the almonds to the air fryer basket and shake so they are in a single layer. Set the air fryer to 300ºF (149ºC) for 8 minutes, stirring the almonds halfway through the cooking time. 3. Let cool completely before serving.

## Lemon Raspberry Muffins

### Prep time: 5 minutes | Cook time: 15 minutes | Serves 6

◄ 2 cups almond flour
◄ ¾ cup Swerve
◄ 1¼ teaspoons baking powder
◄ ⅓ teaspoon ground allspice
◄ ⅓ teaspoon ground anise star
◄ ½ teaspoon grated lemon
zest
◄ ¼ teaspoon salt
◄ 2 eggs
◄ 1 cup sour cream
◄ ½ cup coconut oil
◄ ½ cup raspberries

1. Preheat the air fryer to 345ºF (174ºC). Line a muffin pan with 6 paper liners. 2. In a mixing bowl, mix the almond flour, Swerve, baking powder, allspice, anise, lemon zest, and salt. 3. In another mixing bowl, beat the eggs, sour cream, and coconut oil until well mixed. Add the egg mixture to the flour mixture and stir to combine. Mix in the raspberries. 4. Scrape the batter into the prepared muffin cups, filling each about three-quarters full. 5. Air Fry for 15 minutes, or until the tops are golden and a toothpick inserted in the middle comes out clean. 6. Allow the muffins to cool for 10 minutes in the muffin pan before removing and serving.

## Indian Toast and Milk

### Prep time: 10 minutes | Cook time: 20 minutes | Serves 4

◄ 1 cup sweetened condensed milk
◄ 1 cup evaporated milk
◄ 1 cup half-and-half
◄ 1 teaspoon ground cardamom, plus additional for garnish
◄ 1 pinch saffron threads
◄ 4 slices white bread
◄ 2 to 3 tablespoons ghee or butter, softened
◄ 2 tablespoons crushed pistachios, for garnish (optional)

1. In a baking pan, combine the condensed milk, evaporated milk, half-and-half, cardamom, and saffron. Stir until well combined.

2. Place the pan in the air fryer basket. Set the air fryer to 350ºF (177ºC) for 15 minutes, stirring halfway through the cooking time. Remove the sweetened milk from the air fryer and set aside. 3. Cut each slice of bread into two triangles. Brush each side with ghee. Place the bread in the air fryer basket. Set the air fryer to 350ºF (177ºC) for 5 minutes or until golden brown and toasty. 4. Remove the bread from the air fryer. Arrange two triangles in each of four wide, shallow bowls. Pour the hot milk mixture on top of the bread and let soak for 30 minutes. 5. Garnish with pistachios if using, and sprinkle with additional cardamom.

## Zucchini Nut Muffins

### Prep time: 15 minutes | Cook time: 15 minutes | Serves 4

◄ ¼ cup vegetable oil, plus more for greasing
◄ ¾ cup all-purpose flour
◄ ¾ teaspoon ground cinnamon
◄ ¼ teaspoon kosher salt
◄ ¼ teaspoon baking soda
◄ ¼ teaspoon baking powder
◄ 2 large eggs
◄ ½ cup sugar
◄ ½ cup grated zucchini
◄ ¼ cup chopped walnuts

1. Generously grease four 4 ounces (113-g) ramekins or a baking pan with vegetable oil. 2. In a medium bowl, sift together the flour, cinnamon, salt, baking soda, and baking powder. 3. In a separate medium bowl, beat together the eggs, sugar, and vegetable oil. Add the dry ingredients to the wet ingredients. Add the zucchini and nuts and stir gently until well combined. Transfer the batter to the prepared ramekins or baking pan. 4. Place the ramekins or pan in the air fryer basket. Set the air fryer to 325ºF (163ºC) for 15 minutes, or until a cake tester or toothpick inserted into the center comes out clean. If it doesn't, cook for 3 to 5 minutes more and test again. 5. Let cool in the ramekins or pan on a wire rack for 10 minutes. Carefully remove from the ramekins or pan and let cool completely on the rack before serving.

## Fried Oreos

### Prep time: 7 minutes | Cook time: 6 minutes per batch | Makes 12 cookies

◄ Oil for misting or nonstick spray
◄ 1 cup complete pancake and waffle mix
◄ 1 teaspoon vanilla extract
◄ ½ cup water, plus 2
tablespoons
◄ 12 Oreos or other chocolate sandwich cookies
◄ 1 tablespoon confectioners' sugar

1. Spray baking pan with oil or nonstick spray and place in basket. 2. Preheat the air fryer to 390ºF (199ºC). 3. In a medium bowl, mix together the pancake mix, vanilla, and water. 4. Dip 4 cookies in batter and place in baking pan. 5. Cook for 6 minutes, until browned. 6. Repeat steps 4 and 5 for the remaining cookies. 7. Sift sugar over warm cookies.

## Strawberry Scone Shortcake

### Prep time: 10 minutes | Cook time: 20 minutes | Serves 4 to 6

- ◄ 1⅓ cups all-purpose flour
- ◄ 3 tablespoons granulated sugar
- ◄ 1½ teaspoons baking powder
- ◄ 1 teaspoon kosher salt
- ◄ 8 tablespoons (1 stick) unsalted butter, cubed and chilled
- ◄ 1⅓ cups heavy cream,
- ◄ chilled
- ◄ Turbinado sugar, for sprinkling
- ◄ 2 tablespoons powdered sugar, plus more for dusting
- ◄ ½ teaspoon vanilla extract
- ◄ 1 cup quartered fresh strawberries

1. In a large bowl, whisk together the flour, granulated sugar, baking powder, and salt. Add the butter and use your fingers to break apart the butter pieces while working them into the flour mixture, until pea-size pieces form. Pour ⅔ cup of the cream over the flour mixture and, using a rubber spatula, mix the ingredients together until just combined. 2. Transfer the dough to a work surface and form into a 7-inch-wide disk. Brush the top with water, then sprinkle with some turbinado sugar. Using a large metal spatula, transfer the dough to the air fryer and Air Fry at 350°F (177°C) until golden brown and fluffy, about 20 minutes. Let cool in the air fryer basket for 5 minutes, then turn out onto a wire rack, right-side up, to cool completely. 3. Meanwhile, in a bowl, beat the remaining ⅔ cup cream, the powdered sugar, and vanilla until stiff peaks form. Split the scone like a hamburger bun and spread the strawberries over the bottom. Top with the whipped cream and cover with the top of the scone. Dust with powdered sugar and cut into wedges to serve.

## Pumpkin Cookie with Cream Cheese Frosting

### Prep time: 10 minutes | Cook time: 7 minutes | Serves 6

- ◄ ½ cup blanched finely ground almond flour
- ◄ ½ cup powdered erythritol, divided
- ◄ 2 tablespoons butter, softened
- ◄ 1 large egg
- ◄ ½ teaspoon unflavored gelatin
- ◄ ½ teaspoon baking powder
- ◄ ½ teaspoon vanilla extract
- ◄ ½ teaspoon pumpkin pie spice
- ◄ 2 tablespoons pure pumpkin purée
- ◄ ½ teaspoon ground cinnamon, divided
- ◄ ¼ cup low-carb, sugar-free chocolate chips
- ◄ 3 ounces (85 g) full-fat cream cheese, softened

1. In a large bowl, mix almond flour and ¼ cup erythritol. Stir in butter, egg, and gelatin until combined. 2. Stir in baking powder, vanilla, pumpkin pie spice, pumpkin purée, and ¼ teaspoon cinnamon, then fold in chocolate chips. 3. Pour batter into a round baking pan. Place pan into the air fryer basket. 4. Adjust the temperature to 300°F (149°C) and Air Fry for 7 minutes. 5. When fully cooked, the top will be golden brown and a toothpick inserted in center will come out clean. Let cool at least 20 minutes. 6. To make the frosting: mix cream cheese, remaining ¼ teaspoon cinnamon, and remaining ¼ cup erythritol in a large bowl. Using an electric mixer, beat until it becomes fluffy. Spread onto the cooled cookie. Garnish with additional cinnamon if desired.

## Crumbly Coconut-Pecan Cookies

### Prep time: 10 minutes | Cook time: 25 minutes | Serves 10

- ◄ 1½ cups coconut flour
- ◄ 1½ cups extra-fine almond flour
- ◄ ½ teaspoon baking powder
- ◄ ⅓ teaspoon baking soda
- ◄ 3 eggs plus an egg yolk, beaten
- ◄ ¾ cup coconut oil, at room temperature
- ◄ 1 cup unsalted pecan nuts,
- ◄ roughly chopped
- ◄ ¾ cup monk fruit
- ◄ ¼ teaspoon freshly grated nutmeg
- ◄ ⅓ teaspoon ground cloves
- ◄ ½ teaspoon pure vanilla extract
- ◄ ½ teaspoon pure coconut extract
- ◄ ⅛ teaspoon fine sea salt

1. Preheat the air fryer to 370°F (188°C). Line the air fryer basket with parchment paper. 2. Mix the coconut flour, almond flour, baking powder, and baking soda in a large mixing bowl. 3. In another mixing bowl, stir together the eggs and coconut oil. Add the wet mixture to the dry mixture. 4. Mix in the remaining ingredients and stir until a soft dough forms. 5. Drop about 2 tablespoons of dough on the parchment paper for each cookie and flatten each biscuit until it's 1 inch thick. 6. Air Fry for about 25 minutes until the cookies are golden and firm to the touch. Remove from the basket to a plate. Let the cookies cool to room temperature and serve.

## Pecan Butter Cookies

### Prep time: 5 minutes | Cook time: 24 minutes | Makes 12 cookies

- ◄ 1 cup chopped pecans
- ◄ ½ cup salted butter, melted
- ◄ ½ cup coconut flour
- ◄ ¾ cup erythritol, divided
- ◄ 1 teaspoon vanilla extract

1. In a food processor, blend together pecans, butter, flour, ½ cup erythritol, and vanilla 1 minute until a dough forms. 2. Form dough into twelve individual cookie balls, about 1 tablespoon each. 3. Cut three pieces of parchment to fit air fryer basket. Place four cookies on each ungreased parchment and place one piece parchment with cookies into air fryer basket. Adjust air fryer temperature to 325°F (163°C) and set the timer for 8 minutes. Repeat cooking with remaining batches. 4. When the timer goes off, allow cookies to cool 5 minutes on a large serving plate until cool enough to handle. While still warm, dust cookies with remaining erythritol. Allow to cool completely, about 15 minutes, before serving.

# Glazed Cherry Turnovers

◄ 2 sheets frozen puff pastry, thawed
◄ 1 (21 ounces / 595 g) can premium cherry pie filling
◄ 2 teaspoons ground cinnamon
◄ 1 egg, beaten

◄ 1 cup sliced almonds
◄ 1 cup powdered sugar
◄ 2 tablespoons milk

1. Roll a sheet of puff pastry out into a square that is approximately 10-inches by 10-inches. Cut this large square into quarters. 2. Mix the cherry pie filling and cinnamon together in a bowl. Spoon ¼ cup of the cherry filling into the center of each puff pastry square. Brush the perimeter of the pastry square with the egg wash. Fold one corner of the puff pastry over the cherry pie filling towards the opposite corner, forming a triangle. Seal the two edges of the pastry together with the tip of a fork, making a design with the tines. Brush the top of the turnovers with the egg wash and sprinkle sliced almonds over each one. Repeat these steps with the second sheet of puff pastry. You should have eight turnovers at the end. 3. Preheat the air fryer to 370ºF (188ºC). 4. Air fry two turnovers at a time for 14 minutes, carefully turning them over halfway through the cooking time. 5. While the turnovers are cooking, make the glaze by whisking the powdered sugar and milk together in a small bowl until smooth. Let the glaze sit for a minute so the sugar can absorb the milk. If the consistency is still too thick to drizzle, add a little more milk, a drop at a time, and stir until smooth. 6. Let the cooked cherry turnovers sit for at least 10 minutes. Then drizzle the glaze over each turnover in a zigzag motion. Serve warm or at room temperature.

# Pecan Brownies

◄ ½ cup blanched finely ground almond flour
◄ ½ cup powdered erythritol
◄ 2 tablespoons unsweetened cocoa powder
◄ ½ teaspoon baking powder

◄ ¼ cup unsalted butter, softened
◄ 1 large egg
◄ ¼ cup chopped pecans
◄ ¼ cup low-carb, sugar-free chocolate chips

1. In a large bowl, mix almond flour, erythritol, cocoa powder, and baking powder. Stir in butter and egg. 2. Fold in pecans and chocolate chips. Scoop mixture into a round baking pan. Place pan into the air fryer basket. 3. Adjust the temperature to 300ºF (149ºC) and Air Fry for 20 minutes. 4. When fully cooked a toothpick inserted in center will come out clean. Allow 20 minutes to fully cool and firm up.

# Chocolate Lava Cakes

◄ 2 large eggs, whisked
◄ ¼ cup blanched finely ground almond flour

◄ ½ teaspoon vanilla extract
◄ 2 ounces (57 g) low-carb chocolate chips, melted

1. In a medium bowl, mix eggs with flour and vanilla. Fold in chocolate until fully combined. 2. Pour batter into two ramekins greased with cooking spray. Place ramekins into air fryer basket. Adjust the temperature to 320ºF (160ºC) and Air Fry for 15 minutes. Cakes will be set at the edges and firm in the center when done. Let cool 5 minutes before serving.

# Chapter 3

# Fish and Seafood

# Chapter 3 Fish and Seafood

## Cilantro Lime Air Fryd Salmon

### Prep time: 10 minutes | Cook time: 12 minutes | Serves 2

- 2 (3-ounce / 85-g) salmon fillets, skin removed
- 1 tablespoon salted butter, melted
- 1 teaspoon chili powder
- ½ teaspoon finely minced garlic
- ¼ cup sliced pickled jalapeños
- ½ medium lime, juiced
- 2 tablespoons chopped cilantro

1. Place salmon fillets into a round baking pan. Brush each with butter and sprinkle with chili powder and garlic. 2. Place jalapeño slices on top and around salmon. Pour half of the lime juice over the salmon and cover with foil. Place pan into the air fryer basket. 3. Adjust the temperature to 370°F (188°C) and Air Fry for 12 minutes. 4. When fully cooked, salmon should flake easily with a fork and reach an internal temperature of at least 145°F (63°C). 5. To serve, spritz with remaining lime juice and garnish with cilantro.

## Crab and Bell Pepper Cakes

### Prep time: 5 minutes | Cook time: 10 minutes | Serves 4

- 8 ounces (227 g) jumbo lump crabmeat
- 1 tablespoon Old Bay seasoning
- ⅓ cup bread crumbs
- ¼ cup diced red bell pepper
- ¼ cup diced green bell pepper
- 1 egg
- ¼ cup mayonnaise
- Juice of ½ lemon
- 1 teaspoon all-purpose flour
- Cooking oil spray

1. Sort through the crabmeat, picking out any bits of shell or cartilage. 2. In a large bowl, stir together the Old Bay seasoning, bread crumbs, red and green bell peppers, egg, mayonnaise, and lemon juice. Gently stir in the crabmeat. 3. Insert the crisper plate into the basket and the basket into the unit. Preheat the unit by selecting AIR FRY, setting the temperature to 375°F (191°C), and setting the time to 3 minutes. Select START/PAUSE to begin. 4. Form the mixture into 4 patties. Sprinkle ¼ teaspoon of flour on top of each patty. 5. Once the unit is preheated, spray the crisper plate with cooking oil. Place the crab cakes into the basket and spray them with cooking oil. 6. Select AIR FRY, set the temperature to 375°F (191°C), and set the time to 10 minutes. Select START/PAUSE to begin. 7. When the cooking is complete, the crab cakes will be golden brown and firm.

## Tuna Casserole

### Prep time: 15 minutes | Cook time: 15 minutes | Serves 4

- 2 tablespoons salted butter
- ¼ cup diced white onion
- ¼ cup chopped white mushrooms
- 2 stalks celery, finely chopped
- ½ cup heavy cream
- ½ cup vegetable broth
- 2 tablespoons full-fat mayonnaise
- ¼ teaspoon xanthan gum
- ½ teaspoon red pepper flakes
- 2 medium zucchini, spiralized
- 2 (5 ounces / 142 g) cans albacore tuna
- 1 ounce (28 g) pork rinds, finely ground

1. In a large saucepan over medium heat, melt butter. Add onion, mushrooms, and celery and sauté until fragrant, about 3 to 5 minutes. 2. Pour in heavy cream, vegetable broth, mayonnaise, and xanthan gum. Reduce heat and continue cooking an additional 3 minutes, until the mixture begins to thicken. 3. Add red pepper flakes, zucchini, and tuna. Turn off heat and stir until zucchini noodles are coated. 4. Pour into a round baking dish. Top with ground pork rinds and cover the top of the dish with foil. Place into the air fryer basket. 5. Adjust the temperature to 370°F (188°C) and set the timer for 15 minutes. 6. When 3 minutes remain, remove the foil to brown the top of the casserole. Serve warm.

## Easy Scallops

### Prep time: 5 minutes | Cook time: 4 minutes | Serves 2

- 12 medium sea scallops, rinsed and patted dry
- 1 teaspoon fine sea salt
- ¾ teaspoon ground black pepper, plus more for garnish
- Fresh thyme leaves, for garnish (optional)
- Avocado oil spray

1. Preheat the air fryer to 390°F (199°C). Coat the air fryer basket with avocado oil spray. 2. Place the scallops in a medium bowl and spritz with avocado oil spray. Sprinkle the salt and pepper to season. 3. Transfer the seasoned scallops to the air fryer basket, spacing them apart. You may need to work in batches to avoid overcrowding. 4. Air fry for 4 minutes, flipping the scallops halfway through, or until the scallops are firm and reach an internal temperature of just 145°F (63°C) on a meat thermometer. 5. Remove from the basket and repeat with the remaining scallops. 6. Sprinkle the pepper and thyme leaves on top for garnish, if desired. Serve immediately.

# Cayenne Flounder Cutlets

## Prep time: 15 minutes | Cook time: 10 minutes | Serves 2

- 1 egg
- 1 cup Pecorino Romano cheese, grated
- Sea salt and white pepper, to taste
- ½ teaspoon cayenne pepper
- 1 teaspoon dried parsley flakes
- 2 flounder fillets

1. To make a breading station, whisk the egg until frothy. 2. In another bowl, mix Pecorino Romano cheese, and spices. 3. Dip the fish in the egg mixture and turn to coat evenly; then, dredge in the cracker crumb mixture, turning a couple of times to coat evenly. 4. Cook in the preheated air fryer at 390ºF (199ºC) for 5 minutes; turn them over and cook another 5 minutes. Enjoy!

# Sesame-Crusted Tuna Steak

## Prep time: 5 minutes | Cook time: 8 minutes | Serves 2

- 2 (6 ounces / 170 g) tuna steaks
- 1 tablespoon coconut oil, melted
- ½ teaspoon garlic powder
- 2 teaspoons white sesame seeds
- 2 teaspoons black sesame seeds

1. Brush each tuna steak with coconut oil and sprinkle with garlic powder. 2. In a large bowl, mix sesame seeds and then press each tuna steak into them, covering the steak as completely as possible. Place tuna steaks into the air fryer basket. 3. Adjust the temperature to 400ºF (204ºC) and air fry for 8 minutes. 4. Flip the steaks halfway through the cooking time. Steaks will be well-done at 145ºF (63ºC) internal temperature. Serve warm.

# Cod Tacos with Mango Salsa

## Prep time: 15 minutes | Cook time: 17 minutes | Serves 4

- 1 mango, peeled and diced
- 1 small jalapeño pepper, diced
- ½ red bell pepper, diced
- ½ red onion, minced
- Pinch chopped fresh cilantro
- Juice of ½ lime
- ¼ teaspoon salt
- ¼ teaspoon ground black pepper
- ½ cup Mexican beer
- 1 egg
- ¾ cup cornstarch
- ¾ cup all-purpose flour
- ½ teaspoon ground cumin
- ¼ teaspoon chili powder
- 1 pound (454 g) cod, cut into 4 pieces
- Olive oil spray
- 4 corn tortillas, or flour tortillas, at room temperature

1. In a small bowl, stir together the mango, jalapeño, red bell pepper, red onion, cilantro, lime juice, salt, and pepper. Set aside. 2. In a medium bowl, whisk the beer and egg. 3. In another medium bowl, stir together the cornstarch, flour, cumin, and chili powder. 4. Insert the crisper plate into the basket and the basket into the unit. Preheat the unit by selecting AIR FRY, setting the temperature to 375ºF (191ºC), and setting the time to 3 minutes. Select START/ PAUSE to begin. 5. Dip the fish pieces into the egg mixture and in the flour mixture to coat completely. 6. Once the unit is preheated, place a parchment paper liner into the basket. Place the fish on the liner in a single layer. 7. Select AIR FRY, set the temperature to 375ºF (191ºC), and set the time to 17 minutes. Select START/ PAUSE to begin. 8. After about 9 minutes, spray the fish with olive oil. Reinsert the basket to resume cooking. 9. When the cooking is complete, the fish should be golden and crispy. Place the pieces in the tortillas, top with the mango salsa, and serve.

# Crab Cakes

## Prep time: 10 minutes | Cook time: 10 minutes | Serves 4

- 2 (6 ounces / 170 g) cans lump crab meat
- ¼ cup blanched finely ground almond flour
- 1 large egg
- 2 tablespoons full-fat mayonnaise
- ½ teaspoon Dijon mustard
- ½ tablespoon lemon juice
- ½ medium green bell pepper, seeded and chopped
- ¼ cup chopped green onion
- ½ teaspoon Old Bay seasoning

1. In a large bowl, combine all ingredients. Form into four balls and flatten into patties. Place patties into the air fryer basket. 2. Adjust the temperature to 350ºF (177ºC) and air fry for 10 minutes. 3. Flip patties halfway through the cooking time. Serve warm.

# Air Fryd Monkfish

## Prep time: 20 minutes | Cook time: 12 minutes | Serves 2

- 2 teaspoons olive oil
- 1 cup celery, sliced
- 2 bell peppers, sliced
- 1 teaspoon dried thyme
- ½ teaspoon dried marjoram
- ½ teaspoon dried rosemary
- 2 monkfish fillets
- 1 tablespoon coconut aminos
- 2 tablespoons lime juice
- Coarse salt and ground black pepper, to taste
- 1 teaspoon cayenne pepper
- ½ cup Kalamata olives, pitted and sliced

1. In a nonstick skillet, heat the olive oil for 1 minute. Once hot, sauté the celery and peppers until tender, about 4 minutes. Sprinkle with thyme, marjoram, and rosemary and set aside. 2. Toss the fish fillets with the coconut aminos, lime juice, salt, black pepper, and cayenne pepper. Place the fish fillets in the lightly greased air fryer basket and Air Fry at 390ºF (199ºC) for 8 minutes. 3. Turn them over, add the olives, and cook an additional 4 minutes. Serve with the sautéed vegetables on the side. Bon appétit!

# Smoky Shrimp and Chorizo Tapas

## Prep time: 15 minutes | Cook time: 10 minutes | Serves 2 to 4

- 4 ounces (113 g) Spanish (cured) chorizo, halved horizontally and sliced crosswise
- ½ pound (227 g) raw medium shrimp, peeled and deveined
- 1 tablespoon extra-virgin olive oil
- 1 small shallot, halved and thinly sliced
- 1 garlic clove, minced
- 1 tablespoon finely chopped fresh oregano
- ½ teaspoon smoked Spanish paprika
- ¼ teaspoon kosher salt
- ¼ teaspoon black pepper
- 3 tablespoons fresh orange juice
- 1 tablespoon minced fresh parsley

1. Place the chorizo in a baking pan. Set the pan in the air fryer basket. Set the air fryer to 375ºF (191ºC) for 5 minutes, or until the chorizo has started to brown and render its fat. 2. Meanwhile, in a large bowl, combine the shrimp, olive oil, shallot, garlic, oregano, paprika, salt, and pepper. Toss until the shrimp is well coated. 3. Transfer the shrimp to the pan with the chorizo. Stir to combine. Place the pan in the air fryer basket. Cook for 10 minutes, stirring halfway through the cooking time. 4. Transfer the shrimp and chorizo to a serving dish. Drizzle with the orange juice and toss to combine. Sprinkle with the parsley.

# Sole and Asparagus Bundles

## Prep time: 10 minutes | Cook time: 14 minutes | Serves 2

- 8 ounces (227 g) asparagus, trimmed
- 1 teaspoon extra-virgin olive oil, divided
- Salt and pepper, to taste
- 4 (3-ounce / 85-g) skinless sole or flounder fillets, ⅛ to ¼ inch thick
- 4 tablespoons unsalted butter, softened
- 1 small shallot, minced
- 1 tablespoon chopped fresh tarragon
- ¼ teaspoon lemon zest plus ½ teaspoon juice
- Vegetable oil spray

1. Preheat the air fryer to 300ºF (149ºC). 2. Toss asparagus with ½ teaspoon oil, pinch salt, and pinch pepper in a bowl. Cover and microwave until bright green and just tender, about 3 minutes, tossing halfway through microwaving. Uncover and set aside to cool slightly. 3. Make foil sling for air fryer basket by folding 1 long sheet of aluminum foil so it is 4 inches wide. Lay sheet of foil widthwise across basket, pressing foil into and up sides of basket. Fold excess foil as needed so that edges of foil are flush with top of basket. Lightly spray foil and basket with vegetable oil spray. 4. Pat sole dry with paper towels and season with salt and pepper. Arrange fillets skinned side up on cutting board, with thicker ends closest to you. Arrange asparagus evenly across base of each fillet, then tightly roll fillets away from you around asparagus to form tidy bundles. 5. Rub bundles evenly with remaining ½ teaspoon oil and

arrange seam side down on sling in prepared basket. Air Fry until asparagus is tender and sole flakes apart when gently prodded with a paring knife, 14 to 18 minutes, using a sling to rotate bundles halfway through cooking. 6. Combine butter, shallot, tarragon, and lemon zest and juice in a bowl. Using sling, carefully remove sole bundles from air fryer and transfer to individual plates. Top evenly with butter mixture and serve.

# Country Shrimp

## Prep time: 10 minutes | Cook time: 15 to 20 minutes | Serves 4

- 1 pound (454 g) large shrimp, deveined, with tails on
- 1 pound (454 g) smoked turkey sausage, cut into thick slices
- 2 corn cobs, quartered
- 1 zucchini, cut into bite-
- sized pieces
- 1 red bell pepper, cut into chunks
- 1 tablespoon Old Bay seasoning
- 2 tablespoons olive oil
- Cooking spray

1. Preheat the air fryer to 400ºF (204ºC). Spray the air fryer basket lightly with cooking spray. 2. In a large bowl, mix the shrimp, turkey sausage, corn, zucchini, bell pepper, and Old Bay seasoning, and toss to coat with the spices. Add the olive oil and toss again until evenly coated. 3. Spread the mixture in the air fryer basket in a single layer. You will need to cook in batches. 4. Air fry for 15 to 20 minutes, or until cooked through, shaking the basket every 5 minutes for even cooking. 5. Serve immediately.

# Fish Gratin

## Prep time: 30 minutes | Cook time: 17 minutes | Serves 4

- 1 tablespoon avocado oil
- 1 pound (454 g) hake fillets
- 1 teaspoon garlic powder
- Sea salt and ground white pepper, to taste
- 2 tablespoons shallots, chopped
- 1 bell pepper, seeded and
- chopped
- ½ cup Cottage cheese
- ½ cup sour cream
- 1 egg, well whisked
- 1 teaspoon yellow mustard
- 1 tablespoon lime juice
- ½ cup Swiss cheese, shredded

1. Brush the bottom and sides of a casserole dish with avocado oil. Add the hake fillets to the casserole dish and sprinkle with garlic powder, salt, and pepper. 2. Add the chopped shallots and bell peppers. 3. In a mixing bowl, thoroughly combine the Cottage cheese, sour cream, egg, mustard, and lime juice. Pour the mixture over fish and spread evenly. 4. Cook in the preheated air fryer at 370ºF (188ºC) for 10 minutes. 5. Top with the Swiss cheese and cook an additional 7 minutes. Let it rest for 10 minutes before slicing and serving. Bon appétit!

# Blackened Red Snapper

## Prep time: 13 minutes | Cook time: 8 to 10 minutes | Serves 4

- 1½ teaspoons black pepper
- ¼ teaspoon thyme
- ¼ teaspoon garlic powder
- ⅛ teaspoon cayenne pepper
- 1 teaspoon olive oil
- 4 (4 ounces / 113 g) red snapper fillet portions, skin on
- 4 thin slices lemon
- Cooking spray

1. Mix the spices and oil together to make a paste. Rub into both sides of the fish. 2. Spray the air fryer basket with nonstick cooking spray and lay snapper steaks in basket, skin-side down. 3. Place a lemon slice on each piece of fish. 4. Roast at 390ºF (199ºC) for 8 to 10 minutes. The fish will not flake when done, but it should be white through the center.

# Pesto Shrimp with Wild Rice Pilaf

## Prep time: 5 minutes | Cook time: 5 minutes | Serves 4

- 1 pound (454 g) medium shrimp, peeled and deveined
- ¼ cup pesto sauce
- 1 lemon, sliced
- 2 cups cooked wild rice pilaf

1. Preheat the air fryer to 360ºF(182ºC). 2. In a medium bowl, toss the shrimp with the pesto sauce until well coated. 3. Place the shrimp in a single layer in the air fryer basket. Put the lemon slices over the shrimp and roast for 5 minutes. 4. Remove the lemons and discard. Serve a quarter of the shrimp over ½ cup wild rice with some favorite steamed vegetables.

# Crab Cakes with Lettuce and Apple Salad

## Prep time: 10 minutes | Cook time: 13 minutes | Serves 2

- 8 ounces (227 g) lump crab meat, picked over for shells
- 2 tablespoons panko bread crumbs
- 1 scallion, minced
- 1 large egg
- 1 tablespoon mayonnaise
- 1½ teaspoons Dijon mustard
- Pinch of cayenne pepper
- 2 shallots, sliced thin
- 1 tablespoon extra-virgin
- olive oil, divided
- 1 teaspoon lemon juice, plus lemon wedges for serving
- ⅛ teaspoon salt
- Pinch of pepper
- ½ (3 ounces / 85 g) small head Bibb lettuce, torn into bite-size pieces
- ½ apple, cored and sliced thin

1. Preheat the air fryer to 400ºF (204ºC). 2. Line large plate with triple layer of paper towels. Transfer crab meat to prepared plate and pat dry with additional paper towels. Combine panko, scallion, egg, mayonnaise, mustard, and cayenne in a bowl. Using a rubber spatula, gently fold in crab meat until combined; discard paper towels. Divide crab mixture into 4 tightly packed balls, then flatten each into 1-inch-thick cake (cakes will be delicate). Transfer cakes to plate and refrigerate until firm, about 10 minutes. 3. Toss shallots with ½ teaspoon oil in separate bowl; transfer to air fryer basket. Air fry until shallots are browned, 5 to 7 minutes, tossing once halfway through cooking. Return shallots to now-empty bowl and set aside. 4. Arrange crab cakes in air fryer basket, spaced evenly apart. Return basket to air fryer and air fry until crab cakes are light golden brown on both sides, 8 to 10 minutes, flipping and rotating cakes halfway through cooking. 5. Meanwhile, whisk remaining 2½ teaspoons oil, lemon juice, salt, and pepper together in large bowl. Add lettuce, apple, and shallots and toss to coat. Serve crab cakes with salad, passing lemon wedges separately.

# Ahi Tuna Steaks

## Prep time: 5 minutes | Cook time: 14 minutes | Serves 2

- 2 (6 ounces / 170 g) ahi tuna steaks
- 2 tablespoons olive oil
- 3 tablespoons everything bagel seasoning

1. Drizzle both sides of each steak with olive oil. Place seasoning on a medium plate and press each side of tuna steaks into seasoning to form a thick layer. 2. Place steaks into ungreased air fryer basket. Adjust the temperature to 400ºF (204ºC) and air fry for 14 minutes, turning steaks halfway through cooking. Steaks will be done when internal temperature is at least 145ºF (63ºC) for well-done. Serve warm.

# Lemon Mahi-Mahi

## Prep time: 5 minutes | Cook time: 14 minutes | Serves 2

- Oil, for spraying
- 2 (6 ounces / 170 g) mahi-mahi fillets
- 1 tablespoon lemon juice
- 1 tablespoon olive oil
- ¼ teaspoon salt
- ¼ teaspoon freshly ground black pepper
- 1 tablespoon chopped fresh dill
- 2 lemon slices

1. Line the air fryer basket with parchment and spray lightly with oil. 2. Place the mahi-mahi in the prepared basket. 3. In a small bowl, whisk together the lemon juice and olive oil. Brush the mixture evenly over the mahi-mahi. 4. Sprinkle the mahi-mahi with the salt and black pepper and top with the dill. 5. Air fry at 400ºF (204ºC) for 12 to 14 minutes, depending on the thickness of the fillets, until they flake easily. 6. Transfer to plates, top each with a lemon slice, and serve.

## Salmon Patties

**Prep time: 5 minutes | Cook time: 8 minutes | Serves 4**

- 12 ounces (340 g) pouched pink salmon
- 3 tablespoons mayonnaise
- ⅓ cup blanched finely
- ground almond flour
- ½ teaspoon Cajun seasoning
- 1 medium avocado, peeled, pitted, and sliced

1. In a medium bowl, mix salmon, mayonnaise, flour, and Cajun seasoning. Form mixture into four patties. 2. Place patties into ungreased air fryer basket. Adjust the temperature to 400ºF (204ºC) and air fry for 8 minutes, turning patties halfway through cooking. Patties will be done when firm and golden brown. 3. Transfer patties to four medium plates and serve warm with avocado slices.

## Air Fried Crab Bun

**Prep time: 15 minutes | Cook time: 20 minutes | Serves 2**

- 5 ounces (142 g) crab meat, chopped
- 2 eggs, beaten
- 2 tablespoons coconut flour
- ¼ teaspoon baking powder
- ½ teaspoon coconut aminos
- ½ teaspoon ground black pepper
- 1 tablespoon coconut oil, softened

1. In the mixing bowl, mix crab meat with eggs, coconut flour, baking powder, coconut aminos, ground black pepper, and coconut oil. 2. Knead the smooth dough and cut it into pieces. 3. Make the buns from the crab mixture and put them in the air fryer basket. 4. Cook the crab buns at 365ºF (185ºC) for 20 minutes.

## Lemon-Dill Salmon Burgers

**Prep time: 10 minutes | Cook time: 8 minutes | Serves 4**

- 2 (6 ounces / 170 g) fillets of salmon, finely chopped by hand or in a food processor
- 1 cup fine bread crumbs
- 1 teaspoon freshly grated lemon zest
- 2 tablespoons chopped fresh dill weed
- 1 teaspoon salt
- Freshly ground black pepper, to taste
- 2 eggs, lightly beaten
- 4 brioche or hamburger buns
- Lettuce, tomato, red onion, avocado, mayonnaise or mustard, for serving

1. Preheat the air fryer to 400ºF (204ºC). 2. Combine all the ingredients in a bowl. Mix together well and divide into four balls. Flatten the balls into patties, making an indentation in the center of each patty with your thumb (this will help the burger stay flat as it cooks) and flattening the sides of the burgers so that they fit nicely into the air fryer basket. 3. Transfer the burgers to the air fryer basket and air fry for 4 minutes. Flip the burgers over and air fry for another 3 to 4 minutes, until nicely browned and firm to the touch. 4. Serve on soft brioche buns with your choice of topping: lettuce, tomato, red onion, avocado, mayonnaise or mustard

## Roasted Fish with Almond-Lemon Crumbs

**Prep time: 10 minutes | Cook time: 7 to 8 minutes | Serves 4**

- ½ cup raw whole almonds
- 1 scallion, finely chopped
- Grated zest and juice of 1 lemon
- ½ tablespoon extra-virgin olive oil
- ¾ teaspoon kosher salt,
- divided
- Freshly ground black pepper, to taste
- 4 (6 ounces / 170 g each) skinless fish fillets
- Cooking spray
- 1 teaspoon Dijon mustard

1. In a food processor, pulse the almonds to coarsely chop. Transfer to a small bowl and add the scallion, lemon zest, and olive oil. Season with ¼ teaspoon of the salt and pepper to taste and mix to combine. 2. Spray the top of the fish with oil and squeeze the lemon juice over the fish. Season with the remaining ½ teaspoon salt and pepper to taste. Spread the mustard on top of the fish. Dividing evenly, press the almond mixture onto the top of the fillets to adhere. 3. Preheat the air fryer to 375ºF (191ºC). 4. Working in batches, place the fillets in the air fryer basket in a single layer. Air fry for 7 to 8 minutes, until the crumbs start to brown and the fish is cooked through. 5. Serve immediately.

## Sea Bass with Roasted Root Vegetables

**Prep time: 10 minutes | Cook time: 15 minutes | Serves 4**

- 1 carrot, diced small
- 1 parsnip, diced small
- 1 rutabaga, diced small
- ¼ cup olive oil
- 1 teaspoon salt, divided
- 4 sea bass fillets
- ½ teaspoon onion powder
- 2 garlic cloves, minced
- 1 lemon, sliced, plus additional wedges for serving

1. Preheat the air fryer to 380ºF(193ºC). 2. In a small bowl, toss the carrot, parsnip, and rutabaga with olive oil and 1 teaspoon salt. 3. Lightly season the sea bass with the remaining 1 teaspoon of salt and the onion powder, then place it into the air fryer basket in a single layer. 4. Spread the garlic over the top of each fillet, then cover with lemon slices. 5. Pour the prepared vegetables into the basket around and on top of the fish. Roast for 15 minutes. 6. Serve with additional lemon wedges if desired.

# Crab-Stuffed Avocado Boats

## Prep time: 5 minutes | Cook time: 7 minutes | Serves 4

◀ 2 medium avocados, halved and pitted
◀ 8 ounces (227 g) cooked crab meat
◀ ¼ teaspoon Old Bay

seasoning
◀ 2 tablespoons peeled and diced yellow onion
◀ 2 tablespoons mayonnaise

1. Scoop out avocado flesh in each avocado half, leaving ½ inch around edges to form a shell. Chop scooped-out avocado. 2. In a medium bowl, combine crab meat, Old Bay seasoning, onion, mayonnaise, and chopped avocado. Place ¼ mixture into each avocado shell. 3. Place avocado boats into ungreased air fryer basket. Adjust the temperature to 350ºF (177ºC) and air fry for 7 minutes. Avocado will be browned on the top and mixture will be bubbling when done. Serve warm.

# Lemon-Pepper Trout

## Prep time: 5 minutes | Cook time: 15 minutes | Serves 4

◀ 4 trout fillets
◀ 2 tablespoons olive oil
◀ ½ teaspoon salt
◀ 1 teaspoon black pepper

◀ 2 garlic cloves, sliced
◀ 1 lemon, sliced, plus additional wedges for serving

1. Preheat the air fryer to 380°F(193ºC). 2. Brush each fillet with olive oil on both sides and season with salt and pepper. Place the fillets in an even layer in the air fryer basket. 3. Place the sliced garlic over the tops of the trout fillets, then top the garlic with lemon slices and roast for 12 to 15 minutes, or until it has reached an internal temperature of 145°F(63ºC). 4. Serve with fresh lemon wedges.

# Garlicky Cod Fillets

## Prep time: 10 minutes | Cook time: 10 to 12 minutes | Serves 4

◀ 1 teaspoon olive oil
◀ 4 cod fillets
◀ ¼ teaspoon fine sea salt
◀ ¼ teaspoon ground black pepper, or more to taste
◀ 1 teaspoon cayenne pepper
◀ ½ cup fresh Italian parsley,

coarsely chopped
◀ ½ cup nondairy milk
◀ 1 Italian pepper, chopped
◀ 4 garlic cloves, minced
◀ 1 teaspoon dried basil
◀ ½ teaspoon dried oregano

1. Lightly coat the sides and bottom of a baking dish with the olive oil. Set aside. 2. In a large bowl, sprinkle the fillets with salt, black pepper, and cayenne pepper. 3. In a food processor, pulse the remaining ingredients until smoothly puréed. 4. Add the purée to the bowl of fillets and toss to coat, then transfer to the prepared baking dish. 5. Preheat the air fryer to 380ºF (193ºC). 6. Put the baking dish in the air fryer basket and Air Fry for 10 to 12 minutes, or until the fish flakes when pressed lightly with a fork. 7. Remove from the basket and serve warm.

# Maple Balsamic Glazed Salmon

## Prep time: 5 minutes | Cook time: 10 minutes | Serves 4

◀ 4 (6 ounces / 170 g) fillets of salmon
◀ Salt and freshly ground black pepper, to taste
◀ Vegetable oil

◀ ¼ cup pure maple syrup
◀ 3 tablespoons balsamic vinegar
◀ 1 teaspoon Dijon mustard

1. Preheat the air fryer to 400ºF (204ºC). 2. Season the salmon well with salt and freshly ground black pepper. Spray or brush the bottom of the air fryer basket with vegetable oil and place the salmon fillets inside. Air fry the salmon for 5 minutes. 3. While the salmon is air frying, combine the maple syrup, balsamic vinegar and Dijon mustard in a small saucepan over medium heat and stir to blend well. Let the mixture simmer while the fish is cooking. It should start to thicken slightly, but keep your eye on it so it doesn't burn. 4. Brush the glaze on the salmon fillets and air fry for an additional 5 minutes. The salmon should feel firm to the touch when finished and the glaze should be nicely browned on top. Brush a little more glaze on top before removing and serving with rice and vegetables, or a nice green salad.

# Mustard-Crusted Fish Fillets

## Prep time: 5 minutes | Cook time: 8 to 11 minutes | Serves 4

◀ 5 teaspoons low-sodium yellow mustard
◀ 1 tablespoon freshly squeezed lemon juice
◀ 4 (3½-ounce / 99-g) sole fillets
◀ ½ teaspoon dried thyme

◀ ½ teaspoon dried marjoram
◀ ⅛ teaspoon freshly ground black pepper
◀ 1 slice low-sodium whole-wheat bread, crumbled
◀ 2 teaspoons olive oil

1. In a small bowl, mix the mustard and lemon juice. Spread this evenly over the fillets. Place them in the air fryer basket. 2. In another small bowl, mix the thyme, marjoram, pepper, bread crumbs, and olive oil. Mix until combined. 3. Gently but firmly press the spice mixture onto the top of each fish fillet. 4. Air Fry at 320ºF (160ºC) for 8 to 11 minutes, or until the fish reaches an internal temperature of at least 145ºF (63ºC) on a meat thermometer and the topping is browned and crisp. Serve immediately.

## Lemon Pepper Shrimp

**Prep time: 15 minutes | Cook time: 8 minutes | Serves 2**

◄ Oil, for spraying
◄ 12 ounces (340 g) medium raw shrimp, peeled and deveined
◄ 3 tablespoons lemon juice
◄ 1 tablespoon olive oil
◄ 1 teaspoon lemon pepper
◄ ¼ teaspoon paprika
◄ ¼ teaspoon granulated garlic

1. Preheat the air fryer to 400°F (204°C). Line the air fryer basket with parchment and spray lightly with oil. 2. In a medium bowl, toss together the shrimp, lemon juice, olive oil, lemon pepper, paprika, and garlic until evenly coated. 3. Place the shrimp in the prepared basket. 4. Cook for 6 to 8 minutes, or until pink and firm. Serve immediately.

## Honey-Glazed Salmon

**Prep time: 5 minutes | Cook time: 12 minutes | Serves 4**

◄ ¼ cup raw honey
◄ 4 garlic cloves, minced
◄ 1 tablespoon olive oil
◄ ½ teaspoon salt
◄ Olive oil cooking spray
◄ 4 (1½-inch-thick) salmon fillets

1. Preheat the air fryer to 380°F(193°C). 2. In a small bowl, mix together the honey, garlic, olive oil, and salt. 3. Spray the bottom of the air fryer basket with olive oil cooking spray, and place the salmon in a single layer on the bottom of the air fryer basket. 4. Brush the top of each fillet with the honey-garlic mixture, and roast for 10 to 12 minutes, or until the internal temperature reaches 145°F(63°C).

## Orange-Mustard Glazed Salmon

**Prep time: 10 minutes | Cook time: 10 minutes | Serves 2**

◄ 1 tablespoon orange marmalade
◄ ¼ teaspoon grated orange zest plus 1 tablespoon juice
◄ 2 teaspoons whole-grain mustard
◄ 2 (8-ounce / 227 -g) skin-on salmon fillets, 1½ inches thick
◄ Salt and pepper, to taste
◄ Vegetable oil spray

1. Preheat the air fryer to 400°F (204°C). 2. Make foil sling for air fryer basket by folding 1 long sheet of aluminum foil so it is 4 inches wide. Lay sheet of foil widthwise across basket, pressing foil into and up sides of basket. Fold excess foil as needed so that edges of foil are flush with top of basket. Lightly spray foil and basket with vegetable oil spray. 3. Combine marmalade, orange zest and juice, and mustard in bowl. Pat salmon dry with paper towels and season with salt and pepper. Brush tops and sides of fillets evenly with glaze. Arrange fillets skin side down on sling in prepared basket, spaced evenly apart. Air fry salmon until center is still translucent when checked with the tip of a paring knife and registers 125°F (52°C) (for medium-rare), 10 to 14 minutes, using sling to rotate fillets halfway through cooking. 4. Using the sling, carefully remove salmon from air fryer. Slide fish spatula along underside of fillets and transfer to individual serving plates, leaving skin behind. Serve.

## Fried Catfish with Dijon Sauce

**Prep time: 20 minutes | Cook time: 7 minutes | Serves 4**

◄ 4 tablespoons butter, melted
◄ 2 teaspoons Worcestershire sauce, divided
◄ 1 teaspoon lemon pepper
◄ 1 cup panko bread crumbs
◄ 4 (4 ounces / 113 g) catfish fillets
◄ Cooking spray
◄ ½ cup sour cream
◄ 1 tablespoon Dijon mustard

1. In a shallow bowl, stir together the melted butter, 1 teaspoon of Worcestershire sauce, and the lemon pepper. Place the bread crumbs in another shallow bowl. 2. One at a time, dip both sides of the fillets in the butter mixture, then the bread crumbs, coating thoroughly. 3. Preheat the air fryer to 300°F (149°C). Line the air fryer basket with parchment paper. 4. Place the coated fish on the parchment and spritz with oil. 5. Air Fry for 4 minutes. Flip the fish, spritz it with oil, and Air Fry for 3 to 6 minutes more, depending on the thickness of the fillets, until the fish flakes easily with a fork. 6. In a small bowl, stir together the sour cream, Dijon, and remaining 1 teaspoon of Worcestershire sauce. This sauce can be made 1 day in advance and refrigerated before serving. Serve with the fried fish.

## Fish Taco Bowl

**Prep time: 10 minutes | Cook time: 12 minutes | Serves 4**

◄ ½ teaspoon salt
◄ ¼ teaspoon garlic powder
◄ ¼ teaspoon ground cumin
◄ 4 (4 ounces / 113 g) cod fillets
◄ 4 cups finely shredded green
cabbage
◄ ⅓ cup mayonnaise
◄ ¼ teaspoon ground black pepper
◄ ¼ cup chopped pickled jalapeños

1. Sprinkle salt, garlic powder, and cumin over cod and place into ungreased air fryer basket. Adjust the temperature to 350°F (177°C) and air fry for 12 minutes, turning fillets halfway through cooking. Cod will flake easily and have an internal temperature of at least 145°F (63°C) when done. 2. In a large bowl, toss cabbage with mayonnaise, pepper, and jalapeños until fully coated. Serve cod warm over cabbage slaw on four medium plates.

# Tandoori Shrimp

**Prep time: 25 minutes | Cook time: 6 minutes | Serves 4**

- 1 pound (454 g) jumbo raw shrimp (21 to 25 count), peeled and deveined
- 1 tablespoon minced fresh ginger
- 3 cloves garlic, minced
- ¼ cup chopped fresh cilantro or parsley, plus more for garnish
- 1 teaspoon ground turmeric
- 1 teaspoon garam masala
- 1 teaspoon smoked paprika
- 1 teaspoon kosher salt
- ½ to 1 teaspoon cayenne pepper
- 2 tablespoons olive oil (for Paleo) or melted ghee
- 2 teaspoons fresh lemon juice

1. In a large bowl, combine the shrimp, ginger, garlic, cilantro, turmeric, garam masala, paprika, salt, and cayenne. Toss well to coat. Add the oil or ghee and toss again. Marinate at room temperature for 15 minutes, or cover and refrigerate for up to 8 hours. 2. Place the shrimp in a single layer in the air fryer basket. Set the air fryer to 325ºF (163ºC) for 6 minutes. Transfer the shrimp to a serving platter. Cover and let the shrimp finish cooking in the residual heat, about 5 minutes. 3. Sprinkle the shrimp with the lemon juice and toss to coat. Garnish with additional cilantro and serve.

# Pesto Fish Pie

**Prep time: 15 minutes | Cook time: 15 minutes | Serves 4**

- 2 tablespoons prepared pesto
- ¼ cup half-and-half
- ¼ cup grated Parmesan cheese
- 1 teaspoon kosher salt
- 1 teaspoon black pepper
- Vegetable oil spray
- 1 (10 ounces / 283 g) package frozen chopped spinach, thawed and
- squeezed dry
- 1 pound (454 g) firm white fish, cut into 2-inch chunks
- ½ cup cherry tomatoes, quartered
- All-purpose flour
- ½ sheet frozen puff pastry (from a 17.3 ounces / 490 g package), thawed

1. In a small bowl, combine the pesto, half-and-half, Parmesan, salt, and pepper. Stir until well combined; set aside. 2. Spray a baking pan with vegetable oil spray. Arrange the spinach evenly across the bottom of the pan. Top with the fish and tomatoes. Pour the pesto mixture evenly over everything. 3. On a lightly floured surface, roll the puff pastry sheet into a circle. Place the pastry on top of the pan and tuck it in around the edges of the pan. (Or, do what I do and stretch it with your hands and then pat it into place.) 4. Place the pan in the air fryer basket. Set the air fryer to 400ºF (204ºC) for 15 minutes, or until the pastry is well browned. Let stand 5 minutes before serving.

# Breaded Shrimp Tacos

**Prep time: 10 minutes | Cook time: 9 minutes | Makes 8 tacos**

- 2 large eggs
- 1 teaspoon prepared yellow mustard
- 1 pound (454 g) small shrimp, peeled, deveined, and tails removed
- ½ cup finely shredded Gouda or Parmesan cheese
- ½ cup pork dust
- For Serving:
- 8 large Boston lettuce leaves
- ¼ cup pico de gallo
- ¼ cup shredded purple cabbage
- 1 lemon, sliced
- Guacamole (optional)

1. Preheat the air fryer to 400ºF (204ºC). 2. Crack the eggs into a large bowl, add the mustard, and whisk until well combined. Add the shrimp and stir well to coat. 3. In a medium-sized bowl, mix together the cheese and pork dust until well combined. 4. One at a time, roll the coated shrimp in the pork dust mixture and use your hands to press it onto each shrimp. Spray the coated shrimp with avocado oil and place them in the air fryer basket, leaving space between them. 5. Air fry the shrimp for 9 minutes, or until cooked through and no longer translucent, flipping after 4 minutes. 6. To serve, place a lettuce leaf on a serving plate, place several shrimp on top, and top with 1½ teaspoons each of pico de gallo and purple cabbage. Squeeze some lemon juice on top and serve with guacamole, if desired. 7. Store leftover shrimp in an airtight container in the refrigerator for up to 3 days. Reheat in a preheated 400ºF (204ºC) air fryer for 5 minutes, or until warmed through.

# Steamed Cod with Garlic and Swiss Chard

**Prep time: 5 minutes | Cook time: 12 minutes | Serves 4**

- 1 teaspoon salt
- ½ teaspoon dried oregano
- ½ teaspoon dried thyme
- ½ teaspoon garlic powder
- 4 cod fillets
- ½ white onion, thinly sliced
- 2 cups Swiss chard, washed, stemmed, and torn into pieces
- ¼ cup olive oil
- 1 lemon, quartered

1. Preheat the air fryer to 380°F(193ºC). 2. In a small bowl, whisk together the salt, oregano, thyme, and garlic powder. 3. Tear off four pieces of aluminum foil, with each sheet being large enough to envelop one cod fillet and a quarter of the vegetables. 4. Place a cod fillet in the middle of each sheet of foil, then sprinkle on all sides with the spice mixture. 5. In each foil packet, place a quarter of the onion slices and ½ cup Swiss chard, then drizzle 1 tablespoon olive oil and squeeze ¼ lemon over the contents of each foil packet. 6. Fold and seal the sides of the foil packets and then place them into the air fryer basket. Steam for 12 minutes. 7. Remove from the basket, and carefully open each packet to avoid a steam burn.

# Dukkah-Crusted Halibut

## Prep time: 15 minutes | Cook time: 17 minutes | Serves 2

Dukkah:
- 1 tablespoon coriander seeds
- 1 tablespoon sesame seeds
- 1½ teaspoons cumin seeds

Fish:
- 2 (5 ounces / 142 g) halibut fillets
- 2 tablespoons mayonnaise

- ⅓ cup roasted mixed nuts
- ¼ teaspoon kosher salt
- ¼ teaspoon black pepper

- Vegetable oil spray
- Lemon wedges, for serving

1. For the dukkah: Combine the coriander, sesame seeds, and cumin in a small baking pan. Place the pan in the air fryer basket. Set the air fryer to 400°F (204°C) for 5 minutes. Toward the end of the cooking time, you will hear the seeds popping. Transfer to a plate and let cool for 5 minutes. 2. Transfer the toasted seeds to a food processor or spice grinder and add the mixed nuts. Pulse until coarsely chopped. Add the salt and pepper and stir well. 3. For the fish: Spread each fillet with 1 tablespoon of the mayonnaise. Press a heaping tablespoon of the dukkah into the mayonnaise on each fillet, pressing lightly to adhere. 4. Spray the air fryer basket with vegetable oil spray. Place the fish in the basket. Set the air fryer to 400°F (204°C) for 12 minutes, or until the fish flakes easily with a fork. 5. Serve the fish with lemon wedges.

# Roasted Halibut Steaks with Parsley

## Prep time: 5 minutes | Cook time: 10 minutes | Serves 4

- 1 pound (454 g) halibut steaks
- ¼ cup vegetable oil
- 2½ tablespoons Worcester sauce
- 2 tablespoons honey
- 2 tablespoons vermouth

- 1 tablespoon freshly squeezed lemon juice
- 1 tablespoon fresh parsley leaves, coarsely chopped
- Salt and pepper, to taste
- 1 teaspoon dried basil

1. Preheat the air fryer to 390°F (199°C). 2. Put all the ingredients in a large mixing dish and gently stir until the fish is coated evenly. 3. Transfer the fish to the air fryer basket and roast for 10 minutes, flipping the fish halfway through, or until the fish reaches an internal temperature of at least 145°F (63°C) on a meat thermometer. 4. Let the fish cool for 5 minutes and serve.

# Snapper Scampi

## Prep time: 5 minutes | Cook time: 8 to 10 minutes | Serves 4

- 4 (6 ounces / 170 g) skinless snapper or arctic char fillets
- 1 tablespoon olive oil
- 3 tablespoons lemon juice, divided
- ½ teaspoon dried basil

- Pinch salt
- Freshly ground black pepper, to taste
- 2 tablespoons butter
- 2 cloves garlic, minced

1. Rub the fish fillets with olive oil and 1 tablespoon of the lemon juice. Sprinkle with the basil, salt, and pepper, and place in the air fryer basket. 2. Air fry the fish at 380°F (193°C) for 7 to 8 minutes or until the fish just flakes when tested with a fork. Remove the fish from the basket and put on a serving plate. Cover to keep warm. 3. In a baking pan, combine the butter, remaining 2 tablespoons lemon juice, and garlic. Air Fry in the air fryer for 1 to 2 minutes or until the garlic is sizzling. Pour this mixture over the fish and serve

# Chapter 4

## Poultry

## Bacon-Wrapped Chicken Breasts Rolls

**Prep time: 10 minutes | Cook time: 15 minutes | Serves 4**

- ◄ ¼ cup chopped fresh chives
- ◄ 2 tablespoons lemon juice
- ◄ 1 teaspoon dried sage
- ◄ 1 teaspoon fresh rosemary leaves
- ◄ ½ cup fresh parsley leaves
- ◄ 4 cloves garlic, peeled
- ◄ 1 teaspoon ground fennel
- ◄ 3 teaspoons sea salt
- ◄ ½ teaspoon red pepper flakes
- ◄ 4 (4 ounces / 113 g) boneless, skinless chicken breasts, pounded to ¼ inch thick
- ◄ 8 slices bacon
- ◄ Sprigs of fresh rosemary, for garnish
- ◄ Cooking spray

1. Preheat the air fryer to 340ºF (171ºC). Spritz the air fryer basket with cooking spray. 2. Put the chives, lemon juice, sage, rosemary, parsley, garlic, fennel, salt, and red pepper flakes in a food processor, then pulse to purée until smooth. 3. Unfold the chicken breasts on a clean work surface, then brush the top side of the chicken breasts with the sauce. 4. Roll the chicken breasts up from the shorter side, then wrap each chicken rolls with 2 bacon slices to cover. Secure with toothpicks. 5. Arrange the rolls in the preheated air fryer, then cook for 10 minutes. Flip the rolls halfway through. 6. Increase the heat to 390ºF (199ºC) and air fry for 5 more minutes or until the bacon is browned and crispy. 7. Transfer the rolls to a large plate. Discard the toothpicks and spread with rosemary sprigs before serving.

## Italian Chicken with Sauce

**Prep time: 15 minutes | Cook time: 20 minutes | Serves 4**

- ◄ 2 large skinless chicken breasts (about 1¼ pounds / 567 g)
- ◄ Salt and freshly ground black pepper
- ◄ ½ cup almond meal
- ◄ ½ cup grated Parmesan cheese
- ◄ 2 teaspoons Italian seasoning
- ◄ 1 egg, lightly beaten
- ◄ 1 tablespoon olive oil
- ◄ 1 cup no-sugar-added marinara sauce
- ◄ 4 slices Mozzarella cheese or ½ cup shredded Mozzarella

1. Preheat the air fryer to 360ºF (182ºC). 2. Slice the chicken breasts in half horizontally to create 4 thinner chicken breasts. Working with one piece at a time, place the chicken between two pieces of parchment paper and pound with a meat mallet or rolling pin to flatten to an even thickness. Season both sides with salt and freshly ground black pepper. 3. In a large shallow bowl, combine the almond meal, Parmesan, and Italian seasoning; stir until thoroughly combined. Place the egg in another large shallow bowl. 4. Dip the chicken in the egg, followed by the almond meal mixture, pressing the mixture firmly into the chicken to create an even coating. 5. Working in batches if necessary, arrange the chicken breasts in a single layer in the air fryer basket and coat both sides lightly with olive oil. Pausing halfway through the cooking time to flip the chicken, air fry for 15 minutes, or until a thermometer inserted into the thickest part registers 165ºF (74ºC). 6. Spoon the marinara sauce over each piece of chicken and top with the Mozzarella cheese. Air fry for an additional 3 to 5 minutes until the cheese is melted.

## Greek Chicken Souvlaki

**Prep time: 30 minutes | Cook time: 15 minutes | Serves 3 to 4**

Chicken:
- ◄ Grated zest and juice of 1 lemon
- ◄ 2 tablespoons extra-virgin olive oil
- ◄ 1 tablespoon Greek souvlaki

For Serving:
- ◄ Warm pita bread or hot cooked rice
- ◄ Sliced ripe tomatoes
- ◄ Sliced cucumbers

- seasoning
- ◄ 1 pound (454 g) boneless, skinless chicken breast, cut into 2-inch chunks
- ◄ Vegetable oil spray

- ◄ Thinly sliced red onion
- ◄ Kalamata olives
- ◄ Tzatziki

1. For the chicken: In a small bowl, combine the lemon zest, lemon juice, olive oil, and souvlaki seasoning. Place the chicken in a gallon-size resealable plastic bag. Pour the marinade over chicken. Seal bag and massage to coat. Place the bag in a large bowl and marinate for 30 minutes, or cover and refrigerate up to 24 hours, turning the bag occasionally. 2. Place the chicken a single layer in the air fryer basket. Set the air fryer to 350ºF (177ºC) for 10 minutes, turning the chicken and spraying with a little vegetable oil spray halfway through the cooking time. Increase the air fryer temperature to 400ºF (204ºC) for 5 minutes to allow the chicken to crisp and brown a little. 3. Transfer the chicken to a serving platter and serve with pita bread or rice, tomatoes, cucumbers, onion, olives and tzatziki.

# Yellow Curry Chicken Thighs with Peanuts

**Prep time: 10 minutes | Cook time: 20 minutes | Serves 6**

- ◄ ½ cup unsweetened full-fat coconut milk
- ◄ 2 tablespoons yellow curry paste
- ◄ 1 tablespoon minced fresh ginger
- ◄ 1 tablespoon minced garlic
- ◄ 1 teaspoon kosher salt
- ◄ 1 pound (454 g) boneless, skinless chicken thighs, halved crosswise
- ◄ 2 tablespoons chopped peanuts

1. In a large bowl, stir together the coconut milk, curry paste, ginger, garlic, and salt until well blended. Add the chicken; toss well to coat. Marinate at room temperature for 30 minutes, or cover and refrigerate for up to 24 hours. 2. Preheat the air fryer to 375ºF (191ºC). 3. Place the chicken (along with marinade) in a baking pan. Place the pan in the air fryer basket. Air Fry for 20 minutes, turning the chicken halfway through the cooking time. Use a meat thermometer to ensure the chicken has reached an internal temperature of 165ºF (74ºC). 4. Sprinkle the chicken with the chopped peanuts and serve.

# Sesame Chicken

**Prep time: 10 minutes | Cook time: 18 minutes | Serves 6**

- ◄ Oil, for spraying
- ◄ 2 (6 ounces / 170 g) boneless, skinless chicken breasts, cut into bite-size pieces
- ◄ ½ cup cornstarch, plus 1 tablespoon
- ◄ ¼ cup soy sauce
- ◄ 2 tablespoons packed light brown sugar
- ◄ 2 tablespoons pineapple juice
- ◄ 1 tablespoon molasses
- ◄ ½ teaspoon ground ginger
- ◄ 1 tablespoon water
- ◄ 2 teaspoons sesame seeds

1. Line the air fryer basket with parchment and spray lightly with oil. 2. Place the chicken and ½ cup of cornstarch in a zip-top plastic bag, seal, and shake well until evenly coated. 3. Place the chicken in an even layer in the prepared basket and spray liberally with oil. You may need to work in batches, depending on the size of your fryer. 4. Air fry at 390ºF (199ºC) for 9 minutes, flip, spray with more oil, and cook for another 8 to 9 minutes, or until the internal temperature reaches 165ºF (74ºC). 5. In a small saucepan, combine the soy sauce, brown sugar, pineapple juice, molasses, and ginger over medium heat and cook, stirring frequently, until the brown sugar has dissolved. 6. In a small bowl, mix together the water and remaining 1 tablespoon of cornstarch. Pour it into the soy sauce mixture. 7. Bring the mixture to a boil, stirring frequently, until the sauce thickens. Remove from the heat. 8. Transfer the chicken to a large bowl, add the sauce, and toss until evenly coated. Sprinkle with the sesame seeds and serve.

# Brazilian Tempero Baiano Chicken Drumsticks

**Prep time: 30 minutes | Cook time: 20 minutes | Serves 4**

- ◄ 1 teaspoon cumin seeds
- ◄ 1 teaspoon dried oregano
- ◄ 1 teaspoon dried parsley
- ◄ 1 teaspoon ground turmeric
- ◄ ½ teaspoon coriander seeds
- ◄ 1 teaspoon kosher salt
- ◄ ½ teaspoon black
- peppercorns
- ◄ ½ teaspoon cayenne pepper
- ◄ ¼ cup fresh lime juice
- ◄ 2 tablespoons olive oil
- ◄ 1½ pounds (680 g) chicken drumsticks

1. In a clean coffee grinder or spice mill, combine the cumin, oregano, parsley, turmeric, coriander seeds, salt, peppercorns, and cayenne. Process until finely ground. 2. In a small bowl, combine the ground spices with the lime juice and oil. Place the chicken in a resealable plastic bag. Add the marinade, seal, and massage until the chicken is well coated. Marinate at room temperature for 30 minutes or in the refrigerator for up to 24 hours. 3. When you are ready to cook, place the drumsticks skin side up in the air fryer basket. Set the air fryer to 400ºF (204ºC) for 20 to 25 minutes, turning the legs halfway through the cooking time. Use a meat thermometer to ensure that the chicken has reached an internal temperature of 165ºF (74ºC). 4. Serve with plenty of napkins.

# Golden Tenders

**Prep time: 10 minutes | Cook time: 15 minutes | Serves 4**

- ◄ 1 cup panko bread crumbs
- ◄ 1 tablespoon paprika
- ◄ ½ teaspoon salt
- ◄ ¼ teaspoon freshly ground
- black pepper
- ◄ 16 chicken tenders
- ◄ ½ cup mayonnaise
- ◄ Olive oil spray

1. In a medium bowl, stir together the panko, paprika, salt, and pepper. 2. In a large bowl, toss together the chicken tenders and mayonnaise to coat. Transfer the coated chicken pieces to the bowl of seasoned panko and dredge to coat thoroughly. Press the coating onto the chicken with your fingers. 3. Insert the crisper plate into the basket and the basket into the unit. Preheat the unit by selecting AIR FRY, setting the temperature to 350ºF (177ºC), and setting the time to 3 minutes. Select START/PAUSE to begin. 4. Once the unit is preheated, place a parchment paper liner into the basket. Place the chicken into the basket and spray it with olive oil. 5. Select AIR FRY, set the temperature to 350ºF (177ºC), and set the time to 15 minutes. Select START/PAUSE to begin. 6. When the cooking is complete, the tenders will be golden brown and a food thermometer inserted into the chicken should register 165ºF (74ºC). For more even browning, remove the basket halfway through cooking and flip the tenders. Give them an extra spray of olive oil and reinsert the basket to resume cooking. This ensures they are crispy and brown all over. 7. When the cooking is complete, serve.

# Cornish Hens with Honey-Lime Glaze

**Prep time: 15 minutes | Cook time: 25 to 30 minutes | Serves 2 to 3**

- 1 Cornish game hen (1½ to 2 pounds / 680 to 907 g)
- 1 tablespoon honey
- 1 tablespoon lime juice
- 1 teaspoon poultry seasoning
- Salt and pepper, to taste
- Cooking spray

1. To split the hen into halves, cut through breast bone and down one side of the backbone. 2. Mix the honey, lime juice, and poultry seasoning together and brush or rub onto all sides of the hen. Season to taste with salt and pepper. 3. Spray the air fryer basket with cooking spray and place hen halves in the basket, skin-side down. 4. Air fry at 330°F (166°C) for 25 to 30 minutes. Hen will be done when juices run clear when pierced at leg joint with a fork. Let hen rest for 5 to 10 minutes before cutting.

# Lemon-Basil Turkey Breasts

**Prep time: 30 minutes | Cook time: 58 minutes | Serves 4**

- 2 tablespoons olive oil
- 2 pounds (907 g) turkey breasts, bone-in, skin-on
- Coarse sea salt and ground black pepper, to taste
- 1 teaspoon fresh basil leaves, chopped
- 2 tablespoons lemon zest, grated

1. Rub olive oil on all sides of the turkey breasts; sprinkle with salt, pepper, basil, and lemon zest. 2. Place the turkey breasts skin side up on the parchment-lined air fryer basket. 3. Cook in the preheated air fryer at 330°F (166°C) for 30 minutes. Now, turn them over and cook an additional 28 minutes. 4. Serve with lemon wedges, if desired. Bon appétit!

# Gold Livers

**Prep time: 10 minutes | Cook time: 20 minutes | Serves 4**

- 2 eggs
- 2 tablespoons water
- ¾ cup flour
- 2 cups panko breadcrumbs
- 1 teaspoon salt
- ½ teaspoon ground black pepper
- 20 ounces (567 g) chicken livers
- Cooking spray

1. Preheat the air fryer to 390°F (199°C). Spritz the air fryer basket with cooking spray. 2. Whisk the eggs with water in a large bowl.

Pour the flour in a separate bowl. Pour the panko on a shallow dish and sprinkle with salt and pepper. 3. Dredge the chicken livers in the flour. Shake the excess off, then dunk the livers in the whisked eggs, and then roll the livers over the panko to coat well. 4. Arrange the livers in the preheated air fryer and spritz with cooking spray. Work in batches to avoid overcrowding. 5. Air fry for 10 minutes or until the livers are golden and crispy. Flip the livers halfway through. Repeat with remaining livers. 6. Serve immediately.

# Breaded Turkey Cutlets

**Prep time: 5 minutes | Cook time: 8 minutes | Serves 4**

- ½ cup whole wheat bread crumbs
- ¼ teaspoon paprika
- ¼ teaspoon salt
- ¼ teaspoon black pepper
- ⅛ teaspoon dried sage
- ⅛ teaspoon garlic powder
- 1 egg
- 4 turkey breast cutlets
- Chopped fresh parsley, for serving

1. Preheat the air fryer to 380°F (193°C). 2. In a medium shallow bowl, whisk together the bread crumbs, paprika, salt, black pepper, sage, and garlic powder. 3. In a separate medium shallow bowl, whisk the egg until frothy. 4. Dip each turkey cutlet into the egg mixture, then into the bread crumb mixture, coating the outside with the crumbs. Place the breaded turkey cutlets in a single layer in the bottom of the air fryer basket, making sure that they don't touch each other. 5. Air Fry for 4 minutes. Turn the cutlets over, then Air Fry for 4 minutes more, or until the internal temperature reaches 165°F (74°C). Sprinkle on the parsley and serve.

# Cajun-Breaded Chicken Bites

**Prep time: 10 minutes | Cook time: 12 minutes | Serves 4**

- 1 pound (454 g) boneless, skinless chicken breasts, cut into 1-inch cubes
- ½ cup heavy whipping cream
- ½ teaspoon salt
- ¼ teaspoon ground black
- pepper
- 1 ounce (28 g) plain pork rinds, finely crushed
- ¼ cup unflavored whey protein powder
- ½ teaspoon Cajun seasoning

1. Place chicken in a medium bowl and pour in cream. Stir to coat. Sprinkle with salt and pepper. 2. In a separate large bowl, combine pork rinds, protein powder, and Cajun seasoning. Remove chicken from cream, shaking off any excess, and toss in dry mix until fully coated. 3. Place bites into ungreased air fryer basket. Adjust the temperature to 400°F (204°C) and air fry for 12 minutes, shaking the basket twice during cooking. Bites will be done when golden brown and have an internal temperature of at least 165°F (74°C). Serve warm.

# Chicken Shawarma

## Prep time: 30 minutes | Cook time: 15 minutes | Serves 4

Shawarma Spice:
- 2 teaspoons dried oregano
- 1 teaspoon ground cinnamon
- 1 teaspoon ground cumin
- 1 teaspoon ground coriander
- 1 teaspoon kosher salt
- ½ teaspoon ground allspice
- ½ teaspoon cayenne pepper

Chicken:
- 1 pound (454 g) boneless, skinless chicken thighs, cut into large bite-size chunks
- 2 tablespoons vegetable oil
- For Serving:
- Tzatziki
- Pita bread

1. For the shawarma spice: In a small bowl, combine the oregano, cayenne, cumin, coriander, salt, cinnamon, and allspice. 2. For the chicken: In a large bowl, toss together the chicken, vegetable oil, and shawarma spice to coat. Marinate at room temperature for 30 minutes or cover and refrigerate for up to 24 hours. 3. Place the chicken in the air fryer basket. Set the air fryer to 350ºF (177ºC) for 15 minutes, or until the chicken reaches an internal temperature of 165ºF (74ºC). 4. Transfer the chicken to a serving platter. Serve with tzatziki and pita bread.

# Thai Tacos with Peanut Sauce

## Prep time: 10 minutes | Cook time: 6 minutes | Serves 4

- 1 pound (454 g) ground chicken
- ¼ cup diced onions (about 1 small onion)
- 2 cloves garlic, minced
- ¼ teaspoon fine sea salt

Sauce:
- ¼ cup creamy peanut butter, room temperature
- 2 tablespoons chicken broth, plus more if needed
- 2 tablespoons lime juice
- 2 tablespoons grated fresh ginger
- 2 tablespoons wheat-free tamari or coconut aminos
- 1½ teaspoons hot sauce
- 5 drops liquid stevia (optional)

For Serving:
- 2 small heads butter lettuce, leaves separated
- Lime slices (optional)
- For Garnish (Optional):
- Cilantro leaves
- Shredded purple cabbage
- Sliced green onions

1. Preheat the air fryer to 350ºF (177ºC). 2. Place the ground chicken, onions, garlic, and salt in a pie pan or a dish that will fit in your air fryer. Break up the chicken with a spatula. Place in the air fryer and Air Fry for 5 minutes, or until the chicken is browned and cooked through. Break up the chicken again into small crumbles. 3. Make the sauce: In a medium-sized bowl, stir together the peanut butter, broth, lime juice, ginger, tamari, hot sauce, and stevia (if using) until well combined. If the sauce is too thick, add another tablespoon or two of broth. Taste and add more hot sauce if desired.

4. Add half of the sauce to the pan with the chicken. Cook for another minute, until heated through, and stir well to combine. 5. Assemble the tacos: Place several lettuce leaves on a serving plate. Place a few tablespoons of the chicken mixture in each lettuce leaf and garnish with cilantro leaves, purple cabbage, and sliced green onions, if desired. Serve the remaining sauce on the side. Serve with lime slices, if desired. 6. Store leftover meat mixture in an airtight container in the refrigerator for up to 4 days; store leftover sauce, lettuce leaves, and garnishes separately. Reheat the meat mixture in a lightly greased pie pan in a preheated 350ºF (177ºC) air fryer for 3 minutes, or until heated through.

# Bell Pepper Stuffed Chicken Roll-Ups

## Prep time: 10 minutes | Cook time: 12 minutes | Serves 4

- 2 (4 ounces / 113 g) boneless, skinless chicken breasts, slice in half horizontally
- 1 tablespoon olive oil
- Juice of ½ lime
- 2 tablespoons taco seasoning
- ½ green bell pepper, cut into strips
- ½ red bell pepper, cut into strips
- ¼ onion, sliced

1. Preheat the air fryer to 400ºF (204ºC). 2. Unfold the chicken breast slices on a clean work surface. Rub with olive oil, then drizzle with lime juice and sprinkle with taco seasoning. 3. Top the chicken slices with equal amount of bell peppers and onion. Roll them up and secure with toothpicks. 4. Arrange the chicken roll-ups in the preheated air fryer. Air fry for 12 minutes or until the internal temperature of the chicken reaches at least 165ºF (74ºC). Flip the chicken roll-ups halfway through. 5. Remove the chicken from the air fryer. Discard the toothpicks and serve immediately.

# Blackened Cajun Chicken Tenders

## Prep time: 10 minutes | Cook time: 17 minutes | Serves 4

- 2 teaspoons paprika
- 1 teaspoon chili powder
- ½ teaspoon garlic powder
- ½ teaspoon dried thyme
- ¼ teaspoon onion powder
- ⅛ teaspoon ground cayenne
- pepper
- 2 tablespoons coconut oil
- 1 pound (454 g) boneless, skinless chicken tenders
- ¼ cup full-fat ranch dressing

1. In a small bowl, combine all seasonings. 2. Drizzle oil over chicken tenders and then generously coat each tender in the spice mixture. Place tenders into the air fryer basket. 3. Adjust the temperature to 375ºF (191ºC) and air fry for 17 minutes. 4. Tenders will be 165ºF (74ºC) internally when fully cooked. Serve with ranch dressing for dipping.

# Nacho Chicken Fries

## Prep time: 20 minutes | Cook time: 6 to 7 minutes per batch | Serves 4 to 6

- 1 pound (454 g) chicken tenders
- Salt, to taste
- ¼ cup flour
- 2 eggs
- ¾ cup panko bread crumbs
- ¾ cup crushed organic nacho cheese tortilla chips
- Oil for misting or cooking spray
- Seasoning Mix:
- 1 tablespoon chili powder
- 1 teaspoon ground cumin
- ½ teaspoon garlic powder
- ½ teaspoon onion powder

1. Stir together all seasonings in a small cup and set aside. 2. Cut chicken tenders in half crosswise, then cut into strips no wider than about ½ inch. 3. Preheat the air fryer to 390ºF (199ºC). 4. Salt chicken to taste. Place strips in large bowl and sprinkle with 1 tablespoon of the seasoning mix. Stir well to distribute seasonings. 5. Add flour to chicken and stir well to coat all sides. 6. Beat eggs together in a shallow dish. 7. In a second shallow dish, combine the panko, crushed chips, and the remaining 2 teaspoons of seasoning mix. 8. Dip chicken strips in eggs, then roll in crumbs. Mist with oil or cooking spray. 9. Chicken strips will cook best if done in two batches. They can be crowded and overlapping a little but not stacked in double or triple layers. 10. Cook for 4 minutes. Shake basket, mist with oil, and cook 2 to 3 more minutes, until chicken juices run clear and outside is crispy. 11. Repeat step 10 to cook remaining chicken fries.

# Chicken, Zucchini, and Spinach Salad

## Prep time: 10 minutes | Cook time: 20 minutes | Serves 4

- 3 (5 ounces / 142 g) boneless, skinless chicken breasts, cut into 1-inch cubes
- 5 teaspoons extra-virgin olive oil
- ½ teaspoon dried thyme
- 1 medium red onion, sliced
- 1 red bell pepper, sliced
- 1 small zucchini, cut into strips
- 3 tablespoons freshly squeezed lemon juice
- 6 cups fresh baby spinach leaves

1. Insert the crisper plate into the basket and the basket into the unit. Preheat the unit by selecting ROAST, setting the temperature to 375ºF (191ºC), and setting the time to 3 minutes. Select START/PAUSE to begin. 2. In a large bowl, combine the chicken, olive oil, and thyme. Toss to coat. Transfer to a medium metal bowl that fits into the basket. 3. Once the unit is preheated, place the bowl into the basket. 4. Select ROAST, set the temperature to 375ºF (191ºC), and set the time to 20 minutes. Select START/PAUSE to begin. 5. After 8 minutes, add the red onion, red bell pepper, and zucchini to the bowl. Resume cooking. After about 6 minutes more, stir the chicken and vegetables. Resume cooking. 6. When the cooking

is complete, a food thermometer inserted into the chicken should register at least 165ºF (74ºC). Remove the bowl from the unit and stir in the lemon juice. 7. Put the spinach in a serving bowl and top with the chicken mixture. Toss to combine and serve immediately.

# Yakitori

## Prep time: 10 minutes | Cook time: 15 minutes | Serves 4

- ½ cup mirin
- ¼ cup dry white wine
- ½ cup soy sauce
- 1 tablespoon light brown sugar
- 1½ pounds (680 g) boneless, skinless chicken thighs, cut into 1½-inch pieces, fat trimmed
- 4 medium scallions, trimmed, cut into 1½-inch pieces
- Cooking spray
- Special Equipment:
- 4 (4-inch) bamboo skewers, soaked in water for at least 30 minutes

1. Combine the mirin, dry white wine, soy sauce, and brown sugar in a saucepan. Bring to a boil over medium heat. Keep stirring. 2. Boil for another 2 minutes or until it has a thick consistency. Turn off the heat. 3. Preheat the air fryer to 400ºF (204ºC). Spritz the air fryer basket with cooking spray. 4. Run the bamboo skewers through the chicken pieces and scallions alternatively. 5. Arrange the skewers in the preheated air fryer, then brush with mirin mixture on both sides. Spritz with cooking spray. 6. Air fry for 10 minutes or until the chicken and scallions are glossy. Flip the skewers halfway through. 7. Serve immediately.

# Celery Chicken

## Prep time: 10 minutes | Cook time: 15 minutes | Serves 4

- ½ cup soy sauce
- 2 tablespoons hoisin sauce
- 4 teaspoons minced garlic
- 1 teaspoon freshly ground black pepper
- 8 boneless, skinless chicken
- tenderloins
- 1 cup chopped celery
- 1 medium red bell pepper, diced
- Olive oil spray

1. Preheat the air fryer to 375ºF (191ºC). Spray the air fryer basket lightly with olive oil spray. 2. In a large bowl, mix together the soy sauce, hoisin sauce, garlic, and black pepper to make a marinade. Add the chicken, celery, and bell pepper and toss to coat. 3. Shake the excess marinade off the chicken, place it and the vegetables in the air fryer basket, and lightly spray with olive oil spray. You may need to cook them in batches. Reserve the remaining marinade. 4. Air fry for 8 minutes. Turn the chicken over and brush with some of the remaining marinade. Air fry for an additional 5 to 7 minutes, or until the chicken reaches an internal temperature of at least 165ºF (74ºC). Serve.

# Smoky Chicken Leg Quarters

## Prep time: 30 minutes | Cook time: 23 to 27 minutes | Serves 6

- ◄ ½ cup avocado oil
- ◄ 2 teaspoons smoked paprika
- ◄ 1 teaspoon sea salt
- ◄ 1 teaspoon garlic powder
- ◄ ½ teaspoon dried rosemary
- ◄ ½ teaspoon dried thyme
- ◄ ½ teaspoon freshly ground black pepper
- ◄ 2 pounds (907 g) bone-in, skin-on chicken leg quarters

1. In a blender or small bowl, combine the avocado oil, smoked paprika, salt, garlic powder, rosemary, thyme, and black pepper. 2. Place the chicken in a shallow dish or large zip-top bag. Pour the marinade over the chicken, making sure all the legs are coated. Cover and marinate for at least 2 hours or overnight. 3. Place the chicken in a single layer in the air fryer basket, working in batches if necessary. Set the air fryer to 400ºF (204ºC) and air fry for 15 minutes. Flip the chicken legs, then reduce the temperature to 350ºF (177ºC). Cook for 8 to 12 minutes more, until an instant-read thermometer reads 160ºF (71ºC) when inserted into the thickest piece of chicken. 4. Allow to rest for 5 to 10 minutes before serving.

# Personal Cauliflower Pizzas

## Prep time: 10 minutes | Cook time: 25 minutes | Serves 2

- ◄ 1 (12 ounces / 340 g) bag frozen riced cauliflower
- ◄ ⅓ cup shredded Mozzarella cheese
- ◄ ¼ cup almond flour
- ◄ ¼ grated Parmesan cheese
- ◄ 1 large egg
- ◄ ½ teaspoon salt
- ◄ 1 teaspoon garlic powder
- ◄ 1 teaspoon dried oregano
- ◄ 4 tablespoons no-sugar-
- added marinara sauce, divided
- ◄ 4 ounces (113 g) fresh Mozzarella, chopped, divided
- ◄ 1 cup cooked chicken breast, chopped, divided
- ◄ ½ cup chopped cherry tomatoes, divided
- ◄ ¼ cup fresh baby arugula, divided

1. Preheat the air fryer to 400ºF (204ºC). Cut 4 sheets of parchment paper to fit the basket of the air fryer. Brush with olive oil and set aside. 2. In a large glass bowl, microwave the cauliflower according to package directions. Place the cauliflower on a clean towel, draw up the sides, and squeeze tightly over a sink to remove the excess moisture. Return the cauliflower to the bowl and add the shredded Mozzarella along with the almond flour, Parmesan, egg, salt, garlic powder, and oregano. Stir until thoroughly combined. 3. Divide the dough into two equal portions. Place one piece of dough on the prepared parchment paper and pat gently into a thin, flat disk 7 to 8 inches in diameter. Air fry for 15 minutes until the crust begins to brown. Let cool for 5 minutes. 4. Transfer the parchment paper with the crust on top to a baking sheet. Place a second sheet of parchment paper over the crust. While holding the edges of both sheets together, carefully lift the crust off the baking sheet, flip it, and place it back in the air fryer basket. The new sheet of parchment paper is now on the bottom. Remove the top piece of paper and air fry the crust for another 15 minutes until the top begins to brown. Remove the basket from the air fryer. 5. Spread 2 tablespoons of the marinara sauce on top of the crust, followed by half the fresh Mozzarella, chicken, cherry tomatoes, and arugula. Air fry for 5 to 10 minutes longer, until the cheese is melted and beginning to brown. Remove the pizza from the oven and let it sit for 10 minutes before serving. Repeat with the remaining ingredients to make a second pizza.

# Chicken Cordon Bleu

## Prep time: 20 minutes | Cook time: 15 to 20 minutes | Serves 4

- ◄ 4 small boneless, skinless chicken breasts
- ◄ Salt and pepper, to taste
- ◄ 4 slices deli ham
- ◄ 4 slices deli Swiss cheese
- (about 3 to 4 inches square)
- ◄ 2 tablespoons olive oil
- ◄ 2 teaspoons marjoram
- ◄ ¼ teaspoon paprika

1. Split each chicken breast horizontally almost in two, leaving one edge intact. 2. Lay breasts open flat and sprinkle with salt and pepper to taste. 3. Place a ham slice on top of each chicken breast. 4. Cut cheese slices in half and place one half atop each breast. Set aside remaining halves of cheese slices. 5. Roll up chicken breasts to enclose cheese and ham and secure with toothpicks. 6. Mix together the olive oil, marjoram, and paprika. Rub all over outsides of chicken breasts. 7. Place chicken in air fryer basket and air fry at 360ºF (182ºC) for 15 to 20 minutes, until well done and juices run clear. 8. Remove all toothpicks. To avoid burns, place chicken breasts on a plate to remove toothpicks, then immediately return them to the air fryer basket. 9. Place a half cheese slice on top of each chicken breast and cook for a minute or so just to melt cheese.

# Lemon Thyme Roasted Chicken

## Prep time: 10 minutes | Cook time: 60 minutes | Serves 6

- ◄ 1 (4 pounds / 1.8 kg) chicken
- ◄ 2 teaspoons dried thyme
- ◄ 1 teaspoon garlic powder
- ◄ ½ teaspoon onion powder
- ◄ 2 teaspoons dried parsley
- ◄ 1 teaspoon baking powder
- ◄ 1 medium lemon
- ◄ 2 tablespoons salted butter, melted

1. Rub chicken with thyme, garlic powder, onion powder, parsley, and baking powder. 2. Slice lemon and place four slices on top of chicken, breast side up, and secure with toothpicks. Place remaining slices inside of the chicken. 3. Place entire chicken into the air fryer basket, breast side down. 4. Adjust the temperature to 350ºF (177ºC) and air fry for 60 minutes. 5. After 30 minutes, flip chicken so breast side is up. 6. When done, internal temperature should be 165ºF (74ºC) and the skin golden and crispy. To serve, pour melted butter over entire chicken.

## Barbecue Chicken

**Prep time: 10 minutes | Cook time: 18 to 20 minutes | Serves 4**

- ◄ ⅓ cup no-salt-added tomato sauce
- ◄ 2 tablespoons low-sodium grainy mustard
- ◄ 2 tablespoons apple cider vinegar
- ◄ 1 tablespoon honey
- ◄ 2 garlic cloves, minced
- ◄ 1 jalapeño pepper, minced
- ◄ 3 tablespoons minced onion
- ◄ 4 (5 ounces / 142 g) low-sodium boneless, skinless chicken breasts

1. Preheat the air fryer to 370ºF (188ºC). 2. In a small bowl, stir together the tomato sauce, mustard, cider vinegar, honey, garlic, jalapeño, and onion. 3. Brush the chicken breasts with some sauce and air fry for 10 minutes. 4. Remove the air fryer basket and turn the chicken; brush with more sauce. Air fry for 5 minutes more. 5. Remove the air fryer basket and turn the chicken again; brush with more sauce. Air fry for 3 to 5 minutes more, or until the chicken reaches an internal temperature of 165ºF (74ºC) on a meat thermometer. Discard any remaining sauce. Serve immediately.

## Cilantro Lime Chicken Thighs

**Prep time: 15 minutes | Cook time: 22 minutes | Serves 4**

- ◄ 4 bone-in, skin-on chicken thighs
- ◄ 1 teaspoon baking powder
- ◄ ½ teaspoon garlic powder
- ◄ 2 teaspoons chili powder
- ◄ 1 teaspoon cumin
- ◄ 2 medium limes
- ◄ ¼ cup chopped fresh cilantro

1. Pat chicken thighs dry and sprinkle with baking powder. 2. In a small bowl, mix garlic powder, chili powder, and cumin and sprinkle evenly over thighs, gently rubbing on and under chicken skin. 3. Cut one lime in half and squeeze juice over thighs. Place chicken into the air fryer basket. 4. Adjust the temperature to 380ºF (193ºC) and roast for 22 minutes. 5. Cut other lime into four wedges for serving and garnish cooked chicken with wedges and cilantro.

## Apricot Chicken

**Prep time: 15 minutes | Cook time: 10 to 12 minutes | Serves 4**

- ◄ ⅔ cup apricot preserves
- ◄ 2 tablespoons freshly squeezed lemon juice
- ◄ 1 teaspoon soy sauce
- ◄ ¼ teaspoon salt
- ◄ ¾ cup panko bread crumbs
- ◄ 2 whole boneless, skinless chicken breasts (1 pound / 454 g each), halved
- ◄ 1 to 2 tablespoons oil

1. In a shallow bowl, stir together the apricot preserves, lemon

juice, soy sauce, and salt. Place the bread crumbs in a second shallow bowl. 2. Roll the chicken in the preserves mixture and then the bread crumbs, coating thoroughly. 3. Preheat the air fryer to 350ºF (177ºC). Line the air fryer basket with parchment paper. 4. Place the coated chicken on the parchment and spritz with oil. 5. Cook for 5 minutes. Flip the chicken, spritz it with oil, and cook for 5 to 7 minutes more until the internal temperature reaches 165ºF (74ºC) and the chicken is no longer pink inside. Let sit for 5 minutes.

## Almond-Crusted Chicken

**Prep time: 15 minutes | Cook time: 25 minutes | Serves 4**

- ◄ ¼ cup slivered almonds
- ◄ 2 (6 ounces / 170 g) boneless, skinless chicken breasts
- ◄ 2 tablespoons full-fat mayonnaise
- ◄ 1 tablespoon Dijon mustard

1. Pulse the almonds in a food processor or chop until finely chopped. Place almonds evenly on a plate and set aside. 2. Completely slice each chicken breast in half lengthwise. 3. Mix the mayonnaise and mustard in a small bowl and then coat chicken with the mixture. 4. Lay each piece of chicken in the chopped almonds to fully coat. Carefully move the pieces into the air fryer basket. 5. Adjust the temperature to 350ºF (177ºC) and air fry for 25 minutes. 6. Chicken will be done when it has reached an internal temperature of 165ºF (74ºC) or more. Serve warm.

## Curried Orange Honey Chicken

**Prep time: 10 minutes | Cook time: 16 to 19 minutes | Serves 4**

- ◄ ¾ pound (340 g) boneless, skinless chicken thighs, cut into 1-inch pieces
- ◄ 1 yellow bell pepper, cut into 1½-inch pieces
- ◄ 1 small red onion, sliced
- ◄ Olive oil for misting
- ◄ ¼ cup chicken stock
- ◄ 2 tablespoons honey
- ◄ ¼ cup orange juice
- ◄ 1 tablespoon cornstarch
- ◄ 2 to 3 teaspoons curry powder

1. Preheat the air fryer to 370ºF (188ºC). 2. Put the chicken thighs, pepper, and red onion in the air fryer basket and mist with olive oil. 3. Roast for 12 to 14 minutes or until the chicken is cooked to 165ºF (74ºC), shaking the basket halfway through cooking time. 4. Remove the chicken and vegetables from the air fryer basket and set aside. 5. In a metal bowl, combine the stock, honey, orange juice, cornstarch, and curry powder, and mix well. Add the chicken and vegetables, stir, and put the bowl in the basket. 6. Return the basket to the air fryer and roast for 2 minutes. Remove and stir, then roast for 2 to 3 minutes or until the sauce is thickened and bubbly. 7. Serve warm.

# Crunchy Chicken with Roasted Carrots

## Prep time: 10 minutes | Cook time: 22 minutes | Serves 4

- 4 bone-in, skin-on chicken thighs
- 2 carrots, cut into 2-inch pieces
- 2 tablespoons extra-virgin olive oil
- 2 teaspoons poultry spice
- 1 teaspoon sea salt, divided
- 2 teaspoons chopped fresh rosemary leaves
- Cooking oil spray
- 2 cups cooked white rice

1. Brush the chicken thighs and carrots with olive oil. Sprinkle both with the poultry spice, salt, and rosemary. 2. Insert the crisper plate into the basket and the basket into the unit. Preheat the unit by selecting AIR FRY, setting the temperature to 400ºF (204ºC), and setting the time to 3 minutes. Select START/PAUSE to begin. 3. Once the unit is preheated, spray the crisper plate with cooking oil. Place the carrots into the basket. Add the wire rack and arrange the chicken thighs on the rack. 4. Select AIR FRY, set the temperature to 400ºF (204ºC), and set the time to 20 minutes. Select START/PAUSE to begin. 5. When the cooking is complete, check the chicken temperature. If a food thermometer inserted into the chicken registers 165ºF (74ºC), remove the chicken from the air fryer, place it on a clean plate, and cover with aluminum foil to keep warm. Otherwise, resume cooking for 1 to 2 minutes longer. 6. The carrots can cook for 18 to 22 minutes and will be tender and caramelized; cooking time isn't as crucial for root vegetables. 7. Serve the chicken and carrots with the hot cooked rice.

# African Piri-Piri Chicken Drumsticks

## Prep time: 30 minutes | Cook time: 20 minutes | Serves 2

Chicken:
- 1 tablespoon chopped fresh thyme leaves
- 1 tablespoon minced fresh ginger
- 1 small shallot, finely chopped
- 2 garlic cloves, minced
- ⅓ cup piri-piri sauce or hot

sauce
- 3 tablespoons extra-virgin olive oil
- Zest and juice of 1 lemon
- 1 teaspoon smoked paprika
- ½ teaspoon kosher salt
- ½ teaspoon black pepper
- 4 chicken drumsticks

Glaze:
- 2 tablespoons butter or ghee
- 1 teaspoon chopped fresh thyme leaves
- 1 garlic clove, minced
- 1 tablespoon piri-piri sauce
- 1 tablespoon fresh lemon juice

1. For the chicken: In a small bowl, stir together all the ingredients except the chicken. Place the chicken and the marinade in a gallon-size resealable plastic bag. Seal the bag and massage to coat.

Refrigerate for at least 2 hours or up to 24 hours, turning the bag occasionally. 2. Place the chicken legs in the air fryer basket. Set the air fryer to 400ºF (204ºC) for 20 minutes, turning the chicken halfway through the cooking time. 3. Meanwhile, for the glaze: Melt the butter in a small saucepan over medium-high heat. Add the thyme and garlic. Cook, stirring, until the garlic just begins to brown, 1 to 2 minutes. Add the piri-piri sauce and lemon juice. Reduce the heat to medium-low and simmer for 1 to 2 minutes. 4. Transfer the chicken to a serving platter. Pour the glaze over the chicken. Serve immediately.

# Classic Whole Chicken

## Prep time: 5 minutes | Cook time: 50 minutes | Serves 4

- Oil, for spraying
- 1 (4 pounds / 1.8 kg) whole chicken, giblets removed
- 1 tablespoon olive oil
- 1 teaspoon paprika
- ½ teaspoon granulated garlic
- ½ teaspoon salt
- ½ teaspoon freshly ground black pepper
- ¼ teaspoon finely chopped fresh parsley, for garnish

1. Line the air fryer basket with parchment and spray lightly with oil. 2. Pat the chicken dry with paper towels. Rub it with the olive oil until evenly coated. 3. In a small bowl, mix together the paprika, garlic, salt, and black pepper and sprinkle it evenly over the chicken. 4. Place the chicken in the prepared basket, breast-side down. 5. Air fry at 360ºF (182ºC) for 30 minutes, flip, and cook for another 20 minutes, or until the internal temperature reaches 165ºF (74ºC) and the juices run clear. 6. Sprinkle with the parsley before serving.

# Cranberry Curry Chicken

## Prep time: 12 minutes | Cook time: 18 minutes | Serves 4

- 3 (5 ounces / 142 g) low-sodium boneless, skinless chicken breasts, cut into 1½-inch cubes
- 2 teaspoons olive oil
- 2 tablespoons cornstarch
- 1 tablespoon curry powder
- 1 tart apple, chopped
- ½ cup low-sodium chicken broth
- ⅓ cup dried cranberries
- 2 tablespoons freshly squeezed orange juice
- Brown rice, cooked (optional)

1. Preheat the air fryer to 380ºF (193ºC). 2. In a medium bowl, mix the chicken and olive oil. Sprinkle with the cornstarch and curry powder. Toss to coat. Stir in the apple and transfer to a metal pan. Air Fry in the air fryer for 8 minutes, stirring once during cooking. 3. Add the chicken broth, cranberries, and orange juice. Air Fry for about 10 minutes more, or until the sauce is slightly thickened and the chicken reaches an internal temperature of 165ºF (74ºC) on a meat thermometer. Serve over hot cooked brown rice, if desired.

# Chicken Croquettes with Creole Sauce

**Prep time: 30 minutes | Cook time: 10 minutes | Serves 4**

- 2 cups shredded cooked chicken
- ½ cup shredded Cheddar cheese
- 2 eggs

Creole Sauce:
- ¼ cup mayonnaise
- ¼ cup sour cream
- 1½ teaspoons Dijon mustard
- 1½ teaspoons fresh lemon

- ¼ cup finely chopped onion
- ¼ cup almond meal
- 1 tablespoon poultry seasoning
- Olive oil

  juice
- ½ teaspoon garlic powder
- ½ teaspoon Creole seasoning

1. In a large bowl, combine the chicken, Cheddar, eggs, onion, almond meal, and poultry seasoning. Stir gently until thoroughly combined. Cover and refrigerate for 30 minutes. 2. Meanwhile, to make the Creole sauce: In a small bowl, whisk together the mayonnaise, sour cream, Dijon mustard, lemon juice, garlic powder, and Creole seasoning until thoroughly combined. Cover and refrigerate until ready to serve. 3. Preheat the air fryer to 400°F (204°C). Divide the chicken mixture into 8 portions and shape into patties. 4. Working in batches if necessary, arrange the patties in a single layer in the air fryer basket and coat both sides lightly with olive oil. Pausing halfway through the cooking time to flip the patties, air fry for 10 minutes, or until lightly browned and the cheese is melted. Serve with the Creole sauce.

# Piri-Piri Chicken Thighs

**Prep time: 5 minutes | Cook time: 25 minutes | Serves 4**

- ¼ cup piri-piri sauce
- 1 tablespoon freshly squeezed lemon juice
- 2 tablespoons brown sugar, divided
- 2 cloves garlic, minced
- 1 tablespoon extra-virgin

  olive oil
- 4 bone-in, skin-on chicken thighs, each weighing approximately 7 to 8 ounces (198 to 227 g)
- ½ teaspoon cornstarch

1. To make the marinade, whisk together the piri-piri sauce, lemon juice, 1 tablespoon of brown sugar, and the garlic in a small bowl. While whisking, slowly pour in the oil in a steady stream and continue to whisk until emulsified. Using a skewer, poke holes in the chicken thighs and place them in a small glass dish. Pour the marinade over the chicken and turn the thighs to coat them with the sauce. Cover the dish and refrigerate for at least 15 minutes and up to 1 hour. 2. Preheat the air fryer to 375°F (191°C). Remove the chicken thighs from the dish, reserving the marinade, and place them skin-side down in the air fryer basket. Air fry until the internal temperature reaches 165°F (74°C), 15 to 20 minutes. 3. Meanwhile,

whisk the remaining brown sugar and the cornstarch into the marinade and microwave it on high power for 1 minute until it is bubbling and thickened to a glaze. 4. Once the chicken is cooked, turn the thighs over and brush them with the glaze. Air fry for a few additional minutes until the glaze browns and begins to char in spots. 5. Remove the chicken to a platter and serve with additional piri-piri sauce, if desired.

# Easy Chicken Nachos

**Prep time: 5 minutes | Cook time: 5 minutes | Serves 8**

- Oil, for spraying
- 3 cups shredded cooked chicken
- 1 (1 ounces / 28 g) package ranch seasoning
- ¼ cup sour cream

- 2 cups corn tortilla chips
- ⅓ cup bacon bits
- 1 cup shredded Cheddar cheese
- 1 tablespoon chopped scallions

1. Line the air fryer basket with parchment and spray lightly with oil. 2. In a small bowl, mix together the chicken, ranch seasoning, and sour cream. 3. Place the tortilla chips in the prepared basket and top with the chicken mixture. Add the bacon bits, Cheddar cheese, and scallions. 4. Air fry at 425°F (218°C) for 3 to 5 minutes, or until heated through and the cheese is melted.

# Bruschetta Chicken

**Prep time: 10 minutes | Cook time: 20 minutes | Serves 4**

Bruschetta Stuffing:
- 1 tomato, diced
- 3 tablespoons balsamic vinegar
- 1 teaspoon Italian seasoning
- 2 tablespoons chopped fresh

Chicken:
- 4 (4 ounces / 113 g) boneless, skinless chicken breasts, cut 4 slits each
- 1 teaspoon Italian seasoning

  basil
- 3 garlic cloves, minced
- 2 tablespoons extra-virgin olive oil

- Chicken seasoning or rub, to taste
- Cooking spray

1. Preheat the air fryer to 370°F (188°C). Spritz the air fryer basket with cooking spray. 2. Combine the ingredients for the bruschetta stuffing in a bowl. Stir to mix well. Set aside. 3. Rub the chicken breasts with Italian seasoning and chicken seasoning on a clean work surface. 4. Arrange the chicken breasts, slits side up, in a single layer in the air fryer basket and spritz with cooking spray. You may need to work in batches to avoid overcrowding. 5. Air fry for 7 minutes, then open the air fryer and fill the slits in the chicken with the bruschetta stuffing. Cook for another 3 minutes or until the chicken is well browned. 6. Serve immediately.

# Italian Chicken Thighs

**Prep time: 5 minutes | Cook time: 20 minutes | Serves 2**

◀ 4 bone-in, skin-on chicken thighs
◀ 2 tablespoons unsalted butter, melted
◀ 1 teaspoon dried parsley
◀ 1 teaspoon dried basil

◀ ½ teaspoon garlic powder
◀ ¼ teaspoon onion powder
◀ ¼ teaspoon dried oregano

1. Brush chicken thighs with butter and sprinkle remaining ingredients over thighs. Place thighs into the air fryer basket. 2. Adjust the temperature to 380ºF (193ºC) and roast for 20 minutes. 3. Halfway through the cooking time, flip the thighs. 4. When fully cooked, internal temperature will be at least 165ºF (74ºC) and skin will be crispy. Serve warm.

# Chicken and Broccoli Casserole

**Prep time: 5 minutes | Cook time: 20 to 25 minutes | Serves 4**

◀ ½ pound (227 g) broccoli, chopped into florets
◀ 2 cups shredded cooked chicken
◀ 4 ounces (113 g) cream cheese
◀ ⅓ cup heavy cream
◀ 1½ teaspoons Dijon mustard

◀ ½ teaspoon garlic powder
◀ Salt and freshly ground black pepper, to taste
◀ 2 tablespoons chopped fresh basil
◀ 1 cup shredded Cheddar cheese

1. Preheat the air fryer to 390ºF (199ºC). Lightly coat a casserole dish that will fit in air fryer, with olive oil and set aside. 2. Place the broccoli in a large glass bowl with 1 tablespoon of water and cover with a microwavable plate. Microwave on high for 2 to 3 minutes until the broccoli is bright green but not mushy. Drain if necessary and add to another large bowl along with the shredded chicken. 3. In the same glass bowl used to microwave the broccoli, combine the cream cheese and cream. Microwave for 30 seconds to 1 minute on high and stir until smooth. Add the mustard and garlic powder and season to taste with salt and freshly ground black pepper. Whisk until the sauce is smooth. 4. Pour the warm sauce over the broccoli and chicken mixture and then add the basil. Using a silicone spatula, gently fold the mixture until thoroughly combined. 5. Transfer the chicken mixture to the prepared casserole dish and top with the cheese. Air fry for 20 to 25 minutes until warmed through and the cheese has browned.

# Chicken Nuggets

**Prep time: 10 minutes | Cook time: 15 minutes | Serves 4**

◀ 1 pound (454 g) ground chicken thighs
◀ ½ cup shredded Mozzarella cheese
◀ 1 large egg, whisked

◀ ½ teaspoon salt
◀ ¼ teaspoon dried oregano
◀ ¼ teaspoon garlic powder

1. In a large bowl, combine all ingredients. Form mixture into twenty nugget shapes, about 2 tablespoons each. 2. Place nuggets into ungreased air fryer basket, working in batches if needed. Adjust the temperature to 375ºF (191ºC) and air fry for 15 minutes, turning nuggets halfway through cooking. Let cool 5 minutes before serving.

# Chapter 4

# Beef, Pork, and Lamb

# Chapter 5 Beef, Pork, and Lamb

## Saucy Beef Fingers

**Prep time: 30 minutes | Cook time: 14 minutes | Serves 4**

- 1½ pounds (680 g) sirloin steak
- ¼ cup red wine
- ¼ cup fresh lime juice
- 1 teaspoon garlic powder
- 1 teaspoon shallot powder
- 1 teaspoon celery seeds
- 1 teaspoon mustard seeds
- Coarse sea salt and ground black pepper, to taste
- 1 teaspoon red pepper flakes
- 2 eggs, lightly whisked
- 1 cup Parmesan cheese
- 1 teaspoon paprika

1. Place the steak, red wine, lime juice, garlic powder, shallot powder, celery seeds, mustard seeds, salt, black pepper, and red pepper in a large ceramic bowl; let it marinate for 3 hours. 2. Tenderize the cube steak by pounding with a mallet; cut into 1-inch strips. 3. In a shallow bowl, whisk the eggs. In another bowl, mix the Parmesan cheese and paprika. 4. Dip the beef pieces into the whisked eggs and coat on all sides. Now, dredge the beef pieces in the Parmesan mixture. 5. Cook at 400°F (204°C) for 14 minutes, flipping halfway through the cooking time. 6. Meanwhile, make the sauce by heating the reserved marinade in a saucepan over medium heat; let it simmer until thoroughly warmed. Serve the steak fingers with the sauce on the side. Enjoy!

## Sumptuous Pizza Tortilla Rolls

**Prep time: 10 minutes | Cook time: 6 minutes | Serves 4**

- 1 teaspoon butter
- ½ medium onion, slivered
- ½ red or green bell pepper, julienned
- 4 ounces (113 g) fresh white mushrooms, chopped
- ½ cup pizza sauce
- 8 flour tortillas
- 8 thin slices deli ham
- 24 pepperoni slices
- 1 cup shredded Mozzarella cheese
- Cooking spray

1. Preheat the air fryer to 390°F (199°C). 2. Put butter, onions, bell pepper, and mushrooms in a baking pan. Air Fry in the preheated air fryer for 3 minutes. Stir and cook 3 to 4 minutes longer until just crisp and tender. Remove pan and set aside. 3. To assemble rolls, spread about 2 teaspoons of pizza sauce on one half of each tortilla. Top with a slice of ham and 3 slices of pepperoni. Divide sautéed vegetables among tortillas and top with cheese. 4. Roll up tortillas, secure with toothpicks if needed, and spray with oil. 5. Put 4 rolls in air fryer basket and air fry for 4 minutes. Turn and air fry

4 minutes, until heated through and lightly browned. 6. Repeat step 4 to air fry remaining pizza rolls. 7. Serve immediately.

## Beef Loin with Thyme and Parsley

**Prep time: 5 minutes | Cook time: 15 minutes | Serves 4**

- 1 tablespoon butter, melted
- ¼ dried thyme
- 1 teaspoon garlic salt
- ¼ teaspoon dried parsley
- 1 pound (454 g) beef loin

1. Preheat the air fryer to 400°F (204°C). 2. In a bowl, combine the melted butter, thyme, garlic salt, and parsley. 3. Cut the beef loin into slices and generously apply the seasoned butter using a brush. Transfer to the air fryer basket. 4. Air fry the beef for 15 minutes. 5. Take care when removing it and serve hot.

## Cantonese BBQ Pork

**Prep time: 30 minutes | Cook time: 15 minutes | Serves 4**

- ¼ cup honey
- 2 tablespoons dark soy sauce
- 1 tablespoon sugar
- 1 tablespoon Shaoxing wine (rice cooking wine)
- 1 tablespoon hoisin sauce
- 2 teaspoons minced garlic
- 2 teaspoons minced fresh ginger
- 1 teaspoon Chinese five-spice powder
- 1 pound (454 g) fatty pork shoulder, cut into long, 1-inch-thick pieces

1. In a small microwave-safe bowl, combine the honey, soy sauce, sugar, wine, hoisin, garlic, ginger, and five-spice powder. Microwave in 10-second intervals, stirring in between, until the honey has dissolved. 2. Use a fork to pierce the pork slices to allow the marinade to penetrate better. Place the pork in a large bowl or resealable plastic bag and pour in half the marinade; set aside the remaining marinade to use for the sauce. Toss to coat. Marinate the pork at room temperature for 30 minutes, or cover and refrigerate for up 24 hours. 3. Place the pork in a single layer in the air fryer basket. Set the air fryer to 400°F (204°C) for 15 minutes, turning and basting the pork halfway through the cooking time. 4. While the pork is cooking, microwave the reserved marinade on high for 45 to 60 seconds, stirring every 15 seconds, to thicken it slightly to the consistency of a sauce. 5. Transfer the pork to a cutting board and let rest for 10 minutes. Brush with the sauce and serve.

## Cheesy Low-Carb Lasagna

**Prep time: 10 minutes | Cook time: 10 minutes | Serves 4**

Meat Layer:
- Extra-virgin olive oil
- 1 pound (454 g) 85% lean ground beef
- 1 cup prepared marinara sauce

Cheese Layer:
- 8 ounces (227 g) ricotta cheese
- 1 cup shredded Mozzarella cheese
- ½ cup grated Parmesan cheese

- ¼ cup diced celery
- ¼ cup diced red onion
- ½ teaspoon minced garlic
- Kosher salt and black pepper, to taste

- 2 large eggs
- 1 teaspoon dried Italian seasoning, crushed
- ½ teaspoon each minced garlic, garlic powder, and black pepper

1. For the meat layer: Grease a cake pan with 1 teaspoon olive oil. 2. In a large bowl, combine the ground beef, marinara, celery, onion, garlic, salt, and pepper. Place the seasoned meat in the pan. 3. Place the pan in the air fryer basket. Set the air fryer to 375°F (191°C) for 10 minutes. 4. Meanwhile, for the cheese layer: In a medium bowl, combine the ricotta, half the Mozzarella, the Parmesan, lightly beaten eggs, Italian seasoning, minced garlic, garlic powder, and pepper. Stir until well blended. 5. At the end of the cooking time, spread the cheese mixture over the meat mixture. Sprinkle with the remaining ½ cup Mozzarella. Set the air fryer to 375°F (191°C) for 10 minutes, or until the cheese is browned and bubbling. 6. At the end of the cooking time, use a meat thermometer to ensure the meat has reached an internal temperature of 160°F (71°C). 7. Drain the fat and liquid from the pan. Let stand for 5 minutes before serving.

## Beef Egg Rolls

**Prep time: 15 minutes | Cook time: 12 minutes | Makes 8 egg rolls**

- ½ chopped onion
- 2 garlic cloves, chopped
- ½ packet taco seasoning
- Salt and ground black pepper, to taste
- 1 pound (454 g) lean ground beef

- ½ can cilantro lime rotel
- 16 egg roll wrappers
- 1 cup shredded Mexican cheese
- 1 tablespoon olive oil
- 1 teaspoon cilantro

1. Preheat the air fryer to 400°F (205°C). 2. Add onions and garlic to a skillet, cooking until fragrant. Then add taco seasoning, pepper, salt, and beef, cooking until beef is broke up into tiny pieces and cooked thoroughly. 3. Add rotel and stir well. 4. Lay out egg wrappers and brush with a touch of water to soften a bit. 5. Load wrappers with beef filling and add cheese to each. 6. Fold diagonally to close and use water to secure edges. 7. Brush filled egg wrappers with olive oil and add to the air fryer. 8. Air fry 8 minutes, flip, and air fry for another 4 minutes. 9. Serve sprinkled with cilantro.

## German Rouladen-Style Steak

**Prep time: 20 minutes | Cook time: 15 minutes | Serves 4**

Onion Sauce:
- 2 medium onions, cut into ½-inch-thick slices
- Kosher salt and black pepper, to taste

Rouladen:
- ¼ cup Dijon mustard
- 1 pound (454 g) flank or skirt steak, ¼ to ½ inch thick

- ½ cup sour cream
- 1 tablespoon tomato paste
- 2 teaspoons chopped fresh parsley

- 1 teaspoon black pepper
- 4 slices bacon
- ¼ cup chopped fresh parsley

1. For the sauce: In a small bowl, mix together the onions with salt and pepper to taste. Place the onions in the air fryer basket. Set the air fryer to 400°F (204°C) for 6 minutes, or until the onions are softened and golden brown. 2. Set aside half of the onions to use in the rouladen. Place the rest in a small bowl and add the sour cream, tomato paste, parsley, ½ teaspoon salt, and ½ teaspoon pepper. Stir until well combined, adding 1 to 2 tablespoons of water, if necessary, to thin the sauce slightly. Set the sauce aside. 3. For the rouladen: Evenly spread the mustard over the meat. Sprinkle with the pepper. Top with the bacon slices, reserved onions, and parsley. Starting at the long end, roll up the steak as tightly as possible, ending seam side down. Use 2 or 3 wooden toothpicks to hold the roll together. Using a sharp knife, cut the roll in half so that it better fits in the air fryer basket. 4. Place the steak, seam side down, in the air fryer basket. Set the air fryer to 400°F (204°C) for 9 minutes. Use a meat thermometer to ensure the steak has reached an internal temperature of 145°F (63°C). (It is critical to not overcook flank steak, so as to not toughen the meat.) 5. Let the steak rest for 10 minutes before cutting into slices. Serve with the sauce.

## Cajun Bacon Pork Loin Fillet

**Prep time: 30 minutes | Cook time: 20 minutes | Serves 6**

- 1½ pounds (680 g) pork loin fillet or pork tenderloin
- 3 tablespoons olive oil
- 2 tablespoons Cajun spice

- mix
- Salt, to taste
- 6 slices bacon
- Olive oil spray

1. Cut the pork in half so that it will fit in the air fryer basket. 2. Place both pieces of meat in a resealable plastic bag. Add the oil, Cajun seasoning, and salt to taste, if using. Seal the bag and massage to coat all of the meat with the oil and seasonings. Marinate in the refrigerator for at least 1 hour or up to 24 hours. 3. Remove the pork from the bag and wrap 3 bacon slices around each piece. Spray the air fryer basket with olive oil spray. Place the meat in the air fryer. Set the air fryer to 350°F (177°C) for 15 minutes. Increase the temperature to 400°F (204°C) for 5 minutes. Use a meat thermometer to ensure the meat has reached an internal temperature of 145°F (63°C). 4. Let the meat rest for 10 minutes. Slice into 6 medallions and serve.

# Smoky Pork Tenderloin

## Prep time: 5 minutes | Cook time: 19 to 22 minutes | Serves 6

- ◄ 1½ pounds (680 g) pork tenderloin
- ◄ 1 tablespoon avocado oil
- ◄ 1 teaspoon chili powder
- ◄ 1 teaspoon smoked paprika
- ◄ 1 teaspoon garlic powder
- ◄ 1 teaspoon sea salt
- ◄ 1 teaspoon freshly ground black pepper

1. Pierce the tenderloin all over with a fork and rub the oil all over the meat. 2. In a small dish, stir together the chili powder, smoked paprika, garlic powder, salt, and pepper. 3. Rub the spice mixture all over the tenderloin. 4. Set the air fryer to 400ºF (204ºC). Place the pork in the air fryer basket and air fry for 10 minutes. Flip the tenderloin and cook for 9 to 12 minutes more, until an instant-read thermometer reads at least 145ºF (63ºC). 5. Allow the tenderloin to rest for 5 minutes, then slice and serve.

# Spinach and Beef Braciole

## Prep time: 25 minutes | Cook time: 1 hour 32 minutes | Serves 4

- ◄ ½ onion, finely chopped
- ◄ 1 teaspoon olive oil
- ◄ ⅓ cup red wine
- ◄ 2 cups crushed tomatoes
- ◄ 1 teaspoon Italian seasoning
- ◄ ½ teaspoon garlic powder
- ◄ ¼ teaspoon crushed red pepper flakes
- ◄ 2 tablespoons chopped fresh parsley
- ◄ 2 top round steaks (about 1½ pounds / 680 g)
- ◄ salt and freshly ground black pepper
- ◄ 2 cups fresh spinach, chopped
- ◄ 1 clove minced garlic
- ◄ ½ cup roasted red peppers, julienned
- ◄ ½ cup grated pecorino cheese
- ◄ ¼ cup pine nuts, toasted and roughly chopped
- ◄ 2 tablespoons olive oil

1. Preheat the air fryer to 400ºF (204ºC). 2. Toss the onions and olive oil together in a baking pan or casserole dish. Air fry at 400ºF (204ºC) for 5 minutes, stirring a couple times during the cooking process. Add the red wine, crushed tomatoes, Italian seasoning, garlic powder, red pepper flakes and parsley and stir. Cover the pan tightly with aluminum foil, lower the air fryer temperature to 350ºF (177ºC) and continue to air fry for 15 minutes. 3. While the sauce is simmering, prepare the beef. Using a meat mallet, pound the beef until it is ¼-inch thick. Season both sides of the beef with salt and pepper. Combine the spinach, garlic, red peppers, pecorino cheese, pine nuts and olive oil in a medium bowl. Season with salt and freshly ground black pepper. Disperse the mixture over the steaks. Starting at one of the short ends, roll the beef around the filling, tucking in the sides as you roll to ensure the filling is completely enclosed. Secure the beef rolls with toothpicks. 4. Remove the baking pan with the sauce from the air fryer and set it aside. Preheat the air fryer to 400ºF (204ºC). 5. Brush or spray the beef rolls with a little olive oil and air fry at 400ºF (204ºC) for 12 minutes, rotating the beef during the cooking process for even browning. When the beef is browned, submerge the rolls into the sauce in the baking pan, cover the pan with foil and return it to the air fryer. Reduce the temperature of the air fryer to 250ºF (121ºC) and air fry for 60 minutes. 6. Remove the beef rolls from the sauce. Cut each roll into slices and serve, ladling some sauce overtop.

# Hoisin BBQ Pork Chops

## Prep time: 5 minutes | Cook time: 22 minutes | Serves 2 to 3

- ◄ 3 tablespoons hoisin sauce
- ◄ ¼ cup honey
- ◄ 1 tablespoon soy sauce
- ◄ 3 tablespoons rice vinegar
- ◄ 2 tablespoons brown sugar
- ◄ 1½ teaspoons grated fresh ginger
- ◄ 1 to 2 teaspoons Sriracha sauce, to taste
- ◄ 2 to 3 bone-in center cut pork chops, 1-inch thick (about 1¼ pounds / 567 g)
- ◄ Chopped scallions, for garnish

1. Combine the hoisin sauce, honey, soy sauce, rice vinegar, brown sugar, ginger, and Sriracha sauce in a small saucepan. Whisk the ingredients together and bring the mixture to a boil over medium-high heat on the stovetop. Reduce the heat and simmer the sauce until it has reduced in volume and thickened slightly, about 10 minutes. 2. Preheat the air fryer to 400ºF (204ºC). 3. Place the pork chops into the air fryer basket and pour half the hoisin BBQ sauce over the top. Air fry for 6 minutes. Then, flip the chops over, pour the remaining hoisin BBQ sauce on top and air fry for 5 to 6 more minutes, depending on the thickness of the pork chops. The internal temperature of the pork chops should be 155ºF (68ºC) when tested with an instant read thermometer. 4. Let the pork chops rest for 5 minutes before serving. You can spoon a little of the sauce from the bottom drawer of the air fryer over the top if desired. Sprinkle with chopped scallions and serve.

# Simple Ground Beef with Zucchini

## Prep time: 5 minutes | Cook time: 12 minutes | Serves 4

- ◄ 1½ pounds (680 g) ground beef
- ◄ 1 pound (454 g) chopped zucchini
- ◄ 2 tablespoons extra-virgin olive oil
- ◄ 1 teaspoon dried oregano
- ◄ 1 teaspoon dried basil
- ◄ 1 teaspoon dried rosemary
- ◄ 2 tablespoons fresh chives, chopped

1. Preheat the air fryer to 400ºF (204ºC). 2. In a large bowl, combine all the ingredients, except for the chives, until well blended. 3. Place the beef and zucchini mixture in the baking pan. Air fry for 12 minutes, or until the beef is browned and the zucchini is tender. 4. Divide the beef and zucchini mixture among four serving dishes. Top with fresh chives and serve hot.

# Provolone Stuffed Beef and Pork Meatballs

**Prep time: 15 minutes | Cook time: 12 minutes | Serves 4 to 6**

- ◄ 1 tablespoon olive oil
- ◄ 1 small onion, finely chopped
- ◄ 1 to 2 cloves garlic, minced
- ◄ ¾ pound (340 g) ground beef
- ◄ ¾ pound (340 g) ground pork
- ◄ ¾ cup bread crumbs
- ◄ ¼ cup grated Parmesan cheese
- ◄ ¼ cup finely chopped fresh parsley
- ◄ ½ teaspoon dried oregano
- ◄ 1½ teaspoons salt
- ◄ Freshly ground black pepper, to taste
- ◄ 2 eggs, lightly beaten
- ◄ 5 ounces (142 g) sharp or aged provolone cheese, cut into 1-inch cubes

1. Preheat a skillet over medium-high heat. Add the oil and cook the onion and garlic until tender, but not browned. 2. Transfer the onion and garlic to a large bowl and add the beef, pork, bread crumbs, Parmesan cheese, parsley, oregano, salt, pepper and eggs. Mix well until all the ingredients are combined. Divide the mixture into 12 evenly sized balls. Make one meatball at a time, by pressing a hole in the meatball mixture with the finger and pushing a piece of provolone cheese into the hole. Mold the meat back into a ball, enclosing the cheese. 3. Preheat the air fryer to 380ºF (193ºC). 4. Working in two batches, transfer six of the meatballs to the air fryer basket and air fry for 12 minutes, shaking the basket and turning the meatballs twice during the cooking process. Repeat with the remaining 6 meatballs. Serve warm.

# Italian Steak Rolls

**Prep time: 30 minutes | Cook time: 9 minutes | Serves 4**

- ◄ 1 tablespoon vegetable oil
- ◄ 2 cloves garlic, minced
- ◄ 2 teaspoons dried Italian seasoning
- ◄ 1 teaspoon kosher salt
- ◄ 1 teaspoon black pepper
- ◄ 1 pound (454 g) flank or skirt steak, ¼ to ½ inch
- thick
- ◄ 1 (10 ounces / 283 g) package frozen spinach, thawed and squeezed dry
- ◄ ½ cup diced jarred roasted red pepper
- ◄ 1 cup shredded Mozzarella cheese

1. In a large bowl, combine the oil, garlic, Italian seasoning, salt, and pepper. Whisk to combine. Add the steak to the bowl, turning to ensure the entire steak is covered with the seasonings. Cover and marinate at room temperature for 30 minutes or in the refrigerator for up to 24 hours. 2. Lay the steak on a flat surface. Spread the spinach evenly over the steak, leaving a ¼-inch border at the edge. Evenly top each steak with the red pepper and cheese. 3. Starting at a long end, roll up the steak as tightly as possible, ending seam side down. Use 2 or 3 wooden toothpicks to hold the roll together. Using a sharp knife, cut the roll in half so that it better fits in the air fryer basket. 4. Place the steak roll, seam side down, in the air fryer basket. Set the air fryer to 400ºF (204ºC) for 9 minutes. Use a meat thermometer to ensure the steak has reached an internal temperature of 145ºF (63ºC). (It is critical to not overcook flank steak, so as to not toughen the meat.) 5. Let the steak rest for 10 minutes before cutting into slices to serve.

# Korean Beef Tacos

**Prep time: 30 minutes | Cook time: 12 minutes | Serves 6**

- ◄ 2 tablespoons gochujang (Korean red chile paste)
- ◄ 2 cloves garlic, minced
- ◄ 2 teaspoons minced fresh ginger
- ◄ 2 tablespoons toasted sesame oil
- ◄ 1 tablespoon soy sauce
- ◄ 2 tablespoons sesame seeds
- ◄ 2 teaspoons sugar
- ◄ ½ teaspoon kosher salt
- ◄ 1½ pounds (680 g) thinly sliced beef (chuck, rib eye, or sirloin)
- ◄ 1 medium red onion, sliced
- ◄ 12 (6-inch) flour tortillas, warmed; or lettuce leaves
- ◄ ½ cup chopped green onions
- ◄ ¼ cup chopped fresh cilantro (optional)
- ◄ ½ cup kimchi (optional)

1. In a small bowl, combine the gochujang, garlic, ginger, sesame oil, soy sauce, sesame seeds, sugar, and salt. Whisk until well combined. Place the beef and red onion in a resealable plastic bag and pour the marinade over. Seal the bag and massage to coat all of the meat and onion. Marinate at room temperature for 30 minutes or in the refrigerator for up to 24 hours. 2. Place the meat and onion in the air fryer basket, leaving behind as much of the marinade as possible; discard the marinade. Set the air fryer to 400ºF (204ºC) for 12 minutes, shaking halfway through the cooking time. 3. To serve, place meat and onion in the tortillas. Top with the green onions and the cilantro and kimchi, if using, and serve.

# Greek Lamb Rack

**Prep time: 5 minutes | Cook time: 10 minutes | Serves 4**

- ◄ ¼ cup freshly squeezed lemon juice
- ◄ 1 teaspoon oregano
- ◄ 2 teaspoons minced fresh rosemary
- ◄ 1 teaspoon minced fresh
- thyme
- ◄ 2 tablespoons minced garlic
- ◄ Salt and freshly ground black pepper, to taste
- ◄ 2 to 4 tablespoons olive oil
- ◄ 1 lamb rib rack (7 to 8 ribs)

1. Preheat the air fryer to 360ºF (182ºC). 2. In a small mixing bowl, combine the lemon juice, oregano, rosemary, thyme, garlic, salt, pepper, and olive oil and mix well. 3. Rub the mixture over the lamb, covering all the meat. Put the rack of lamb in the air fryer. Roast for 10 minutes. Flip the rack halfway through. 4. After 10 minutes, measure the internal temperature of the rack of lamb reaches at least 145ºF (63ºC). 5. Serve immediately.

# Kielbasa Sausage with Pineapple and Bell Peppers

**Prep time: 15 minutes | Cook time: 10 minutes | Serves 2 to 4**

- ◄ ¾ pound (340 g) kielbasa sausage, cut into ½-inch slices
- ◄ 1 (8-ounce / 227-g) can pineapple chunks in juice, drained
- ◄ 1 cup bell pepper chunks
- ◄ 1 tablespoon barbecue seasoning
- ◄ 1 tablespoon soy sauce
- ◄ Cooking spray

1. Preheat the air fryer to 390ºF (199ºC). Spritz the air fryer basket with cooking spray. 2. Combine all the ingredients in a large bowl. Toss to mix well. 3. Pour the sausage mixture in the preheated air fryer. 4. Air fry for 10 minutes or until the sausage is lightly browned and the bell pepper and pineapple are soft. Shake the basket halfway through. Serve immediately.

# Blue Cheese Steak Salad

**Prep time: 30 minutes | Cook time: 22 minutes | Serves 4**

- ◄ 2 tablespoons balsamic vinegar
- ◄ 2 tablespoons red wine vinegar
- ◄ 1 tablespoon Dijon mustard
- ◄ 1 tablespoon Swerve
- ◄ 1 teaspoon minced garlic
- ◄ Sea salt and freshly ground black pepper, to taste
- ◄ ¾ cup extra-virgin olive oil
- ◄ 1 pound (454 g) boneless
- sirloin steak
- ◄ Avocado oil spray
- ◄ 1 small red onion, cut into ¼-inch-thick rounds
- ◄ 6 ounces (170 g) baby spinach
- ◄ ½ cup cherry tomatoes, halved
- ◄ 3 ounces (85 g) blue cheese, crumbled

1. In a blender, combine the balsamic vinegar, red wine vinegar, Dijon mustard, Swerve, and garlic. Season with salt and pepper and process until smooth. With the blender running, drizzle in the olive oil. Process until well combined. Transfer to a jar with a tight-fitting lid, and refrigerate until ready to serve (it will keep for up to 2 weeks). 2. Season the steak with salt and pepper and let sit at room temperature for at least 45 minutes, time permitting. 3. Set the air fryer to 400ºF (204ºC). Spray the steak with oil and place it in the air fryer basket. Air fry for 6 minutes. Flip the steak and spray it with more oil. Air fry for 6 minutes more for medium-rare or until the steak is done to your liking. 4. Transfer the steak to a plate, tent with a piece of aluminum foil, and allow it to rest. 5. Spray the onion slices with oil and place them in the air fryer basket. Cook at 400ºF (204ºC) for 5 minutes. Flip the onion slices and spray them with more oil. Air fry for 5 minutes more. 6. Slice the steak diagonally into thin strips. Place the spinach, cherry tomatoes, onion slices, and steak in a large bowl. Toss with the desired amount of dressing. Sprinkle with crumbled blue cheese and serve.

# Pork Cutlets with Aloha Salsa

**Prep time: 20 minutes | Cook time: 7 to 9 minutes | Serves 4**

Aloha Salsa:
- ◄ 1 cup fresh pineapple, chopped in small pieces
- ◄ ¼ cup red onion, finely chopped
- ◄ ¼ cup green or red bell pepper, chopped
- ◄ ½ teaspoon ground cinnamon
- ◄ 1 teaspoon low-sodium soy sauce
- ◄ ⅛ teaspoon crushed red pepper
- ◄ ⅛ teaspoon ground black
- pepper
- ◄ 2 eggs
- ◄ 2 tablespoons milk
- ◄ ¼ cup flour
- ◄ ¼ cup panko bread crumbs
- ◄ 4 teaspoons sesame seeds
- ◄ 1 pound (454 g) boneless, thin pork cutlets (⅜- to ½-inch thick)
- ◄ lemon pepper and salt
- ◄ ¼ cup cornstarch
- ◄ Oil for misting or cooking spray

1. In a medium bowl, stir together all ingredients for salsa. Cover and refrigerate while cooking pork. 2. Preheat the air fryer to 390ºF (199ºC). 3. Beat together eggs and milk in shallow dish. 4. In another shallow dish, mix together the flour, panko, and sesame seeds. 5. Sprinkle pork cutlets with lemon pepper and salt to taste. Most lemon pepper seasoning contains salt, so go easy adding extra. 6. Dip pork cutlets in cornstarch, egg mixture, and then panko coating. Spray both sides with oil or cooking spray. 7. Cook cutlets for 3 minutes. Turn cutlets over, spraying both sides, and continue cooking for 4 to 6 minutes or until well done. 8. Serve fried cutlets with salsa on the side.

# Cheese Pork Chops

**Prep time: 15 minutes | Cook time: 9 to 14 minutes | Serves 4**

- ◄ 2 large eggs
- ◄ ½ cup finely grated Parmesan cheese
- ◄ ½ cup finely ground blanched almond flour or finely crushed pork rinds
- ◄ 1 teaspoon paprika
- ◄ ½ teaspoon dried oregano
- ◄ ½ teaspoon garlic powder
- ◄ Salt and freshly ground black pepper, to taste
- ◄ 1¼ pounds (567 g) (1-inch-thick) boneless pork chops
- ◄ Avocado oil spray

1. Beat the eggs in a shallow bowl. In a separate bowl, combine the Parmesan cheese, almond flour, paprika, oregano, garlic powder, and salt and pepper to taste. 2. Dip the pork chops into the eggs, then coat them with the Parmesan mixture, gently pressing the coating onto the meat. Spray the breaded pork chops with oil. 3. Set the air fryer to 400ºF (204ºC). Place the pork chops in the air fryer basket in a single layer, working in batches if necessary. Cook for 6 minutes. Flip the chops and spray them with more oil. Cook for another 3 to 8 minutes, until an instant-read thermometer reads 145ºF (63ºC). 4. Allow the pork chops to rest for at least 5 minutes, then serve.

# Bacon and Cheese Stuffed Pork Chops

**Prep time: 10 minutes | Cook time: 12 minutes | Serves 4**

- ½ ounce (14 g) plain pork rinds, finely crushed
- ½ cup shredded sharp Cheddar cheese
- 4 slices cooked sugar-free bacon, crumbled
- 4 (4 ounces / 113 g) boneless pork chops
- ½ teaspoon salt
- ¼ teaspoon ground black pepper

1. In a small bowl, mix pork rinds, Cheddar, and bacon. 2. Make a 3-inch slit in the side of each pork chop and stuff with ¼ pork rind mixture. Sprinkle each side of pork chops with salt and pepper. 3. Place pork chops into ungreased air fryer basket, stuffed side up. Adjust the temperature to 400ºF (204ºC) and air fry for 12 minutes. Pork chops will be browned and have an internal temperature of at least 145ºF (63ºC) when done. Serve warm.

# Pork Schnitzel with Dill Sauce

**Prep time: 5 minutes | Cook time: 24 minutes | Serves 4 to 6**

- 6 boneless, center cut pork chops (about 1½ pounds / 680 g)
- ½ cup flour
- 1½ teaspoons salt
- Freshly ground black pepper, to taste
- 2 eggs
- ½ cup milk
- 1½ cups toasted fine bread crumbs
- 1 teaspoon paprika
- 3 tablespoons butter, melted
- 2 tablespoons vegetable or olive oil
- lemon wedges
- Dill Sauce:
- 1 cup chicken stock
- 1½ tablespoons cornstarch
- ⅓ cup sour cream
- 1½ tablespoons chopped fresh dill
- Salt and pepper, to taste

1. Trim the excess fat from the pork chops and pound each chop with a meat mallet between two pieces of plastic wrap until they are ½-inch thick. 2. Set up a dredging station. Combine the flour, salt, and black pepper in a shallow dish. Whisk the eggs and milk together in a second shallow dish. Finally, combine the bread crumbs and paprika in a third shallow dish. 3. Dip each flattened pork chop in the flour. Shake off the excess flour and dip each chop into the egg mixture. Finally dip them into the bread crumbs and press the bread crumbs onto the meat firmly. Place each finished chop on a baking sheet until they are all coated. 4. Preheat the air fryer to 400ºF (204ºC). 5. Combine the melted butter and the oil in a small bowl and lightly brush both sides of the coated pork chops. Do not brush the chops too heavily or the breading will not be as crispy. 6. Air fry one schnitzel at a time for 4 minutes, turning it over halfway through the cooking time. Hold the cooked schnitzels warm on a baking pan in a 170ºF (77ºC) oven while you finish air frying the rest. 7. While the schnitzels are cooking, whisk the chicken stock and cornstarch together in a small saucepan over medium-high heat on the stovetop. Bring the mixture to a boil and simmer for 2 minutes. Remove the saucepan from heat and whisk in the sour cream. Add the chopped fresh dill and season with salt and pepper. 8. Transfer the pork schnitzel to a platter and serve with dill sauce and lemon wedges.

# Blackened Cajun Pork Roast

**Prep time: 20 minutes | Cook time: 33 minutes | Serves 4**

- 2 pounds (907 g) bone-in pork loin roast
- 2 tablespoons oil
- ¼ cup Cajun seasoning
- ½ cup diced onion
- ½ cup diced celery
- ½ cup diced green bell pepper
- 1 tablespoon minced garlic

1. Cut 5 slits across the pork roast. Spritz it with oil, coating it completely. Evenly sprinkle the Cajun seasoning over the pork roast. 2. In a medium bowl, stir together the onion, celery, green bell pepper, and garlic until combined. Set aside. 3. Preheat the air fryer to 360ºF (182ºC). Line the air fryer basket with parchment paper. 4. Place the pork roast on the parchment and spritz with oil. 5. Cook for 5 minutes. Flip the roast and cook for 5 minutes more. Continue to flip and cook in 5-minute increments for a total cook time of 20 minutes. 6. Increase the air fryer temperature to 390ºF (199ºC). 7. Cook the roast for 8 minutes more and flip. Add the vegetable mixture to the basket and cook for a final 5 minutes. Let the roast sit for 5 minutes before serving.

# Lemony Pork Loin Chop Schnitzel

**Prep time: 15 minutes | Cook time: 15 minutes | Serves 4**

- 4 thin boneless pork loin chops
- 2 tablespoons lemon juice
- ½ cup flour
- ¼ teaspoon marjoram
- 1 teaspoon salt
- 1 cup panko breadcrumbs
- 2 eggs
- Lemon wedges, for serving
- Cooking spray

1. Preheat the air fryer to 390ºF (199ºC) and spritz with cooking spray. 2. On a clean work surface, drizzle the pork chops with lemon juice on both sides. 3. Combine the flour with marjoram and salt on a shallow plate. Pour the breadcrumbs on a separate shallow dish. Beat the eggs in a large bowl. 4. Dredge the pork chops in the flour, then dunk in the beaten eggs to coat well. Shake the excess off and roll over the breadcrumbs. 5. Arrange the chops in the preheated air fryer and spritz with cooking spray. Air fry for 15 minutes or until the chops are golden and crispy. Flip the chops halfway through. Squeeze the lemon wedges over the fried chops and serve immediately.

## Spicy Flank Steak with Zhoug

**Prep time: 30 minutes | Cook time: 8 minutes | Serves 4**

Marinade and Steak:
- ½ cup dark beer or orange juice
- ¼ cup fresh lemon juice
- 3 cloves garlic, minced
- 2 tablespoons extra-virgin olive oil
- 2 tablespoons Sriracha
- 2 tablespoons brown sugar
- 2 teaspoons ground cumin
- 2 teaspoons smoked paprika
- 1 tablespoon kosher salt
- 1 teaspoon black pepper
- 1½ pounds (680 g) flank steak, trimmed and cut into 3 pieces

Zhoug:
- 1 cup packed fresh cilantro leaves
- 2 cloves garlic, peeled
- 2 jalapeño or serrano chiles, stemmed and coarsely chopped
- ½ teaspoon ground cumin
- ¼ teaspoon ground coriander
- ¼ teaspoon kosher salt
- 2 to 4 tablespoons extra-virgin olive oil

1. For the marinade and steak: In a small bowl, whisk together the beer, lemon juice, garlic, olive oil, Sriracha, brown sugar, cumin, paprika, salt, and pepper. Place the steak in a large resealable plastic bag. Pour the marinade over the steak, seal the bag, and massage the steak to coat. Marinate in the refrigerator for 1 hour or up to 24 hours, turning the bag occasionally. 2. Meanwhile, for the zhoug: In a food processor, combine the cilantro, garlic, jalapeños, cumin, coriander, and salt. Process until finely chopped. Add 2 tablespoons olive oil and pulse to form a loose paste, adding up to 2 tablespoons more olive oil if needed. Transfer the zhoug to a glass container. Cover and store in the refrigerator until 30 minutes before serving if marinating more than 1 hour. 3. Remove the steak from the marinade and discard the marinade. Place the steak in the air fryer basket and set the air fryer to 400°F (204°C) for 8 minutes. Use a meat thermometer to ensure the steak has reached an internal temperature of 150°F / 66°C (for medium). 4. Transfer the steak to a cutting board and let rest for 5 minutes. Slice the steak across the grain and serve with the zhoug.

## Mexican Pork Chops

**Prep time: 5 minutes | Cook time: 15 minutes | Serves 2**

- ¼ teaspoon dried oregano
- 1½ teaspoons taco seasoning mix
- 2 (4 ounces / 113 g) boneless
- pork chops
- 2 tablespoons unsalted butter, divided

1. Preheat the air fryer to 400°F (204°C). 2. Combine the dried oregano and taco seasoning in a small bowl and rub the mixture into the pork chops. Brush the chops with 1 tablespoon butter. 3. In the air fryer, air fry the chops for 15 minutes, turning them over halfway through to air fry on the other side. 4. When the chops are a brown color, check the internal temperature has reached 145°F

(63°C) and remove from the air fryer. Serve with a garnish of remaining butter.

## Pork Meatballs

**Prep time: 10 minutes | Cook time: 12 minutes | Makes 18 meatballs**

- 1 pound (454 g) ground pork
- 1 large egg, whisked
- ½ teaspoon garlic powder
- ½ teaspoon salt
- ½ teaspoon ground ginger
- ¼ teaspoon crushed red pepper flakes
- 1 medium scallion, trimmed and sliced

1. Combine all ingredients in a large bowl. Spoon out 2 tablespoons mixture and roll into a ball. Repeat to form eighteen meatballs total. 2. Place meatballs into ungreased air fryer basket. Adjust the temperature to 400°F (204°C) and air fry for 12 minutes, shaking the basket three times throughout cooking. Meatballs will be browned and have an internal temperature of at least 145°F (63°C) when done. Serve warm.

## Chicken Fried Steak with Cream Gravy

**Prep time: 5 minutes | Cook time: 10 minutes | Serves 4**

- 4 small thin cube steaks (about 1 pound / 454 g)
- ½ teaspoon salt
- ½ teaspoon freshly ground black pepper
- ¼ teaspoon garlic powder
- 1 egg, lightly beaten
- 1 cup crushed pork rinds (about 3 ounces / 85 g)
- Cream Gravy:
- ½ cup heavy cream
- 2 ounces (57 g) cream cheese
- ¼ cup bacon grease
- 2 to 3 tablespoons water
- 2 to 3 dashes Worcestershire sauce
- Salt and freshly ground black pepper, to taste

1. Preheat the air fryer to 400°F (204°C). 2. Working one at a time, place the steak between two sheets of parchment paper and use a meat mallet to pound to an even thickness. 3. In a small bowl, combine the salt, pepper, and garlic power. Season both sides of each steak with the mixture. 4. Place the egg in a small shallow dish and the pork rinds in another small shallow dish. Dip each steak first in the egg wash, followed by the pork rinds, pressing lightly to form an even coating. Working in batches if necessary, arrange the steaks in a single layer in the air fryer basket. Air fry for 10 minutes until crispy and cooked through. 5. To make the cream gravy: In a heavy-bottomed pot, warm the cream, cream cheese, and bacon grease over medium heat, whisking until smooth. Lower the heat if the mixture begins to boil. Continue whisking as you slowly add the water, 1 tablespoon at a time, until the sauce reaches the desired consistency. Season with the Worcestershire sauce and salt and pepper to taste. Serve over the chicken fried steaks.

# Roast Beef with Horseradish Cream

**Prep time: 5 minutes | Cook time: 35 to 45 minutes | Serves 6**

- 2 pounds (907 g) beef roast top round or eye of round
- 1 tablespoon salt
- 2 teaspoons garlic powder

Horseradish Cream:
- ⅓ cup heavy cream
- ⅓ cup sour cream
- ⅓ cup prepared horseradish
- 2 teaspoons fresh lemon
- 1 teaspoon freshly ground black pepper
- 1 teaspoon dried thyme

- juice
- Salt and freshly ground black pepper, to taste

1. Preheat the air fryer to 400ºF (204ºC). 2. Season the beef with the salt, garlic powder, black pepper, and thyme. Place the beef fat-side down in the basket of the air fryer and lightly coat with olive oil. Pausing halfway through the cooking time to turn the meat, air fry for 35 to 45 minutes, until a thermometer inserted into the thickest part indicates the desired doneness, 125ºF (52ºC) (rare) to 150ºF (66ºC) (medium). Let the beef rest for 10 minutes before slicing. 3. To make the horseradish cream: In a small bowl, combine the heavy cream, sour cream, horseradish, and lemon juice. Whisk until thoroughly combined. Season to taste with salt and freshly ground black pepper. Serve alongside the beef.

# Pork and Pinto Bean Gorditas

**Prep time: 20 minutes | Cook time: 21 minutes | Serves 4**

- 1 pound (454 g) lean ground pork
- 2 tablespoons chili powder
- 2 tablespoons ground cumin
- 1 teaspoon dried oregano
- 2 teaspoons paprika
- 1 teaspoon garlic powder
- ½ cup water
- 1 (15 ounces / 425 g) can pinto beans, drained and rinsed
- ½ cup taco sauce
- Salt and freshly ground
- black pepper, to taste
- 2 cups grated Cheddar cheese
- 5 (12-inch) flour tortillas
- 4 (8-inch) crispy corn tortilla shells
- 4 cups shredded lettuce
- 1 tomato, diced
- ⅓ cup sliced black olives
- Sour cream, for serving
- Tomato salsa, for serving
- Cooking spray

1. Preheat the air fryer to 400ºF (204ºC). Spritz the air fryer basket with cooking spray. 2. Put the ground pork in the air fryer basket and air fry at 400ºF (204ºC) for 10 minutes, stirring a few times to gently break up the meat. Combine the chili powder, cumin, oregano, paprika, garlic powder and water in a small bowl. Stir the spice mixture into the browned pork. Stir in the beans and taco sauce and air fry for an additional minute. Transfer the pork mixture to a bowl. Season with salt and freshly ground black pepper. 3.

Sprinkle ½ cup of the grated cheese in the center of the flour tortillas, leaving a 2-inch border around the edge free of cheese and filling. Divide the pork mixture among the four tortillas, placing it on top of the cheese. Put a crunchy corn tortilla on top of the pork and top with shredded lettuce, diced tomatoes, and black olives. Cut the remaining flour tortilla into 4 quarters. These quarters of tortilla will serve as the bottom of the gordita. Put one quarter tortilla on top of each gordita and fold the edges of the bottom flour tortilla up over the sides, enclosing the filling. While holding the seams down, brush the bottom of the gordita with olive oil and place the seam side down on the countertop while you finish the remaining three gorditas. 4. Adjust the temperature to 380ºF (193ºC). 5. Air fry one gordita at a time. Transfer the gordita carefully to the air fryer basket, seam side down. Brush or spray the top tortilla with oil and air fry for 5 minutes. Carefully turn the gordita over and air fry for an additional 4 to 5 minutes until both sides are browned. When finished air frying all four gorditas, layer them back into the air fryer for an additional minute to make sure they are all warm before serving with sour cream and salsa.

# Bo Luc Lac

**Prep time: 50 minutes | Cook time: 8 minutes | Serves 4**

For the Meat:
- 2 teaspoons soy sauce
- 4 garlic cloves, minced
- 1 teaspoon kosher salt
- 2 teaspoons sugar
- ¼ teaspoon ground black pepper

For the Salad:
- 1 head Bibb lettuce, leaves separated and torn into large pieces
- ¼ cup fresh mint leaves
- ½ cup halved grape tomatoes
- ½ red onion, halved and thinly sliced
- 2 tablespoons apple cider

For Serving:
- Lime wedges, for garnish
- Coarse salt and freshly

- 1 teaspoon toasted sesame oil
- 1½ pounds (680 g) top sirloin steak, cut into 1-inch cubes
- Cooking spray

- vinegar
- 1 garlic clove, minced
- 2 teaspoons sugar
- ¼ teaspoon kosher salt
- ¼ teaspoon ground black pepper
- 2 tablespoons vegetable oil

- cracked black pepper, to taste

1. Combine the ingredients for the meat, except for the steak, in a large bowl. Stir to mix well. 2. Dunk the steak cubes in the bowl and press to coat. Wrap the bowl in plastic and marinate under room temperature for at least 30 minutes. 3. Preheat the air fryer to 450ºF (232ºC). Spritz the air fryer basket with cooking spray. 4. Discard the marinade and transfer the steak cubes in the preheated air fryer basket. You need to air fry in batches to avoid overcrowding. 5. Air fry for 4 minutes or until the steak cubes are lightly browned but still have a little pink. Shake the basket halfway through the cooking time. 6. Meanwhile, combine the ingredients for the salad in a separate large bowl. Toss to mix well. 7. Pour the salad in a large serving bowl and top with the steak cubes. Squeeze the lime wedges over and sprinkle with salt and black pepper before serving.

## Sausage and Pork Meatballs

**Prep time: 15 minutes | Cook time: 8 to 12 minutes | Serves 8**

- ◀ 1 large egg
- ◀ 1 teaspoon gelatin
- ◀ 1 pound (454 g) ground pork
- ◀ ½ pound (227 g) Italian sausage, casings removed, crumbled
- ◀ ⅓ cup Parmesan cheese
- ◀ ¼ cup finely diced onion
- ◀ 1 tablespoon tomato paste
- ◀ 1 teaspoon minced garlic
- ◀ 1 teaspoon dried oregano
- ◀ ¼ teaspoon red pepper flakes
- ◀ Sea salt and freshly ground black pepper, to taste
- ◀ Keto-friendly marinara sauce, for serving

1. Beat the egg in a small bowl and sprinkle with the gelatin. Allow to sit for 5 minutes. 2. In a large bowl, combine the ground pork, sausage, Parmesan, onion, tomato paste, garlic, oregano, and red pepper flakes. Season with salt and black pepper. 3. Stir the gelatin mixture, then add it to the other ingredients and, using clean hands, mix to ensure that everything is well combined. Form into 1½-inch round meatballs. 4. Set the air fryer to 400ºF (204ºC). Place the meatballs in the air fryer basket in a single layer, cooking in batches as needed. Air fry for 5 minutes. Flip and cook for 3 to 7 minutes more, or until an instant-read thermometer reads 160ºF (71ºC).

## London Broil with Herb Butter

**Prep time: 30 minutes | Cook time: 20 to 25 minutes | Serves 4**

- ◀ 1½ pounds (680 g) London broil top round steak
- ◀ ¼ cup olive oil
- ◀ 2 tablespoons balsamic

Herb Butter:
- ◀ 6 tablespoons unsalted butter, softened
- ◀ 1 tablespoon chopped fresh parsley
- ◀ ¼ teaspoon salt

- vinegar
- ◀ 1 tablespoon Worcestershire sauce
- ◀ 4 cloves garlic, minced

- ◀ ¼ teaspoon dried ground rosemary or thyme
- ◀ ¼ teaspoon garlic powder
- ◀ Pinch of red pepper flakes

1. Place the beef in a gallon-size resealable bag. In a small bowl, whisk together the olive oil, balsamic vinegar, Worcestershire sauce, and garlic. Pour the marinade over the beef, massaging gently to coat, and seal the bag. Let sit at room temperature for an hour or refrigerate overnight. 2. To make the herb butter: In a small bowl, mix the butter with the parsley, salt, rosemary, garlic powder, and red pepper flakes until smooth. Cover and refrigerate until ready to use. 3. Preheat the air fryer to 400ºF (204ºC). 4. Remove the beef from the marinade (discard the marinade) and place the beef in the air fryer basket. Pausing halfway through the cooking time to turn the meat, air fry for 20 to 25 minutes, until a thermometer inserted into the thickest part indicates the desired doneness, 125ºF / 52ºC (rare) to 150ºF / 66ºC (medium). Let the beef rest for 10 minutes before slicing. Serve topped with the herb butter.

## Rack of Lamb with Pistachio Crust

**Prep time: 10 minutes | Cook time: 19 minutes | Serves 2**

- ◀ ½ cup finely chopped pistachios
- ◀ 3 tablespoons panko bread crumbs
- ◀ 1 teaspoon chopped fresh rosemary
- ◀ 2 teaspoons chopped fresh
- oregano
- ◀ Salt and freshly ground black pepper, to taste
- ◀ 1 tablespoon olive oil
- ◀ 1 rack of lamb, bones trimmed of fat and frenched
- ◀ 1 tablespoon Dijon mustard

1. Preheat the air fryer to 380ºF (193ºC). 2. Combine the pistachios, bread crumbs, rosemary, oregano, salt and pepper in a small bowl. (This is a good job for your food processor if you have one.) Drizzle in the olive oil and stir to combine. 3. Season the rack of lamb with salt and pepper on all sides and transfer it to the air fryer basket with the fat side facing up. Air fry the lamb for 12 minutes. Remove the lamb from the air fryer and brush the fat side of the lamb rack with the Dijon mustard. Coat the rack with the pistachio mixture, pressing the bread crumbs onto the lamb with your hands and rolling the bottom of the rack in any of the crumbs that fall off. 4. Return the rack of lamb to the air fryer and air fry for another 3 to 7 minutes or until an instant read thermometer reads 140ºF (60ºC) for medium. Add or subtract a couple of minutes for lamb that is more or less well cooked. (Your time will vary depending on how big the rack of lamb is.) 5. Let the lamb rest for at least 5 minutes. Then, slice into chops and serve.

## Easy Beef Satay

**Prep time: 30 minutes | Cook time: 8 minutes | Serves 4**

- ◀ 1 pound (454 g) beef flank steak, thinly sliced into long strips
- ◀ 2 tablespoons vegetable oil
- ◀ 1 tablespoon fish sauce
- ◀ 1 tablespoon soy sauce
- ◀ 1 tablespoon minced fresh ginger
- ◀ 1 tablespoon minced garlic
- ◀ 1 tablespoon sugar
- ◀ 1 teaspoon Sriracha or other hot sauce
- ◀ 1 teaspoon ground coriander
- ◀ ½ cup chopped fresh cilantro
- ◀ ¼ cup chopped roasted peanuts

1. Place the beef strips in a large bowl or resealable plastic bag. Add the vegetable oil, fish sauce, soy sauce, ginger, garlic, sugar, Sriracha, coriander, and ¼ cup of the cilantro to the bag. Seal and massage the bag to thoroughly coat and combine. Marinate at room temperature for 30 minutes, or cover and refrigerate for up to 24 hours. 2. Using tongs, remove the beef strips from the bag and lay them flat in the air fryer basket, minimizing overlap as much as possible; discard the marinade. Set the air fryer to 400ºF (204ºC) for 8 minutes, turning the beef strips halfway through the cooking time. 3. Transfer the meat to a serving platter. Sprinkle with the remaining ¼ cup cilantro and the peanuts. Serve.

# Beef Burger

**Prep time: 20 minutes | Cook time: 12 minutes | Serves 4**

◄ 1¼ pounds (567 g) lean ground beef
◄ 1 tablespoon coconut aminos
◄ 1 teaspoon Dijon mustard
◄ A few dashes of liquid smoke
◄ 1 teaspoon shallot powder
◄ 1 clove garlic, minced

◄ ½ teaspoon cumin powder
◄ ¼ cup scallions, minced
◄ ⅓ teaspoon sea salt flakes
◄ ⅓ teaspoon freshly cracked mixed peppercorns
◄ 1 teaspoon celery seeds
◄ 1 teaspoon parsley flakes

1. Mix all of the above ingredients in a bowl; knead until everything is well incorporated. 2. Shape the mixture into four patties. Next, make a shallow dip in the center of each patty to prevent them puffing up during air frying. 3. Spritz the patties on all sides using nonstick cooking spray. Cook approximately 12 minutes at 360°F (182°C). 4. Check for doneness, an instant-read thermometer should read 160°F (71°C). Bon appétit!

# Mexican-Style Shredded Beef

**Prep time: 5 minutes | Cook time: 35 minutes | Serves 6**

◄ 1 (2 pounds / 907 g) beef chuck roast, cut into 2-inch cubes
◄ 1 teaspoon salt

◄ ½ teaspoon ground black pepper
◄ ½ cup no-sugar-added chipotle sauce

1. In a large bowl, sprinkle beef cubes with salt and pepper and toss to coat. Place beef into ungreased air fryer basket. Adjust the temperature to 400°F (204°C) and air fry for 30 minutes, shaking the basket halfway through cooking. Beef will be done when internal temperature is at least 160°F (71°C). 2. Place cooked beef into a large bowl and shred with two forks. Pour in chipotle sauce and toss to coat. 3. Return beef to air fryer basket for an additional 5 minutes at 400°F (204°C) to crisp with sauce. Serve warm.

# Sausage and Peppers

**Prep time: 7 minutes | Cook time: 35 minutes | Serves 4**

◄ Oil, for spraying
◄ 2 pounds (907 g) hot or sweet Italian sausage links, cut into thick slices
◄ 4 large bell peppers of any color, seeded and cut into slices

◄ 1 onion, thinly sliced
◄ 1 tablespoon olive oil
◄ 1 tablespoon chopped fresh parsley
◄ 1 teaspoon dried oregano
◄ 1 teaspoon dried basil
◄ 1 teaspoon balsamic vinegar

1. Line the air fryer basket with parchment and spray lightly with oil. 2. In a large bowl, combine the sausage, bell peppers, and onion. 3. In a small bowl, whisk together the olive oil, parsley, oregano, basil, and balsamic vinegar. Pour the mixture over the sausage and peppers and toss until evenly coated. 4. Using a slotted spoon, transfer the mixture to the prepared basket, taking care to drain out as much excess liquid as possible. 5. Air fry at 350°F (177°C) for 20 minutes, stir, and cook for another 15 minutes, or until the sausage is browned and the juices run clear.

# Ham with Sweet Potatoes

**Prep time: 20 minutes | Cook time: 15 to 17 minutes | Serves 4**

◄ 1 cup freshly squeezed orange juice
◄ ½ cup packed light brown sugar
◄ 1 tablespoon Dijon mustard
◄ ½ teaspoon salt
◄ ½ teaspoon freshly ground

black pepper
◄ 3 sweet potatoes, cut into small wedges
◄ 2 ham steaks (8 ounces / 227 g each), halved
◄ 1 to 2 tablespoons oil

1. In a large bowl, whisk the orange juice, brown sugar, Dijon, salt, and pepper until blended. Toss the sweet potato wedges with the brown sugar mixture. 2. Preheat the air fryer to 400°F (204°C). Line the air fryer basket with parchment paper and spritz with oil. 3. Place the sweet potato wedges on the parchment. 4. Cook for 10 minutes. 5. Place ham steaks on top of the sweet potatoes and brush everything with more of the orange juice mixture. 6. Cook for 3 minutes. Flip the ham and cook or 2 to 4 minutes more until the sweet potatoes are soft and the glaze has thickened. Cut the ham steaks in half to serve.

# Cinnamon-Beef Kofta

**Prep time: 10 minutes | Cook time: 13 minutes per batch | Makes 12 koftas**

◄ 1½ pounds (680 g) lean ground beef
◄ 1 teaspoon onion powder
◄ ¾ teaspoon ground cinnamon
◄ ¾ teaspoon ground dried turmeric

◄ 1 teaspoon ground cumin
◄ ¾ teaspoon salt
◄ ¼ teaspoon cayenne
◄ 12 (3½- to 4-inch-long) cinnamon sticks
◄ Cooking spray

1. Preheat the air fryer to 375°F (191°C). Spritz the air fryer basket with cooking spray. 2. Combine all the ingredients, except for the cinnamon sticks, in a large bowl. Toss to mix well. 3. Divide and shape the mixture into 12 balls, then wrap each ball around each cinnamon stick and leave a quarter of the length uncovered. 4. Arrange the beef-cinnamon sticks in the preheated air fryer and spritz with cooking spray. Work in batches to avoid overcrowding. 5. Air fry for 13 minutes or until the beef is browned. Flip the sticks halfway through. 6. Serve immediately.

# Chapter 6
## Vegetables and Sides

# Chapter 6 Vegetables and Sides

## Broccoli Tots

**Prep time: 15 minutes | Cook time: 10 minutes | Makes 24 tots**

- ◀ 2 cups broccoli florets (about ½ pound / 227 g broccoli crowns)
- ◀ 1 egg, beaten
- ◀ ⅛ teaspoon onion powder
- ◀ ¼ teaspoon salt
- ◀ ⅛ teaspoon pepper
- ◀ 2 tablespoons grated Parmesan cheese
- ◀ ¼ cup panko bread crumbs
- ◀ Oil for misting

1. Steam broccoli for 2 minutes. Rinse in cold water, drain well, and chop finely. 2. In a large bowl, mix broccoli with all other ingredients except the oil. 3. Scoop out small portions of mixture and shape into 24 tots. Lay them on a cookie sheet or wax paper as you work. 4. Spray tots with oil and place in air fryer basket in single layer. 5. Air fry at 390ºF (199ºC) for 5 minutes. Shake basket and spray with oil again. Cook 5 minutes longer or until browned and crispy.

## Gorgonzola Mushrooms with Horseradish Mayo

**Prep time: 15 minutes | Cook time: 10 minutes | Serves 5**

- ◀ ½ cup bread crumbs
- ◀ 2 cloves garlic, pressed
- ◀ 2 tablespoons chopped fresh coriander
- ◀ ⅓ teaspoon kosher salt
- ◀ ½ teaspoon crushed red pepper flakes
- ◀ 1½ tablespoons olive oil
- ◀ 20 medium mushrooms,
- stems removed
- ◀ ½ cup grated Gorgonzola cheese
- ◀ ¼ cup low-fat mayonnaise
- ◀ 1 teaspoon prepared horseradish, well-drained
- ◀ 1 tablespoon finely chopped fresh parsley

1. Preheat the air fryer to 380ºF (193ºC). 2. Combine the bread crumbs together with the garlic, coriander, salt, red pepper, and olive oil. 3. Take equal-sized amounts of the bread crumb mixture and use them to stuff the mushroom caps. Add the grated Gorgonzola on top of each. 4. Put the mushrooms in a baking pan and transfer to the air fryer. 5. Air fry for 10 minutes, ensuring the stuffing is warm throughout. 6. In the meantime, prepare the horseradish mayo. Mix the mayonnaise, horseradish and parsley. 7. When the mushrooms are ready, serve with the mayo.

## Spinach and Cheese Stuffed Tomatoes

**Prep time: 20 minutes | Cook time: 15 minutes | Serves 2**

- ◀ 4 ripe beefsteak tomatoes
- ◀ ¾ teaspoon black pepper
- ◀ ½ teaspoon kosher salt
- ◀ 1 (10 ounces / 283 g) package frozen chopped spinach, thawed and squeezed dry
- ◀ 1 (5.2-ounce / 147-g) package garlic-and-herb Boursin cheese
- ◀ 3 tablespoons sour cream
- ◀ ½ cup finely grated Parmesan cheese

1. Cut the tops off the tomatoes. Using a small spoon, carefully remove and discard the pulp. Season the insides with ½ teaspoon of the black pepper and ¼ teaspoon of the salt. Invert the tomatoes onto paper towels and allow to drain while you make the filling. 2. Meanwhile, in a medium bowl, combine the spinach, Boursin cheese, sour cream, ¼ cup of the Parmesan, and the remaining ¼ teaspoon salt and ¼ teaspoon pepper. Stir until ingredients are well combined. Divide the filling among the tomatoes. Top with the remaining ¼ cup Parmesan. 3. Place the tomatoes in the air fryer basket. Set the air fryer to 350ºF (177ºC) for 15 minutes, or until the filling is hot.

## Dinner Rolls

**Prep time: 10 minutes | Cook time: 12 minutes | Serves 6**

- ◀ 1 cup shredded Mozzarella cheese
- ◀ 1 ounce (28 g) full-fat cream cheese
- ◀ 1 cup blanched finely ground
- almond flour
- ◀ ¼ cup ground flaxseed
- ◀ ½ teaspoon baking powder
- ◀ 1 large egg

1. Place Mozzarella, cream cheese, and almond flour in a large microwave-safe bowl. Microwave for 1 minute. Mix until smooth. 2. Add flaxseed, baking powder, and egg until fully combined and smooth. Microwave an additional 15 seconds if it becomes too firm. 3. Separate the dough into six pieces and roll into balls. Place the balls into the air fryer basket. 4. Adjust the temperature to 320ºF (160ºC) and air fry for 12 minutes. 5. Allow rolls to cool completely before serving.

## Golden Garlicky Mushrooms

### Prep time: 10 minutes | Cook time: 10 minutes | Serves 4

- 6 small mushrooms
- 1 tablespoon bread crumbs
- 1 tablespoon olive oil
- 1 ounce (28 g) onion, peeled and diced
- 1 teaspoon parsley
- 1 teaspoon garlic purée
- Salt and ground black pepper, to taste

1. Preheat the air fryer to 350ºF (177ºC). 2. Combine the bread crumbs, oil, onion, parsley, salt, pepper and garlic in a bowl. Cut out the mushrooms' stalks and stuff each cap with the crumb mixture. 3. Air fry in the air fryer for 10 minutes. 4. Serve hot.

## Bacon Potatoes and Green Beans

### Prep time: 10 minutes | Cook time: 25 minutes | Serves 4

- Oil, for spraying
- 2 pounds (907 g) medium russet potatoes, quartered
- ¾ cup bacon bits
- 10 ounces (283 g) fresh
- green beans
- 1 teaspoon salt
- ½ teaspoon freshly ground black pepper

1. Line the air fryer basket with parchment and spray lightly with oil. 2. Place the potatoes in the prepared basket. Top with the bacon bits and green beans. Sprinkle with the salt and black pepper and spray liberally with oil. 3. Air fry at 355ºF (179ºC) for 25 minutes, stirring after 12 minutes and spraying with oil, until the potatoes are easily pierced with a fork.

## Easy Potato Croquettes

### Prep time: 15 minutes | Cook time: 15 minutes | Serves 10

- ¼ cup nutritional yeast
- 2 cups boiled potatoes, mashed
- 1 flax egg
- 1 tablespoon flour
- 2 tablespoons chopped
- chives
- Salt and ground black pepper, to taste
- 2 tablespoons vegetable oil
- ¼ cup bread crumbs

1. Preheat the air fryer to 400ºF (204ºC). 2. In a bowl, combine the nutritional yeast, potatoes, flax egg, flour, and chives. Sprinkle with salt and pepper as desired. 3. In a separate bowl, mix the vegetable oil and bread crumbs to achieve a crumbly consistency. 4. Shape the potato mixture into small balls and dip each one into the bread crumb mixture. 5. Put the croquettes inside the air fryer and air fry for 15 minutes, ensuring the croquettes turn golden brown. 6. Serve immediately.

## Scalloped Potatoes

### Prep time: 5 minutes | Cook time: 20 minutes | Serves 4

- 2 cup sliced frozen potatoes, thawed
- 3 cloves garlic, minced
- Pinch salt
- Freshly ground black pepper, to taste
- ¾ cup heavy cream

1. Preheat the air fryer to 380ºF (193ºC). 2. Toss the potatoes with the garlic, salt, and black pepper in a baking pan until evenly coated. Pour the heavy cream over the top. 3. Place the baking pan in the air fryer basket and Air Fry for 15 minutes, or until the potatoes are tender and top is golden brown. Check for doneness and Air Fry for another 5 minutes as needed. 4. Serve hot.

## Corn Croquettes

### Prep time: 10 minutes | Cook time: 12 to 14 minutes | Serves 4

- ½ cup leftover mashed potatoes
- 2 cups corn kernels (if frozen, thawed, and well drained)
- ¼ teaspoon onion powder
- ⅛ teaspoon ground black pepper
- ¼ teaspoon salt
- ½ cup panko bread crumbs
- Oil for misting or cooking spray

1. Place the potatoes and half the corn in food processor and pulse until corn is well chopped. 2. Transfer mixture to large bowl and stir in remaining corn, onion powder, pepper and salt. 3. Shape mixture into 16 balls. 4. Roll balls in panko crumbs, mist with oil or cooking spray, and place in air fryer basket. 5. Air fry at 360ºF (182ºC) for 12 to 14 minutes, until golden brown and crispy.

## Butter and Garlic Fried Cabbage

### Prep time: 5 minutes | Cook time: 9 minutes | Serves 2

- Oil, for spraying
- ½ head cabbage, cut into bite-size pieces
- 2 tablespoons unsalted butter, melted
- 1 teaspoon granulated garlic
- ½ teaspoon coarse sea salt
- ¼ teaspoon freshly ground black pepper

1. Line the air fryer basket with parchment and spray lightly with oil. 2. In a large bowl, mix together the cabbage, butter, garlic, salt, and black pepper until evenly coated. 3. Transfer the cabbage to the prepared basket and spray lightly with oil. 4. Air fry at 375ºF (191ºC) for 5 minutes, toss, and cook for another 3 to 4 minutes, or until lightly crispy.

## Bacon-Wrapped Asparagus

**Prep time: 10 minutes | Cook time: 10 minutes | Serves 4**

◄ 8 slices reduced-sodium bacon, cut in half
◄ 16 thick (about 1 pound /

454 g) asparagus spears, trimmed of woody ends

1. Preheat the air fryer to 350ºF (177ºC). 2. Wrap a half piece of bacon around the center of each stalk of asparagus. 3. Working in batches, if necessary, arrange seam-side down in a single layer in the air fryer basket. Air fry for 10 minutes until the bacon is crisp and the stalks are tender.

## Mushrooms with Goat Cheese

**Prep time: 10 minutes | Cook time: 10 minutes | Serves 4**

◄ 3 tablespoons vegetable oil
◄ 1 pound (454 g) mixed mushrooms, trimmed and sliced
◄ 1 clove garlic, minced
◄ ¼ teaspoon dried thyme

◄ ½ teaspoon black pepper
◄ 4 ounces (113 g) goat cheese, diced
◄ 2 teaspoons chopped fresh thyme leaves (optional)

1. In a baking pan, combine the oil, mushrooms, garlic, dried thyme, and pepper. Stir in the goat cheese. Place the pan in the air fryer basket. Set the air fryer to 400ºF (204ºC) for 10 minutes, stirring halfway through the cooking time. 2. Sprinkle with fresh thyme, if desired.

## Mole-Braised Cauliflower

**Prep time: 10 minutes | Cook time: 15 minutes | Serves 2**

◄ 8 ounces (227 g) medium cauliflower florets
◄ 1 tablespoon vegetable oil
◄ Kosher salt and freshly ground black pepper, to taste
◄ 1½ cups vegetable broth
◄ 2 tablespoons New Mexico chile powder (or regular chili powder)
◄ 2 tablespoons salted roasted

peanuts
◄ 1 tablespoon toasted sesame seeds, plus more for garnish
◄ 1 tablespoon finely chopped golden raisins
◄ 1 teaspoon kosher salt
◄ 1 teaspoon dark brown sugar
◄ ½ teaspoon dried oregano
◄ ¼ teaspoon cayenne pepper
◄ ⅛ teaspoon ground cinnamon

1. In a large bowl, toss the cauliflower with the oil and season with salt and black pepper. Transfer to a cake pan. Place the pan in the air fryer and roast at 375ºF (191ºC) until the cauliflower is tender and lightly browned at the edges, about 10 minutes, stirring halfway through. 2. Meanwhile, in a small blender, combine the broth, chile powder, peanuts, sesame seeds, raisins, salt, brown sugar, oregano, cayenne, and cinnamon and purée until smooth. Pour into a small saucepan or skillet and bring to a simmer over medium heat, then cook until reduced by half, 3 to 5 minutes. 3. Pour the hot mole sauce over the cauliflower in the pan, stir to coat, then cook until the sauce is thickened and lightly charred on the cauliflower, about 5 minutes more. Sprinkle with more sesame seeds and serve warm.

## Air-Fried Okra

**Prep time: 10 minutes | Cook time: 10 minutes | Serves 4**

◄ 1 egg
◄ ½ cup almond milk
◄ ½ cup crushed pork rinds
◄ ¼ cup grated Parmesan cheese
◄ ¼ cup almond flour

◄ 1 teaspoon garlic powder
◄ ¼ teaspoon freshly ground black pepper
◄ ½ pound (227 g) fresh okra, stems removed and chopped into 1-inch slices

1. Preheat the air fryer to 400ºF (204ºC). 2. In a shallow bowl, whisk together the egg and milk. 3. In a second shallow bowl, combine the pork rinds, Parmesan, almond flour, garlic powder, and black pepper. 4. Working with a few slices at a time, dip the okra into the egg mixture followed by the crumb mixture. Press lightly to ensure an even coating. 5. Working in batches if necessary, arrange the okra in a single layer in the air fryer basket and spray lightly with olive oil. Pausing halfway through the cooking time to turn the okra, air fry for 10 minutes until tender and golden brown. Serve warm.

## Citrus Sweet Potatoes and Carrots

**Prep time: 5 minutes | Cook time: 20 to 25 minutes | Serves 4**

◄ 2 large carrots, cut into 1-inch chunks
◄ 1 medium sweet potato, peeled and cut into 1-inch cubes
◄ ½ cup chopped onion

◄ 2 garlic cloves, minced
◄ 2 tablespoons honey
◄ 1 tablespoon freshly squeezed orange juice
◄ 2 teaspoons butter, melted

1. Insert the crisper plate into the basket and the basket into the unit. Preheat the unit by selecting ROAST, setting the temperature to 400ºF (204ºC), and setting the time to 3 minutes. Select START/PAUSE to begin. 2. In a 6-by-2-inch round pan, toss together the carrots, sweet potato, onion, garlic, honey, orange juice, and melted butter to coat. 3. Once the unit is preheated, place the pan into the basket. 4. Select ROAST, set the temperature to 400ºF (204ºC), and set the time to 25 minutes. Select START/PAUSE to begin. 5. After 15 minutes, remove the basket and shake the vegetables. Reinsert the basket to resume cooking. After 5 minutes, if the vegetables are tender and glazed, they are done. If not, resume cooking. 6. When the cooking is complete, serve immediately.

## Cheesy Loaded Broccoli

**Prep time: 10 minutes | Cook time: 10 minutes | Serves 2**

- 3 cups fresh broccoli florets
- 1 tablespoon coconut oil
- ¼ teaspoon salt
- ½ cup shredded sharp Cheddar cheese
- ¼ cup sour cream
- 4 slices cooked sugar-free bacon, crumbled
- 1 medium scallion, trimmed and sliced on the bias

1. Place broccoli into ungreased air fryer basket, drizzle with coconut oil, and sprinkle with salt. Adjust the temperature to 350ºF (177ºC) and roast for 8 minutes. Shake basket three times during cooking to avoid burned spots. 2. Sprinkle broccoli with Cheddar and cook for 2 additional minutes. When done, cheese will be melted and broccoli will be tender. 3. Serve warm in a large serving dish, topped with sour cream, crumbled bacon, and scallion slices.

## Cauliflower with Lime Juice

**Prep time: 10 minutes | Cook time: 7 minutes | Serves 4**

- 2 cups chopped cauliflower florets
- 2 tablespoons coconut oil, melted
- 2 teaspoons chili powder
- ½ teaspoon garlic powder
- 1 medium lime
- 2 tablespoons chopped cilantro

1. In a large bowl, toss cauliflower with coconut oil. Sprinkle with chili powder and garlic powder. Place seasoned cauliflower into the air fryer basket. 2. Adjust the temperature to 350ºF (177ºC) and set the timer for 7 minutes. 3. Cauliflower will be tender and begin to turn golden at the edges. Place into a serving bowl. 4. Cut the lime into quarters and squeeze juice over cauliflower. Garnish with cilantro.

## Potato with Creamy Cheese

**Prep time: 5 minutes | Cook time: 15 minutes | Serves 2**

- 2 medium potatoes
- 1 teaspoon butter
- 3 tablespoons sour cream
- 1 teaspoon chives
- 1½ tablespoons grated Parmesan cheese

1. Preheat the air fryer to 350ºF (177ºC). 2. Pierce the potatoes with a fork and boil them in water until they are cooked. 3. Transfer to the air fryer and air fry for 15 minutes. 4. In the meantime, combine the sour cream, cheese and chives in a bowl. Cut the potatoes halfway to open them up and fill with the butter and sour cream mixture. 5. Serve immediately.

## Corn on the Cob

**Prep time: 5 minutes | Cook time: 12 to 15 minutes | Serves 4**

- 2 large ears fresh corn
- Olive oil for misting
- Salt, to taste (optional)

1. Shuck corn, remove silks, and wash. 2. Cut or break each ear in half crosswise. 3. Spray corn with olive oil. 4. Air fry at 390ºF (199ºC) for 12 to 15 minutes or until browned as much as you like. 5. Serve plain or with coarsely ground salt.

## Air Fried Potatoes with Olives

**Prep time: 15 minutes | Cook time: 40 minutes | Serves 1**

- 1 medium russet potatoes, scrubbed and peeled
- 1 teaspoon olive oil
- ¼ teaspoon onion powder
- ⅛ teaspoon salt
- Dollop of butter
- Dollop of cream cheese
- 1 tablespoon Kalamata olives
- 1 tablespoon chopped chives

1. Preheat the air fryer to 400ºF (204ºC). 2. In a bowl, coat the potatoes with the onion powder, salt, olive oil, and butter. 3. Transfer to the air fryer and air fry for 40 minutes, turning the potatoes over at the halfway point. 4. Take care when removing the potatoes from the air fryer and serve with the cream cheese, Kalamata olives and chives on top.

## Lemon-Garlic Mushrooms

**Prep time: 10 minutes | Cook time: 10 to 15 minutes | Serves 6**

- 12 ounces (340 g) sliced mushrooms
- 1 tablespoon avocado oil
- Sea salt and freshly ground black pepper, to taste
- 3 tablespoons unsalted butter
- 1 teaspoon minced garlic
- 1 teaspoon freshly squeezed lemon juice
- ½ teaspoon red pepper flakes
- 2 tablespoons chopped fresh parsley

1. Place the mushrooms in a medium bowl and toss with the oil. Season to taste with salt and pepper. 2. Place the mushrooms in a single layer in the air fryer basket. Set your air fryer to 375ºF (191ºC) and roast for 10 to 15 minutes, until the mushrooms are tender. 3. While the mushrooms cook, melt the butter in a small pot or skillet over medium-low heat. Stir in the garlic and cook for 30 seconds. Remove the pot from the heat and stir in the lemon juice and red pepper flakes. 4. Toss the mushrooms with the lemon-garlic butter and garnish with the parsley before serving.

# Burger Bun for One

## Prep time: 2 minutes | Cook time: 5 minutes | Serves 1

◄ 2 tablespoons salted butter, melted
◄ ¼ cup blanched finely ground almond flour
◄ ¼ teaspoon baking powder
◄ ⅛ teaspoon apple cider vinegar
◄ 1 large egg, whisked

1. Pour butter into an ungreased ramekin. Add flour, baking powder, and vinegar to ramekin and stir until combined. Add egg and stir until batter is mostly smooth. 2. Place ramekin into air fryer basket. Adjust the temperature to 350ºF (177ºC) and Air Fry for 5 minutes. When done, the center will be firm and the top slightly browned. Let cool, about 5 minutes, then remove from ramekin and slice in half. Serve.

# Parmesan-Thyme Butternut Squash

## Prep time: 15 minutes | Cook time: 20 minutes | Serves 4

◄ 2½ cups butternut squash, cubed into 1-inch pieces (approximately 1 medium)
◄ 2 tablespoons olive oil
◄ ¼ teaspoon salt
◄ ¼ teaspoon garlic powder
◄ ¼ teaspoon black pepper
◄ 1 tablespoon fresh thyme
◄ ¼ cup grated Parmesan

1. Preheat the air fryer to 360°F(182ºC). 2. In a large bowl, combine the cubed squash with the olive oil, salt, garlic powder, pepper, and thyme until the squash is well coated. 3. Pour this mixture into the air fryer basket, and roast for 10 minutes. Stir and roast another 8 to 10 minutes more. 4. Remove the squash from the air fryer and toss with freshly grated Parmesan before serving.

# Roasted Sweet Potatoes

## Prep time: 10 minutes | Cook time: 25 minutes | Serves 4

◄ Cooking oil spray
◄ 2 sweet potatoes, peeled and cut into 1-inch cubes
◄ 1 tablespoon extra-virgin olive oil
◄ Pinch salt
◄ Freshly ground black pepper, to taste
◄ ½ teaspoon dried thyme
◄ ½ teaspoon dried marjoram
◄ ¼ cup grated Parmesan cheese

1. Insert the crisper plate into the basket and the basket into the unit. Preheat the unit by selecting ROAST, setting the temperature to 330ºF (166ºC), and setting the time to 3 minutes. Select START/PAUSE to begin. 2. Once the unit is preheated, spray the crisper plate with cooking oil. Put the sweet potato cubes into the basket and drizzle with olive oil. Toss gently to coat. Sprinkle with the salt, pepper, thyme, and marjoram and toss again. 3. Select ROAST, set the temperature to 330ºF (166ºC), and set the time to 25 minutes. Select START/PAUSE to begin. 4. After 10 minutes, remove the basket and shake the potatoes. Reinsert the basket to resume cooking. After another 10 minutes, remove the basket and shake the potatoes one more time. Sprinkle evenly with the Parmesan cheese. Reinsert the basket to resume cooking. 5. When the cooking is complete, the potatoes should be tender. Serve immediately.

# "Faux-Tato" Hash

## Prep time: 10 minutes | Cook time: 12 minutes | Serves 4

◄ 1 pound (454 g) radishes, ends removed, quartered
◄ ¼ medium yellow onion, peeled and diced
◄ ½ medium green bell pepper, seeded and chopped
◄ 2 tablespoons salted butter, melted
◄ ½ teaspoon garlic powder
◄ ¼ teaspoon ground black pepper

1. In a large bowl, combine radishes, onion, and bell pepper. Toss with butter. 2. Sprinkle garlic powder and black pepper over mixture in bowl, then spoon into ungreased air fryer basket. 3. Adjust the temperature to 320ºF (160ºC) and air fry for 12 minutes. Shake basket halfway through cooking. Radishes will be tender when done. Serve warm.

# Lemony Broccoli

## Prep time: 10 minutes | Cook time: 9 to 14 minutes per batch | Serves 4

◄ 1 large head broccoli, rinsed and patted dry
◄ 2 teaspoons extra-virgin olive oil
◄ 1 tablespoon freshly squeezed lemon juice
◄ Olive oil spray

1. Cut off the broccoli florets and separate them. You can use the stems, too; peel the stems and cut them into 1-inch chunks. 2. Insert the crisper plate into the basket and the basket into the unit. Preheat the unit by selecting ROAST, setting the temperature to 390ºF (199ºC), and setting the time to 3 minutes. Select START/PAUSE to begin. 3. In a large bowl, toss together the broccoli, olive oil, and lemon juice until coated. 4. Once the unit is preheated, spray the crisper plate with olive oil. Working in batches, place half the broccoli into the basket. 5. Select ROAST, set the temperature to 390ºF (199ºC), and set the time to 14 minutes. Select START/PAUSE to begin. 6. After 5 minutes, remove the basket and shake the broccoli. Reinsert the basket to resume cooking. Check the broccoli after 5 minutes. If it is crisp-tender and slightly brown around the edges, it is done. If not, resume cooking. 7. When the cooking is complete, transfer the broccoli to a serving bowl. Repeat steps 5 and 6 with the remaining broccoli. Serve immediately.

## Grits Casserole

**Prep time: 5 minutes | Cook time: 28 to 30 minutes | Serves 4**

- ◀ 10 fresh asparagus spears, cut into 1-inch pieces
- ◀ 2 cups cooked grits, cooled to room temperature
- ◀ 1 egg, beaten
- ◀ 2 teaspoons Worcestershire sauce
- ◀ ½ teaspoon garlic powder
- ◀ ¼ teaspoon salt
- ◀ 2 slices provolone cheese (about 1½ ounces / 43 g)
- ◀ Oil for misting or cooking spray

1. Mist asparagus spears with oil and air fry at 390ºF (199ºC) for 5 minutes, until crisp-tender. 2. In a medium bowl, mix together the grits, egg, Worcestershire, garlic powder, and salt. 3. Spoon half of grits mixture into a baking pan and top with asparagus. 4. Tear cheese slices into pieces and layer evenly on top of asparagus. 5. Top with remaining grits. 6. Air Fry at 360ºF (182ºC) for 23 to 25 minutes. The casserole will rise a little as it cooks. When done, the top will have browned lightly with just a hint of crispiness.

## Green Peas with Mint

**Prep time: 5 minutes | Cook time: 5 minutes | Serves 4**

- ◀ 1 cup shredded lettuce
- ◀ 1 (10 ounces / 283 g) package frozen green peas, thawed
- ◀ 1 tablespoon fresh mint, shredded
- ◀ 1 teaspoon melted butter

1. Lay the shredded lettuce in the air fryer basket. 2. Toss together the peas, mint, and melted butter and spoon over the lettuce. 3. Air fry at 360ºF (182ºC) for 5 minutes, until peas are warm and lettuce wilts.

## Five-Spice Roasted Sweet Potatoes

**Prep time: 10 minutes | Cook time: 12 minutes | Serves 4**

- ◀ ½ teaspoon ground cinnamon
- ◀ ¼ teaspoon ground cumin
- ◀ ¼ teaspoon paprika
- ◀ 1 teaspoon chile powder
- ◀ ⅛ teaspoon turmeric
- ◀ ½ teaspoon salt (optional)
- ◀ Freshly ground black pepper, to taste
- ◀ 2 large sweet potatoes, peeled and cut into ¾-inch cubes (about 3 cups)
- ◀ 1 tablespoon olive oil

1. In a large bowl, mix together cinnamon, cumin, paprika, chile powder, turmeric, salt, and pepper to taste. 2. Add potatoes and stir well. 3. Drizzle the seasoned potatoes with the olive oil and stir until evenly coated. 4. Place seasoned potatoes in a baking pan or

an ovenproof dish that fits inside your air fryer basket. 5. Cook for 6 minutes at 390ºF (199ºC), PAUSE, and stir well. 6. Cook for an additional 6 minutes.

## Roasted Grape Tomatoes and Asparagus

**Prep time: 5 minutes | Cook time: 12 minutes | Serves 6**

- ◀ 2 cups grape tomatoes
- ◀ 1 bunch asparagus, trimmed
- ◀ 2 tablespoons olive oil
- ◀ 3 garlic cloves, minced
- ◀ ½ teaspoon kosher salt

1. Preheat the air fryer to 380ºF(193ºC). 2. In a large bowl, combine all of the ingredients, tossing until the vegetables are well coated with oil. 3. Pour the vegetable mixture into the air fryer basket and spread into a single layer, then roast for 12 minutes.

## Roasted Eggplant

**Prep time: 15 minutes | Cook time: 15 minutes | Serves 4**

- ◀ 1 large eggplant
- ◀ 2 tablespoons olive oil
- ◀ ¼ teaspoon salt
- ◀ ½ teaspoon garlic powder

1. Remove top and bottom from eggplant. Slice eggplant into ¼-inch-thick round slices. 2. Brush slices with olive oil. Sprinkle with salt and garlic powder. Place eggplant slices into the air fryer basket. 3. Adjust the temperature to 390ºF (199ºC) and set the timer for 15 minutes. 4. Serve immediately.

## Lemon-Thyme Asparagus

**Prep time: 5 minutes | Cook time: 4 to 8 minutes | Serves 4**

- ◀ 1 pound (454 g) asparagus, woody ends trimmed off
- ◀ 1 tablespoon avocado oil
- ◀ ½ teaspoon dried thyme or ½ tablespoon chopped fresh thyme
- ◀ Sea salt and freshly ground
- black pepper, to taste
- ◀ 2 ounces (57 g) goat cheese, crumbled
- ◀ Zest and juice of 1 lemon
- ◀ Flaky sea salt, for serving (optional)

1. In a medium bowl, toss together the asparagus, avocado oil, and thyme, and season with sea salt and pepper. 2. Place the asparagus in the air fryer basket in a single layer. Set the air fryer to 400ºF (204ºC) and air fry for 4 to 8 minutes, to your desired doneness. 3. Transfer to a serving platter. Top with the goat cheese, lemon zest, and lemon juice. If desired, season with a pinch of flaky salt.

## Garlic and Thyme Tomatoes

**Prep time: 10 minutes | Cook time: 15 minutes | Serves 2 to 4**

◄ 4 Roma tomatoes
◄ 1 tablespoon olive oil
◄ Salt and freshly ground

black pepper, to taste
◄ 1 clove garlic, minced
◄ ½ teaspoon dried thyme

1. Preheat the air fryer to 390ºF (199ºC). 2. Cut the tomatoes in half and scoop out the seeds and any pithy parts with your fingers. Place the tomatoes in a bowl and toss with the olive oil, salt, pepper, garlic and thyme. 3. Transfer the tomatoes to the air fryer, cut side up. Air fry for 15 minutes. The edges should just start to brown. Let the tomatoes cool to an edible temperature for a few minutes and then use in pastas, on top of crostini, or as an accompaniment to any poultry, meat or fish.

## Flatbread

**Prep time: 5 minutes | Cook time: 7 minutes | Serves 2**

◄ 1 cup shredded Mozzarella cheese
◄ ¼ cup blanched finely

ground almond flour
◄ 1 ounce (28 g) full-fat cream cheese, softened

1. In a large microwave-safe bowl, melt Mozzarella in the microwave for 30 seconds. Stir in almond flour until smooth and then add cream cheese. Continue mixing until dough forms, gently kneading it with wet hands if necessary. 2. Divide the dough into two pieces and roll out to ¼-inch thickness between two pieces of parchment. Cut another piece of parchment to fit your air fryer basket. 3. Place a piece of flatbread onto your parchment and into the air fryer, working in two batches if needed. 4. Adjust the temperature to 320ºF (160ºC) and air fry for 7 minutes. 5. Halfway through the cooking time flip the flatbread. Serve warm.

## Marinara Pepperoni Mushroom Pizza

**Prep time: 5 minutes | Cook time: 18 minutes | Serves 4**

◄ 4 large portobello mushrooms, stems removed
◄ 4 teaspoons olive oil
◄ 1 cup marinara sauce

◄ 1 cup shredded Mozzarella cheese
◄ 10 slices sugar-free pepperoni

1. Preheat the air fryer to 375ºF (191ºC). 2. Brush each mushroom cap with the olive oil, one teaspoon for each cap. 3. Put on a baking sheet and Air Fry, stem-side down, for 8 minutes. 4. Take out of the air fryer and divide the marinara sauce, Mozzarella cheese and pepperoni evenly among the caps. 5. Air fry for another 10 minutes until browned. 6. Serve hot.

## Blistered Shishito Peppers with Lime Juice

**Prep time: 5 minutes | Cook time: 9 minutes | Serves 3**

◄ ½ pound (227 g) shishito peppers, rinsed
◄ Cooking spray
◄ Sauce:

◄ 1 tablespoon tamari or shoyu
◄ 2 teaspoons fresh lime juice
◄ 2 large garlic cloves, minced

1. Preheat the air fryer to 392ºF (200ºC). Spritz the air fryer basket with cooking spray. 2. Place the shishito peppers in the basket and spritz them with cooking spray. Roast for 3 minutes. 3. Meanwhile, whisk together all the ingredients for the sauce in a large bowl. Set aside. 4. Shake the basket and spritz them with cooking spray again, then roast for an additional 3 minutes. 5. Shake the basket one more time and spray the peppers with cooking spray. Continue roasting for 3 minutes until the peppers are blistered and nicely browned. 6. Remove the peppers from the basket to the bowl of sauce. Toss to coat well and serve immediately.

## Garlic Cauliflower with Tahini

**Prep time: 10 minutes | Cook time: 20 minutes | Serves 4**

Cauliflower:
◄ 5 cups cauliflower florets (about 1 large head)
◄ 6 garlic cloves, smashed and cut into thirds
Sauce:
◄ 2 tablespoons tahini (sesame paste)
◄ 2 tablespoons hot water
◄ 1 tablespoon fresh lemon

◄ 3 tablespoons vegetable oil
◄ ½ teaspoon ground cumin
◄ ½ teaspoon ground coriander
◄ ½ teaspoon kosher salt

juice
◄ 1 teaspoon minced garlic
◄ ½ teaspoon kosher salt

1. For the cauliflower: In a large bowl, combine the cauliflower florets and garlic. Drizzle with the vegetable oil. Sprinkle with the cumin, coriander, and salt. Toss until well coated. 2. Place the cauliflower in the air fryer basket. Set the air fryer to 400ºF (204ºC) for 20 minutes, turning the cauliflower halfway through the cooking time. 3. Meanwhile, for the sauce: In a small bowl, combine the tahini, water, lemon juice, garlic, and salt. (The sauce will appear curdled at first, but keep stirring until you have a thick, creamy, smooth mixture.) 4. Transfer the cauliflower to a large serving bowl. Pour the sauce over and toss gently to coat. Serve immediately.

# Simple Zucchini Crisps

**Prep time: 5 minutes | Cook time: 14 minutes | Serves 4**

◄ 2 zucchini, sliced into ¼ to ½-inch-thick rounds (about 2 cups)
◄ ¼ teaspoon garlic granules
◄ ⅛ teaspoon sea salt
◄ Freshly ground black pepper, to taste (optional)
◄ Cooking spray

1. Preheat the air fryer to 392ºF (200ºC). Spritz the air fryer basket with cooking spray. 2. Put the zucchini rounds in the air fryer basket, spreading them out as much as possible. Top with a sprinkle of garlic granules, sea salt, and black pepper (if desired). Spritz the zucchini rounds with cooking spray. 3. Roast for 14 minutes, flipping the zucchini rounds halfway through, or until the zucchini rounds are crisp-tender. 4. Let them rest for 5 minutes and serve.

# Tofu Bites

**Prep time: 15 minutes | Cook time: 30 minutes | Serves 4**

◄ 1 packaged firm tofu, cubed and pressed to remove excess water
◄ 1 tablespoon soy sauce
◄ 1 tablespoon ketchup
◄ 1 tablespoon maple syrup
◄ ½ teaspoon vinegar
◄ 1 teaspoon liquid smoke
◄ 1 teaspoon hot sauce
◄ 2 tablespoons sesame seeds
◄ 1 teaspoon garlic powder
◄ Salt and ground black pepper, to taste
◄ Cooking spray

1. Preheat the air fryer to 375ºF (191ºC). 2. Spritz a baking dish with cooking spray. 3. Combine all the ingredients to coat the tofu completely and allow the marinade to absorb for half an hour. 4. Transfer the tofu to the baking dish, then air fry for 15 minutes. Flip the tofu over and air fry for another 15 minutes on the other side. 5. Serve immediately.

# Citrus-Roasted Broccoli Florets

**Prep time: 5 minutes | Cook time: 12 minutes | Serves 6**

◄ 4 cups broccoli florets (approximately 1 large head)
◄ 2 tablespoons olive oil
◄ ½ teaspoon salt
◄ ½ cup orange juice
◄ 1 tablespoon raw honey
◄ Orange wedges, for serving (optional)

1. Preheat the air fryer to 360°F(182ºC). 2. In a large bowl, combine the broccoli, olive oil, salt, orange juice, and honey. Toss the broccoli in the liquid until well coated. 3. Pour the broccoli mixture into the air fryer basket and roast for 6 minutes. Stir and roast for 6 minutes more. 4. Serve alone or with orange wedges for additional citrus flavor, if desired.

# Chapter 7

## Vegetarian Mains

# Chapter 7 Vegetarian Mains

## Crispy Tofu

**Prep time: 30 minutes | Cook time: 15 to 20 minutes | Serves 4**

- 1 (16 ounces / 454 g) block extra-firm tofu
- 2 tablespoons coconut aminos
- 1 tablespoon toasted sesame oil
- 1 tablespoon olive oil
- 1 tablespoon chili-garlic sauce
- 1½ teaspoons black sesame seeds
- 1 scallion, thinly sliced

1. Press the tofu for at least 15 minutes by wrapping it in paper towels and setting a heavy pan on top so that the moisture drains. 2. Slice the tofu into bite-size cubes and transfer to a bowl. Drizzle with the coconut aminos, sesame oil, olive oil, and chili-garlic sauce. Cover and refrigerate for 1 hour or up to overnight. 3. Preheat the air fryer to 400ºF (204ºC). 4. Arrange the tofu in a single layer in the air fryer basket. Pausing to shake the pan halfway through the cooking time, air fry for 15 to 20 minutes until crisp. Serve with any juices that accumulate in the bottom of the air fryer, sprinkled with the sesame seeds and sliced scallion.

## Garlic White Zucchini Rolls

**Prep time: 20 minutes | Cook time: 20 minutes | Serves 4**

- 2 medium zucchini
- 2 tablespoons unsalted butter
- ¼ white onion, peeled and diced
- ½ teaspoon finely minced roasted garlic
- ¼ cup heavy cream
- 2 tablespoons vegetable broth
- ⅛ teaspoon xanthan gum
- ½ cup full-fat ricotta cheese
- ¼ teaspoon salt
- ½ teaspoon garlic powder
- ¼ teaspoon dried oregano
- 2 cups spinach, chopped
- ½ cup sliced baby portobello mushrooms
- ¾ cup shredded Mozzarella cheese, divided

1. Using a mandoline or sharp knife, slice zucchini into long strips lengthwise. Place strips between paper towels to absorb moisture. Set aside. 2. In a medium saucepan over medium heat, melt butter. Add onion and sauté until fragrant. Add garlic and sauté 30 seconds. 3. Pour in heavy cream, broth, and xanthan gum. Turn off heat and whisk mixture until it begins to thicken, about 3 minutes. 4. In a medium bowl, add ricotta, salt, garlic powder, and oregano and mix well. Fold in spinach, mushrooms, and ½ cup Mozzarella. 5. Pour half of the sauce into a round baking pan. To assemble the rolls, place two strips of zucchini on a work surface. Spoon 2 tablespoons of ricotta mixture onto the slices and roll up. Place seam side down on top of sauce. Repeat with remaining ingredients. 6. Pour remaining sauce over the rolls and sprinkle with remaining Mozzarella. Cover with foil and place into the air fryer basket. 7. Adjust the temperature to 350ºF (177ºC) and Air Fry for 20 minutes. 8. In the last 5 minutes, remove the foil to brown the cheese. Serve immediately.

## Crispy Eggplant Slices with Parsley

**Prep time: 5 minutes | Cook time: 10 to 12 minutes | Serves 4**

- 1 cup flour
- 4 eggs
- Salt, to taste
- 2 cups bread crumbs
- 1 teaspoon Italian seasoning
- 2 eggplants, sliced
- 2 garlic cloves, sliced
- 2 tablespoons chopped parsley
- Cooking spray

1. Preheat the air fryer to 390ºF (199ºC). Spritz the air fryer basket with cooking spray. 2. On a plate, place the flour. In a shallow bowl, whisk the eggs with salt. In another shallow bowl, combine the bread crumbs and Italian seasoning. 3. Dredge the eggplant slices, one at a time, in the flour, then in the whisked eggs, finally in the bread crumb mixture to coat well. 4. Arrange the coated eggplant slices in the air fryer basket and air fry for 10 to 12 minutes until golden brown and crispy. Flip the eggplant slices halfway through the cooking time. 5. Transfer the eggplant slices to a plate and sprinkle the garlic and parsley on top before serving.

## Crustless Spinach Cheese Pie

**Prep time: 10 minutes | Cook time: 20 minutes | Serves 4**

- 6 large eggs
- ¼ cup heavy whipping cream
- 1 cup frozen chopped
- spinach, drained
- 1 cup shredded sharp Cheddar cheese
- ¼ cup diced yellow onion

1. In a medium bowl, whisk eggs and add cream. Add remaining ingredients to bowl. 2. Pour into a round baking dish. Place into the air fryer basket. 3. Adjust the temperature to 320ºF (160ºC) and Air Fry for 20 minutes. 4. Eggs will be firm and slightly browned when cooked. Serve immediately.

## Cheesy Cabbage Wedges

**Prep time: 5 minutes | Cook time: 20 minutes | Serves 4**

◄ 4 tablespoons melted butter
◄ 1 head cabbage, cut into wedges
◄ 1 cup shredded Parmesan cheese
◄ Salt and black pepper, to taste
◄ ½ cup shredded Mozzarella cheese

1. Preheat the air fryer to 380ºF (193ºC). 2. Brush the melted butter over the cut sides of cabbage wedges and sprinkle both sides with the Parmesan cheese. Season with salt and pepper to taste. 3. Place the cabbage wedges in the air fryer basket and air fry for 20 minutes, flipping the cabbage halfway through, or until the cabbage wedges are lightly browned. 4. Transfer the cabbage wedges to a plate and serve with the Mozzarella cheese sprinkled on top.

## Spaghetti Squash Alfredo

**Prep time: 10 minutes | Cook time: 15 minutes | Serves 2**

◄ ½ large cooked spaghetti squash
◄ 2 tablespoons salted butter, melted
◄ ½ cup low-carb Alfredo sauce
◄ ¼ cup grated vegetarian Parmesan cheese
◄ ½ teaspoon garlic powder
◄ 1 teaspoon dried parsley
◄ ¼ teaspoon ground peppercorn
◄ ½ cup shredded Italian blend cheese

1. Using a fork, remove the strands of spaghetti squash from the shell. Place into a large bowl with butter and Alfredo sauce. Sprinkle with Parmesan, garlic powder, parsley, and peppercorn. 2. Pour into a 4-cup round baking dish and top with shredded cheese. Place dish into the air fryer basket. 3. Adjust the temperature to 320ºF (160ºC) and Air Fry for 15 minutes. When finished, cheese will be golden and bubbling. Serve immediately.

## Mushroom and Pepper Pizza Squares

**Prep time: 10 minutes | Cook time: 10 minutes | Serves 10**

◄ 1 pizza dough, cut into squares
◄ 1 cup chopped oyster mushrooms
◄ 1 shallot, chopped
◄ ¼ red bell pepper, chopped
◄ 2 tablespoons parsley
◄ Salt and ground black pepper, to taste

1. Preheat the air fryer to 400ºF (204ºC). 2. In a bowl, combine the oyster mushrooms, shallot, bell pepper and parsley. Sprinkle some salt and pepper as desired. 3. Spread this mixture on top of the pizza squares. 4. Air Fry in the air fryer for 10 minutes. 5. Serve warm.

## Fried Root Vegetable Medley with Thyme

**Prep time: 10 minutes | Cook time: 22 minutes | Serves 4**

◄ 2 carrots, sliced
◄ 2 potatoes, cut into chunks
◄ 1 rutabaga, cut into chunks
◄ 1 turnip, cut into chunks
◄ 1 beet, cut into chunks
◄ 8 shallots, halved
◄ 2 tablespoons olive oil
◄ Salt and black pepper, to taste
◄ 2 tablespoons tomato pesto
◄ 2 tablespoons water
◄ 2 tablespoons chopped fresh thyme

1. Preheat the air fryer to 400ºF (204ºC). 2. Toss the carrots, potatoes, rutabaga, turnip, beet, shallots, olive oil, salt, and pepper in a large mixing bowl until the root vegetables are evenly coated. 3. Place the root vegetables in the air fryer basket and air fry for 12 minutes. Shake the basket and air fry for another 10 minutes until they are cooked to your preferred doneness. 4. Meanwhile, in a small bowl, whisk together the tomato pesto and water until smooth. 5. When ready, remove the root vegetables from the basket to a platter. Drizzle with the tomato pesto mixture and sprinkle with the thyme. Serve immediately.

## Rosemary Beets with Balsamic Glaze

**Prep time: 5 minutes | Cook time: 10 minutes | Serves 2**

Beet:
◄ 2 beets, cubed
◄ 2 tablespoons olive oil
◄ 2 springs rosemary, chopped
Balsamic Glaze:
◄ ⅓ cup balsamic vinegar
◄ Salt and black pepper, to taste
◄ 1 tablespoon honey

1. Preheat the air fryer to 400ºF (204ºC). 2. Combine the beets, olive oil, rosemary, salt, and pepper in a mixing bowl and toss until the beets are completely coated. 3. Place the beets in the air fryer basket and air fry for 10 minutes until the beets are crisp and browned at the edges. Shake the basket halfway through the cooking time. 4. Meanwhile, make the balsamic glaze: Place the balsamic vinegar and honey in a small saucepan and bring to a boil over medium heat. When the sauce starts to boil, reduce the heat to medium-low heat and simmer until the liquid is reduced by half. 5. When ready, remove the beets from the basket to a platter. Pour the balsamic glaze over the top and serve immediately.

## Russet Potato Gratin

**Prep time: 10 minutes | Cook time: 35 minutes | Serves 6**

- ½ cup milk
- 7 medium russet potatoes, peeled
- Salt, to taste
- 1 teaspoon black pepper
- ½ cup heavy whipping cream
- ½ cup grated semi-mature cheese
- ½ teaspoon nutmeg

1. Preheat the air fryer to 390ºF (199ºC). 2. Cut the potatoes into wafer-thin slices. 3. In a bowl, combine the milk and cream and sprinkle with salt, pepper, and nutmeg. 4. Use the milk mixture to coat the slices of potatoes. Put in a baking dish. Top the potatoes with the rest of the milk mixture. 5. Put the baking dish into the air fryer basket and Air Fry for 25 minutes. 6. Pour the cheese over the potatoes. 7. Air Fry for an additional 10 minutes, ensuring the top is nicely browned before serving.

## Basic Spaghetti Squash

**Prep time: 10 minutes | Cook time: 45 minutes | Serves 2**

- ½ large spaghetti squash
- 1 tablespoon coconut oil
- 2 tablespoons salted butter,
- melted
- ½ teaspoon garlic powder
- 1 teaspoon dried parsley

1. Brush shell of spaghetti squash with coconut oil. Place the skin side down and brush the inside with butter. Sprinkle with garlic powder and parsley. 2. Place squash with the skin side down into the air fryer basket. 3. Adjust the temperature to 350ºF (177ºC) and air fry for 30 minutes. 4. Flip the squash so skin side is up and cook an additional 15 minutes or until fork tender. Serve warm.

## Roasted Veggie Bowl

**Prep time: 10 minutes | Cook time: 15 minutes | Serves 2**

- 1 cup broccoli florets
- 1 cup quartered Brussels sprouts
- ½ cup cauliflower florets
- ¼ medium white onion, peeled and sliced ¼ inch thick
- ½ medium green bell pepper, seeded and sliced ¼ inch thick
- 1 tablespoon coconut oil
- 2 teaspoons chili powder
- ½ teaspoon garlic powder
- ½ teaspoon cumin

1. Toss all ingredients together in a large bowl until vegetables are fully coated with oil and seasoning. 2. Pour vegetables into the air fryer basket. 3. Adjust the temperature to 360ºF (182ºC) and roast for 15 minutes. 4. Shake two or three times during cooking. Serve warm.

## Roasted Spaghetti Squash

**Prep time: 10 minutes | Cook time: 45 minutes | Serves 6**

- 1 (4 pounds / 1.8 kg) spaghetti squash, halved and seeded
- 2 tablespoons coconut oil
- 4 tablespoons salted butter, melted
- 1 teaspoon garlic powder
- 2 teaspoons dried parsley

1. Brush shell of spaghetti squash with coconut oil. Brush inside with butter. Sprinkle inside with garlic powder and parsley. 2. Place squash skin side down into ungreased air fryer basket, working in batches if needed. Adjust the temperature to 350ºF (177ºC) and set the timer for 30 minutes. When the timer beeps, flip squash and cook an additional 15 minutes until fork-tender. 3. Use a fork to remove spaghetti strands from shell and serve warm.

## Mediterranean Pan Pizza

**Prep time: 5 minutes | Cook time: 8 minutes | Serves 2**

- 1 cup shredded Mozzarella cheese
- ¼ medium red bell pepper, seeded and chopped
- ½ cup chopped fresh spinach
- leaves
- 2 tablespoons chopped black olives
- 2 tablespoons crumbled feta cheese

1. Sprinkle Mozzarella into an ungreased round nonstick baking dish in an even layer. Add remaining ingredients on top. 2. Place dish into air fryer basket. Adjust the temperature to 350ºF (177ºC) and Air Fry for 8 minutes, checking halfway through to avoid burning. Top of pizza will be golden brown and the cheese melted when done. 3. Remove dish from fryer and let cool 5 minutes before slicing and serving.

## Quiche-Stuffed Peppers

**Prep time: 5 minutes | Cook time: 15 minutes | Serves 2**

- 2 medium green bell peppers
- 3 large eggs
- ¼ cup full-fat ricotta cheese
- ¼ cup diced yellow onion
- ½ cup chopped broccoli
- ½ cup shredded medium Cheddar cheese

1. Cut the tops off of the peppers and remove the seeds and white membranes with a small knife. 2. In a medium bowl, whisk eggs and ricotta. 3. Add onion and broccoli. Pour the egg and vegetable mixture evenly into each pepper. Top with Cheddar. Place peppers into a 4-cup round baking dish and place into the air fryer basket. 4. Adjust the temperature to 350ºF (177ºC) and Air Fry for 15 minutes. 5. Eggs will be mostly firm and peppers tender when fully cooked. Serve immediately.

# Cauliflower, Chickpea, and Avocado Mash

## Prep time: 10 minutes | Cook time: 25 minutes | Serves 4

- 1 medium head cauliflower, cut into florets
- 1 can chickpeas, drained and rinsed
- 1 tablespoon extra-virgin olive oil
- 2 tablespoons lemon juice
- Salt and ground black pepper, to taste
- 4 flatbreads, toasted
- 2 ripe avocados, mashed

1. Preheat the air fryer to 425°F (218°C). 2. In a bowl, mix the chickpeas, cauliflower, lemon juice and olive oil. Sprinkle salt and pepper as desired. 3. Put inside the air fryer basket and air fry for 25 minutes. 4. Spread on top of the flatbread along with the mashed avocado. Sprinkle with more pepper and salt and serve.

# Parmesan Artichokes

## Prep time: 10 minutes | Cook time: 10 minutes | Serves 4

- 2 medium artichokes, trimmed and quartered, center removed
- 2 tablespoons coconut oil
- 1 large egg, beaten
- ½ cup grated vegetarian Parmesan cheese
- ¼ cup blanched finely ground almond flour
- ½ teaspoon crushed red pepper flakes

1. In a large bowl, toss artichokes in coconut oil and then dip each piece into the egg. 2. Mix the Parmesan and almond flour in a large bowl. Add artichoke pieces and toss to cover as completely as possible, sprinkle with pepper flakes. Place into the air fryer basket. 3. Adjust the temperature to 400°F (204°C) and air fry for 10 minutes. 4. Toss the basket two times during cooking. Serve warm.

# Pesto Spinach Flatbread

## Prep time: 10 minutes | Cook time: 8 minutes | Serves 4

- 1 cup blanched finely ground almond flour
- 2 ounces (57 g) cream cheese
- 2 cups shredded Mozzarella cheese
- 1 cup chopped fresh spinach leaves
- 2 tablespoons basil pesto

1. Place flour, cream cheese, and Mozzarella in a large microwave-safe bowl and microwave on high 45 seconds, then stir. 2. Fold in spinach and microwave an additional 15 seconds. Stir until a soft dough ball forms. 3. Cut two pieces of parchment paper to fit air fryer basket. Separate dough into two sections and press each out on ungreased parchment to create 6-inch rounds. 4. Spread 1 tablespoon pesto over each flatbread and place rounds on parchment into ungreased air fryer basket. Adjust the temperature to 350°F (177°C) and air fry for 8 minutes, turning crusts halfway through cooking. Flatbread will be golden when done. 5. Let cool 5 minutes before slicing and serving.

# Spinach Cheese Casserole

## Prep time: 15 minutes | Cook time: 15 minutes | Serves 4

- 1 tablespoon salted butter, melted
- ¼ cup diced yellow onion
- 8 ounces (227 g) full-fat cream cheese, softened
- ⅓ cup full-fat mayonnaise
- ⅓ cup full-fat sour cream
- ¼ cup chopped pickled jalapeños
- 2 cups fresh spinach, chopped
- 2 cups cauliflower florets, chopped
- 1 cup artichoke hearts, chopped

1. In a large bowl, mix butter, onion, cream cheese, mayonnaise, and sour cream. Fold in jalapeños, spinach, cauliflower, and artichokes. 2. Pour the mixture into a round baking dish. Cover with foil and place into the air fryer basket. 3. Adjust the temperature to 370°F (188°C) and set the timer for 15 minutes. In the last 2 minutes of cooking, remove the foil to brown the top. Serve warm.

# Crispy Eggplant Rounds

## Prep time: 15 minutes | Cook time: 10 minutes | Serves 4

- 1 large eggplant, ends trimmed, cut into ½-inch slices
- ½ teaspoon salt
- 2 ounces (57 g) Parmesan
- 100% cheese crisps, finely ground
- ½ teaspoon paprika
- ¼ teaspoon garlic powder
- 1 large egg

1. Sprinkle eggplant rounds with salt. Place rounds on a kitchen towel for 30 minutes to draw out excess water. Pat rounds dry. 2. In a medium bowl, mix cheese crisps, paprika, and garlic powder. In a separate medium bowl, whisk egg. Dip each eggplant round in egg, then gently press into cheese crisps to coat both sides. 3. Place eggplant rounds into ungreased air fryer basket. Adjust the temperature to 400°F (204°C) and air fry for 10 minutes, turning rounds halfway through cooking. Eggplant will be golden and crispy when done. Serve warm.

# Chapter **8**

## Snacks and Appetizers

# Chapter 8 Snacks and Appetizers

## Buffalo Bites

### Prep time: 15 minutes | Cook time: 11 to 12 minutes per batch | Makes 16 meatballs

- ◄ 1½ cups cooked jasmine or sushi rice
- ◄ ¼ teaspoon salt
- ◄ 1 pound (454 g) ground chicken
- ◄ 8 tablespoons buffalo wing sauce
- ◄ 2 ounces (57 g) Gruyère cheese, cut into 16 cubes
- ◄ 1 tablespoon maple syrup

1. Mix 4 tablespoons buffalo wing sauce into all the ground chicken. 2. Shape chicken into a log and divide into 16 equal portions. 3. With slightly damp hands, mold each chicken portion around a cube of cheese and shape into a firm ball. When you have shaped 8 meatballs, place them in air fryer basket. 4. Air fry at 390ºF (199ºC) for approximately 5 minutes. Shake basket, reduce temperature to 360ºF (182ºC), and cook for 5 to 6 minutes longer. 5. While the first batch is cooking, shape remaining chicken and cheese into 8 more meatballs. 6. Repeat step 4 to cook second batch of meatballs. 7. In a medium bowl, mix the remaining 4 tablespoons of buffalo wing sauce with the maple syrup. Add all the cooked meatballs and toss to coat. 8. Place meatballs back into air fryer basket and air fry at 390ºF (199ºC) for 2 to 3 minutes to set the glaze. Skewer each with a toothpick and serve.

## Shrimp Egg Rolls

### Prep time: 15 minutes | Cook time: 10 minutes per batch | Serves 4

- ◄ 1 tablespoon vegetable oil
- ◄ ½ head green or savoy cabbage, finely shredded
- ◄ 1 cup shredded carrots
- ◄ 1 cup canned bean sprouts, drained
- ◄ 1 tablespoon soy sauce
- ◄ ½ teaspoon sugar
- ◄ 1 teaspoon sesame oil
- ◄ ¼ cup hoisin sauce
- ◄ Freshly ground black pepper, to taste
- ◄ 1 pound (454 g) cooked shrimp, diced
- ◄ ¼ cup scallions
- ◄ 8 egg roll wrappers
- ◄ Vegetable oil
- ◄ Duck sauce

1. Preheat a large sauté pan over medium-high heat. Add the oil and cook the cabbage, carrots and bean sprouts until they start to wilt, about 3 minutes. Add the soy sauce, sugar, sesame oil, hoisin sauce and black pepper. Sauté for a few more minutes. Stir in the shrimp and scallions and cook until the vegetables are just tender. Transfer the mixture to a colander in a bowl to cool. Press or squeeze out any excess water from the filling so that you don't end up with soggy egg rolls. 2. Make the egg rolls: Place the egg roll wrappers on a flat surface with one of the points facing towards you so they look like diamonds. Dividing the filling evenly between the eight wrappers, spoon the mixture onto the center of the egg roll wrappers. Spread the filling across the center of the wrappers from the left corner to the right corner, but leave 2 inches from each corner empty. Brush the empty sides of the wrapper with a little water. Fold the bottom corner of the wrapper tightly up over the filling, trying to avoid making any air pockets. Fold the left corner in toward the center and then the right corner toward the center. It should now look like an envelope. Tightly roll the egg roll from the bottom to the top open corner. Press to seal the egg roll together, brushing with a little extra water if need be. Repeat this technique with all 8 egg rolls. 3. Preheat the air fryer to 370ºF (188ºC). 4. Spray or brush all sides of the egg rolls with vegetable oil. Air fry four egg rolls at a time for 10 minutes, turning them over halfway through the cooking time. 5. Serve hot with duck sauce or your favorite dipping sauce.

## Chile-Brined Fried Calamari

### Prep time: 20 minutes | Cook time: 8 minutes | Serves 2

- ◄ 1 (8 ounces / 227 g) jar sweet or hot pickled cherry peppers
- ◄ ½ pound (227 g) calamari bodies and tentacles, bodies cut into ½-inch-wide rings
- ◄ 1 lemon
- ◄ 2 cups all-purpose flour
- ◄ Kosher salt and freshly
- ◄ ground black pepper, to taste
- ◄ 3 large eggs, lightly beaten
- ◄ Cooking spray
- ◄ ½ cup mayonnaise
- ◄ 1 teaspoon finely chopped rosemary
- ◄ 1 garlic clove, minced

1. Drain the pickled pepper brine into a large bowl and tear the peppers into bite-size strips. Add the pepper strips and calamari to the brine and let stand in the refrigerator for 20 minutes or up to 2 hours. 2. Grate the lemon zest into a large bowl then whisk in the flour and season with salt and pepper. Dip the calamari and pepper strips in the egg, then toss them in the flour mixture until fully coated. Spray the calamari and peppers liberally with cooking spray, then transfer half to the air fryer. Air fry at 400ºF (204ºC), shaking the basket halfway into cooking, until the calamari is cooked through and golden brown, about 8 minutes. Transfer to a plate and repeat with the remaining pieces. 3. In a small bowl, whisk together the mayonnaise, rosemary, and garlic. Squeeze half the zested lemon to get 1 tablespoon of juice and stir it into the sauce. Season with salt and pepper. Cut the remaining zested lemon half into 4 small wedges and serve alongside the calamari, peppers, and sauce.

## Greek Street Tacos

### Prep time: 10 minutes | Cook time: 3 minutes | Makes 8 small tacos

- 8 small flour tortillas (4-inch diameter)
- 8 tablespoons hummus
- 4 tablespoons crumbled feta cheese
- 4 tablespoons chopped kalamata or other olives (optional)
- Olive oil for misting

1. Place 1 tablespoon of hummus or tapenade in the center of each tortilla. Top with 1 teaspoon of feta crumbles and 1 teaspoon of chopped olives, if using. 2. Using your finger or a small spoon, moisten the edges of the tortilla all around with water. 3. Fold tortilla over to make a half-moon shape. Press center gently. Then press the edges firmly to seal in the filling. 4. Mist both sides with olive oil. 5. Place in air fryer basket very close but try not to overlap. 6. Air fry at 390°F (199°C) for 3 minutes, just until lightly browned and crispy.

## Lemony Endive in Curried Yogurt

### Prep time: 5 minutes | Cook time: 10 minutes | Serves 6

- 6 heads endive
- ½ cup plain and fat-free yogurt
- 3 tablespoons lemon juice
- 1 teaspoon garlic powder
- ½ teaspoon curry powder
- Salt and ground black pepper, to taste

1. Wash the endives, and slice them in half lengthwise. 2. In a bowl, mix together the yogurt, lemon juice, garlic powder, curry powder, salt and pepper. 3. Brush the endive halves with the marinade, coating them completely. Allow to sit for at least 30 minutes or up to 24 hours. 4. Preheat the air fryer to 320°F (160°C). 5. Put the endives in the air fryer basket and air fry for 10 minutes. 6. Serve hot.

## Hush Puppies

### Prep time: 45 minutes | Cook time: 10 minutes | Serves 12

- 1 cup self-rising yellow cornmeal
- ½ cup all-purpose flour
- 1 teaspoon sugar
- 1 teaspoon salt
- 1 teaspoon freshly ground black pepper
- 1 large egg
- ⅓ cup canned creamed corn
- 1 cup minced onion
- 2 teaspoons minced jalapeño pepper
- 2 tablespoons olive oil, divided

1. Thoroughly combine the cornmeal, flour, sugar, salt, and pepper in a large bowl. 2. Whisk together the egg and corn in a small bowl.

Pour the egg mixture into the bowl of cornmeal mixture and stir to combine. Stir in the minced onion and jalapeño. Cover the bowl with plastic wrap and place in the refrigerator for 30 minutes. 3. Preheat the air fryer to 375°F (191°C). Line the air fryer basket with parchment paper and lightly brush it with 1 tablespoon of olive oil. 4. Scoop out the cornmeal mixture and form into 24 balls, about 1 inch. 5. Arrange the balls in the parchment paper-lined basket, leaving space between each ball. 6. Air fry in batches for 5 minutes. Shake the basket and brush the balls with the remaining 1 tablespoon of olive oil. Continue cooking for 5 minutes until golden brown. 7. Remove the balls (hush puppies) from the basket and serve on a plate.

## Spinach and Crab Meat Cups

### Prep time: 10 minutes | Cook time: 10 minutes | Makes 30 cups

- 1 (6 ounces / 170 g) can crab meat, drained to yield ⅓ cup meat
- ¼ cup frozen spinach, thawed, drained, and chopped
- 1 clove garlic, minced
- ½ cup grated Parmesan
- cheese
- 3 tablespoons plain yogurt
- ¼ teaspoon lemon juice
- ½ teaspoon Worcestershire sauce
- 30 mini frozen phyllo shells, thawed
- Cooking spray

1. Preheat the air fryer to 390°F (199°C). 2. Remove any bits of shell that might remain in the crab meat. 3. Mix the crab meat, spinach, garlic, and cheese together. 4. Stir in the yogurt, lemon juice, and Worcestershire sauce and mix well. 5. Spoon a teaspoon of filling into each phyllo shell. 6. Spray the air fryer basket with cooking spray and arrange half the shells in the basket. Air fry for 5 minutes. Repeat with the remaining shells. 7. Serve immediately.

## Asian Five-Spice Wings

### Prep time: 30 minutes | Cook time: 13 to 15 minutes | Serves 4

- 2 pounds (907 g) chicken wings
- ½ cup Asian-style salad
- dressing
- 2 tablespoons Chinese five-spice powder

1. Cut off wing tips and discard or freeze for stock. Cut remaining wing pieces in two at the joint. 2. Place wing pieces in a large sealable plastic bag. Pour in the Asian dressing, seal bag, and massage the marinade into the wings until well coated. Refrigerate for at least an hour. 3. Remove wings from bag, drain off excess marinade, and place wings in air fryer basket. 4. Air fry at 360°F (182°C) for 13 to 15 minutes or until juices run clear. About halfway through cooking time, shake the basket or stir wings for more even cooking. 5. Transfer cooked wings to plate in a single layer. Sprinkle half of the Chinese five-spice powder on the wings, turn, and sprinkle other side with remaining seasoning.

## Spicy Chicken Bites

### Prep time: 10 minutes | Cook time: 10 to 12 minutes | Makes 30 bites

- ◄ 8 ounces boneless and skinless chicken thighs, cut into 30 pieces
- ◄ ¼ teaspoon kosher salt
- ◄ 2 tablespoons hot sauce
- ◄ Cooking spray

1. Preheat the air fryer to 390ºF (199ºC). 2. Spray the air fryer basket with cooking spray and season the chicken bites with the kosher salt, then place in the basket and air fry for 10 to 12 minutes or until crispy. 3. While the chicken bites cook, pour the hot sauce into a large bowl. 4. Remove the bites and add to the sauce bowl, tossing to coat. Serve warm.

## Golden Onion Rings

### Prep time: 15 minutes | Cook time: 14 minutes per batch | Serves 4

- ◄ 1 large white onion, peeled and cut into ½ to ¾-inch-thick slices (about 2 cups)
- ◄ ½ cup 2% milk
- ◄ 1 cup whole-wheat pastry flour, or all-purpose flour
- ◄ 2 tablespoons cornstarch
- ◄ ¾ teaspoon sea salt, divided
- ◄ ½ teaspoon freshly ground black pepper, divided
- ◄ ¾ teaspoon granulated garlic, divided
- ◄ 1½ cups whole-grain bread crumbs, or gluten-free bread crumbs
- ◄ Cooking oil spray (coconut, sunflower, or safflower)
- ◄ Ketchup, for serving (optional)

1. Carefully separate the onion slices into rings—a gentle touch is important here. 2. Place the milk in a shallow bowl and set aside. 3. Make the first breading: In a medium bowl, stir together the flour, cornstarch, ¼ teaspoon of salt, ¼ teaspoon of pepper, and ¼ teaspoon of granulated garlic. Set aside. 4. Make the second breading: In a separate medium bowl, stir together the bread crumbs with the remaining ½ teaspoon of salt, the remaining ½ teaspoon of garlic, and the remaining ½ teaspoon of pepper. Set aside. 5. Insert the crisper plate into the basket and the basket into the unit. Preheat the unit by selecting AIR FRY, setting the temperature to 390ºF (199ºC), and setting the time to 3 minutes. Select START/PAUSE to begin. 6. Once the unit is preheated, spray the crisper plate and the basket with cooking oil. 7. To make the onion rings, dip one ring into the milk and into the first breading mixture. Dip the ring into the milk again and back into the first breading mixture, coating thoroughly. Dip the ring into the milk one last time and then into the second breading mixture, coating thoroughly. Gently lay the onion ring in the basket. Repeat with additional rings and, as you place them into the basket, do not overlap them too much. Once all the onion rings are in the basket, generously spray the tops with cooking oil. 8. Select AIR FRY, set the temperature to 390ºF (199ºC), and set the time to 14 minutes. Insert the basket into the unit. Select START/PAUSE to begin. 9. After 4 minutes, open the unit and spray the rings generously with cooking oil. Close the unit to resume cooking. After 3 minutes, remove the basket and spray the onion rings again. Remove the rings, turn them over, and place them back into the basket. Generously spray them again with oil. Reinsert the basket to resume cooking. After 4 minutes, generously spray the rings with oil one last time. Resume cooking for the remaining 3 minutes, or until the onion rings are very crunchy and brown. 10. When the cooking is complete, serve the hot rings with ketchup, or other sauce of choice.

## Air Fryd Ricotta

### Prep time: 10 minutes | Cook time: 15 minutes | Makes 2 cups

- ◄ 1 (15 ounces / 425 g) container whole milk Ricotta cheese
- ◄ 3 tablespoons grated Parmesan cheese, divided
- ◄ 2 tablespoons extra-virgin olive oil
- ◄ 1 teaspoon chopped fresh
- thyme leaves
- ◄ 1 teaspoon grated lemon zest
- ◄ 1 clove garlic, crushed with press
- ◄ ¼ teaspoon salt
- ◄ ¼ teaspoon pepper
- ◄ Toasted baguette slices or crackers, for serving

1. Preheat the air fryer to 380ºF (193ºC). 2. To get the baking dish in and out of the air fryer, create a sling using a 24-inch length of foil, folded lengthwise into thirds. 3. Whisk together the Ricotta, 2 tablespoons of the Parmesan, oil, thyme, lemon zest, garlic, salt, and pepper. Pour into a baking dish. Cover the dish tightly with foil. 4. Place the sling under dish and lift by the ends into the air fryer, tucking the ends of the sling around the dish. Air Fry for 10 minutes. Remove the foil cover and sprinkle with the remaining 1 tablespoon of the Parmesan. Air fry for 5 more minutes, or until bubbly at edges and the top is browned. 5. Serve warm with toasted baguette slices or crackers.

## Lemon-Pepper Chicken Drumsticks

### Prep time: 30 minutes | Cook time: 30 minutes | Serves 2

- ◄ 2 teaspoons freshly ground coarse black pepper
- ◄ 1 teaspoon baking powder
- ◄ ½ teaspoon garlic powder
- ◄ 4 chicken drumsticks (4 ounces / 113 g each)
- ◄ Kosher salt, to taste
- ◄ 1 lemon

1. In a small bowl, stir together the pepper, baking powder, and garlic powder. Place the drumsticks on a plate and sprinkle evenly with the baking powder mixture, turning the drumsticks so they're well coated. Let the drumsticks stand in the refrigerator for at least 1 hour or up to overnight. 2. Sprinkle the drumsticks with salt, then transfer them to the air fryer, standing them bone-end up and leaning against the wall of the air fryer basket. Air fry at 375ºF (191ºC) until cooked through and crisp on the outside, about 30 minutes. 3. Transfer the drumsticks to a serving platter and finely grate the zest of the lemon over them while they're hot. Cut the lemon into wedges and serve with the warm drumsticks.

# Mexican Potato Skins

## Prep time: 10 minutes | Cook time: 55 minutes | Serves 6

- ◄ Olive oil
- ◄ 6 medium russet potatoes, scrubbed
- ◄ Salt and freshly ground black pepper, to taste
- ◄ 1 cup fat-free refried black beans
- ◄ 1 tablespoon taco seasoning
- ◄ ½ cup salsa
- ◄ ¾ cup reduced-fat shredded Cheddar cheese

1. Spray the air fryer basket lightly with olive oil. 2. Spray the potatoes lightly with oil and season with salt and pepper. Pierce each potato a few times with a fork. 3. Place the potatoes in the air fryer basket. Air fry at 400°F (204°C) until fork-tender, 30 to 40 minutes. The cooking time will depend on the size of the potatoes. You can cook the potatoes in the microwave or a standard oven, but they won't get the same lovely crispy skin they will get in the air fryer. 4. While the potatoes are cooking, in a small bowl, mix together the beans and taco seasoning. Set aside until the potatoes are cool enough to handle. 5. Cut each potato in half lengthwise. Scoop out most of the insides, leaving about ¼ inch in the skins so the potato skins hold their shape. 6. Season the insides of the potato skins with salt and black pepper. Lightly spray the insides of the potato skins with oil. You may need to cook them in batches. 7. Place them into the air fryer basket, skin-side down, and air fry until crisp and golden, 8 to 10 minutes. 8. Transfer the skins to a work surface and spoon ½ tablespoon of seasoned refried black beans into each one. Top each with 2 teaspoons salsa and 1 tablespoon shredded Cheddar cheese. 9. Place filled potato skins in the air fryer basket in a single layer. Lightly spray with oil. 10. Air fry until the cheese is melted and bubbly, 2 to 3 minutes.

# Air Fryd Spanakopita Dip

## Prep time: 10 minutes | Cook time: 15 minutes | Serves 2

- ◄ Olive oil cooking spray
- ◄ 3 tablespoons olive oil, divided
- ◄ 2 tablespoons minced white onion
- ◄ 2 garlic cloves, minced
- ◄ 4 cups fresh spinach
- ◄ 4 ounces (113 g) cream cheese, softened
- ◄ 4 ounces (113 g) feta cheese, divided
- ◄ Zest of 1 lemon
- ◄ ¼ teaspoon ground nutmeg
- ◄ 1 teaspoon dried dill
- ◄ ½ teaspoon salt
- ◄ Pita chips, carrot sticks, or sliced bread for serving (optional)

1. Preheat the air fryer to 360°F(182°C). Coat the inside of a 6-inch ramekin or baking dish with olive oil cooking spray. 2. In a large skillet over medium heat, heat 1 tablespoon of the olive oil. Add the onion, then cook for 1 minute. 3. Add in the garlic and cook, stirring for 1 minute more. 4. Reduce the heat to low and mix in the spinach and water. Let this cook for 2 to 3 minutes, or until the spinach has wilted. Remove the skillet from the heat. 5. In a medium bowl, combine the cream cheese, 2 ounces (57 g) of the feta, and the remaining 2 tablespoons of olive oil, along with the lemon zest, nutmeg, dill, and salt. Mix until just combined. 6. Add the vegetables to the cheese base and stir until combined. 7. Pour the dip mixture into the prepared ramekin and top with the remaining 2 ounces (57 g) of feta cheese. 8. Place the dip into the air fryer basket and cook for 10 minutes, or until heated through and bubbling. 9. Serve with pita chips, carrot sticks, or sliced bread.

# Asian Rice Logs

## Prep time: 30 minutes | Cook time: 5 minutes | Makes 8 rice logs

- ◄ 1½ cups cooked jasmine or sushi rice
- ◄ ¼ teaspoon salt
- ◄ 2 teaspoons five-spice powder
- ◄ 2 teaspoons diced shallots
- ◄ 1 tablespoon tamari sauce
- ◄ 1 egg, beaten
- ◄ 1 teaspoon sesame oil
- ◄ 2 teaspoons water
- ◄ ⅓ cup plain bread crumbs
- ◄ ¾ cup panko bread crumbs
- ◄ 2 tablespoons sesame seeds
- ◄ Orange Marmalade Dipping Sauce:
- ◄ ½ cup all-natural orange marmalade
- ◄ 1 tablespoon soy sauce

1. Make the rice according to package instructions. While the rice is cooking, make the dipping sauce by combining the marmalade and soy sauce and set aside. 2. Stir together the cooked rice, salt, five-spice powder, shallots, and tamari sauce. 3. Divide rice into 8 equal pieces. With slightly damp hands, mold each piece into a log shape. Chill in freezer for 10 to 15 minutes. 4. Mix the egg, sesame oil, and water together in a shallow bowl. 5. Place the plain bread crumbs on a sheet of wax paper. 6. Mix the panko bread crumbs with the sesame seeds and place on another sheet of wax paper. 7. Roll the rice logs in plain bread crumbs, then dip in egg wash, and then dip in the panko and sesame seeds. 8. Cook the logs at 390°F (199°C) for approximately 5 minutes, until golden brown. 9. Cool slightly before serving with Orange Marmalade Dipping Sauce.

# Cream Cheese Wontons

## Prep time: 15 minutes | Cook time: 6 minutes | Makes 20 wontons

- ◄ Oil, for spraying
- ◄ 20 wonton wrappers
- ◄ 4 ounces (113 g) cream cheese

1. Line the air fryer basket with parchment and spray lightly with oil. 2. Pour some water in a small bowl. 3. Lay out a wonton wrapper and place 1 teaspoon of cream cheese in the center. 4. Dip your finger in the water and moisten the edge of the wonton wrapper. Fold over the opposite corners to make a triangle and press the edges together. 5. Pinch the corners of the triangle together to form a classic wonton shape. Place the wonton in the prepared basket. Repeat with the remaining wrappers and cream cheese. You may need to work in batches, depending on the size of your air fryer. 6. Air fry at 400°F (204°C) for 6 minutes, or until golden brown around the edges.

## Sea Salt Potato Chips

**Prep time: 30 minutes | Cook time: 27 minutes | Serves 4**

◄ Oil, for spraying
◄ 4 medium yellow potatoes
◄ 1 tablespoon oil
◄ ⅛ to ¼ teaspoon fine sea salt

1. Line the air fryer basket with parchment and spray lightly with oil. 2. Using a mandoline or a very sharp knife, cut the potatoes into very thin slices. 3. Place the slices in a bowl of cold water and let soak for about 20 minutes. 4. Drain the potatoes, transfer them to a plate lined with paper towels, and pat dry. 5. Drizzle the oil over the potatoes, sprinkle with the salt, and toss to combine. Transfer to the prepared basket. 6. Air fry at 200ºF (93ºC) for 20 minutes. Toss the chips, increase the heat to 400ºF (204ºC), and cook for another 5 to 7 minutes, until crispy.

## Taco-Spiced Chickpeas

**Prep time: 5 minutes | Cook time: 17 minutes | Serves 3**

◄ Oil, for spraying
◄ 1 (15½ ounces / 439 g) can chickpeas, drained
◄ 1 teaspoon chili powder
◄ ½ teaspoon ground cumin
◄ ½ teaspoon salt
◄ ½ teaspoon granulated garlic
◄ 2 teaspoons lime juice

1. Line the air fryer basket with parchment and spray lightly with oil. Place the chickpeas in the prepared basket. 2. Air fry at 390ºF (199ºC) for 17 minutes, shaking or stirring the chickpeas and spraying lightly with oil every 5 to 7 minutes. 3. In a small bowl, mix together the chili powder, cumin, salt, and garlic. 4. When 2 to 3 minutes of cooking time remain, sprinkle half of the seasoning mix over the chickpeas. Finish cooking. 5. Transfer the chickpeas to a medium bowl and toss with the remaining seasoning mix and the lime juice. Serve immediately.

## Cheese-Stuffed Blooming Onion

**Prep time: 10 minutes | Cook time: 15 minutes | Serves 2**

◄ 1 large yellow onion (14 ounces / 397 g)
◄ 1 tablespoon olive oil
◄ Kosher salt and freshly ground black pepper, to taste
◄ ¼ cup plus 2 tablespoons panko bread crumbs
◄ ¼ cup grated Parmesan
    cheese
◄ 3 tablespoons mayonnaise
◄ 1 tablespoon fresh lemon juice
◄ 1 tablespoon chopped fresh flat-leaf parsley
◄ 2 teaspoons whole-grain Dijon mustard
◄ 1 garlic clove, minced

1. Place the onion on a cutting board and trim the top off and peel off the outer skin. Turn the onion upside down and use a paring knife, cut vertical slits halfway through the onion at ½-inch intervals around the onion, keeping the root intact. When you turn the onion right side up, it should open up like the petals of a flower. Drizzle the cut sides of the onion with the olive oil and season with salt and pepper. Place petal-side up in the air fryer and air fry at 350ºF (177ºC) for 10 minutes. 2. Meanwhile, in a bowl, stir together the panko, Parmesan, mayonnaise, lemon juice, parsley, mustard, and garlic until incorporated into a smooth paste. 3. Remove the onion from the fryer and stuff the paste all over and in between the onion "petals." Return the onion to the air fryer and air fry at 375ºF (191ºC) until the onion is tender in the center and the bread crumb mixture is golden brown, about 5 minutes. Remove the onion from the air fryer, transfer to a plate, and serve hot.

## Skinny Fries

**Prep time: 10 minutes | Cook time: 15 minutes per batch | Serves 2**

2 to 3 russet potatoes, peeled and cut into ¼-inch sticks
2 to 3 teaspoons olive or vegetable oil
Salt, to taste

1. Cut the potatoes into ¼-inch strips. (A mandolin with a julienne blade is really helpful here.) Rinse the potatoes with cold water several times and let them soak in cold water for at least 10 minutes or as long as overnight. 2. Preheat the air fryer to 380ºF (193ºC). 3. Drain and dry the potato sticks really well, using a clean kitchen towel. Toss the fries with the oil in a bowl and then air fry the fries in two batches at 380ºF (193ºC) for 15 minutes, shaking the basket a couple of times while they cook. 4. Add the first batch of French fries back into the air fryer basket with the finishing batch and let everything warm through for a few minutes. As soon as the fries are done, season them with salt and transfer to a plate or basket. Serve them warm with ketchup or your favorite dip.

## Veggie Salmon Nachos

**Prep time: 10 minutes | Cook time: 9 to 12 minutes | Serves 6**

◄ 2 ounces (57 g) Air Fryd no-salt corn tortilla chips
◄ 1 (5 ounces / 142 g) Air Fryd salmon fillet, flaked
◄ ½ cup canned low-sodium black beans, rinsed and drained
◄ 1 red bell pepper, chopped
◄ ½ cup grated carrot
◄ 1 jalapeño pepper, minced
◄ ⅓ cup shredded low-sodium low-fat Swiss cheese
◄ 1 tomato, chopped

1. Preheat the air fryer to 360ºF (182ºC). 2. In a baking pan, layer the tortilla chips. Top with the salmon, black beans, red bell pepper, carrot, jalapeño, and Swiss cheese. 3. Air Fry in the air fryer for 9 to 12 minutes, or until the cheese is melted and starts to brown. 4. Top with the tomato and serve.

# Grilled Ham and Cheese on Raisin Bread

## Prep time: 5 minutes | Cook time: 10 minutes | Serves 1

◄ 2 slices raisin bread
◄ 2 tablespoons butter, softened
◄ 2 teaspoons honey mustard
◄ 3 slices thinly sliced honey

ham (about 3 ounces / 85 g)
◄ 4 slices Muenster cheese (about 3 ounces / 85 g)
◄ 2 toothpicks

1. Preheat the air fryer to 370ºF (188ºC). 2. Spread the softened butter on one side of both slices of raisin bread and place the bread, buttered side down on the counter. Spread the honey mustard on the other side of each slice of bread. Layer 2 slices of cheese, the ham and the remaining 2 slices of cheese on one slice of bread and top with the other slice of bread. Remember to leave the buttered side of the bread on the outside. 3. Transfer the sandwich to the air fryer basket and secure the sandwich with toothpicks. 4. Air fry for 5 minutes. Flip the sandwich over, remove the toothpicks and air fry for another 5 minutes. Cut the sandwich in half and enjoy!

# Kale Chips with Sesame

## Prep time: 15 minutes | Cook time: 8 minutes | Serves 5

◄ 8 cups deribbed kale leaves, torn into 2-inch pieces
◄ 1½ tablespoons olive oil
◄ ¾ teaspoon chili powder

◄ ¼ teaspoon garlic powder
◄ ½ teaspoon paprika
◄ 2 teaspoons sesame seeds

1. Preheat air fryer to 350ºF (177ºC). 2. In a large bowl, toss the kale with the olive oil, chili powder, garlic powder, paprika, and sesame seeds until well coated. 3. Put the kale in the air fryer basket and air fry for 8 minutes, flipping the kale twice during cooking, or until the kale is crispy. 4. Serve warm.

# Veggie Shrimp Toast

## Prep time: 15 minutes | Cook time: 3 to 6 minutes | Serves 4

◄ 8 large raw shrimp, peeled and finely chopped
◄ 1 egg white
◄ 2 garlic cloves, minced
◄ 3 tablespoons minced red bell pepper
◄ 1 medium celery stalk,

minced
◄ 2 tablespoons cornstarch
◄ ¼ teaspoon Chinese five-spice powder
◄ 3 slices firm thin-sliced no-sodium whole-wheat bread

1. Preheat the air fryer to 350ºF (177ºC). 2. In a small bowl, stir

together the shrimp, egg white, garlic, red bell pepper, celery, cornstarch, and five-spice powder. Top each slice of bread with one-third of the shrimp mixture, spreading it evenly to the edges. With a sharp knife, cut each slice of bread into 4 strips. 3. Place the shrimp toasts in the air fryer basket in a single layer. You may need to cook them in batches. Air fry for 3 to 6 minutes, until crisp and golden brown. 4. Serve hot.

# String Bean Fries

## Prep time: 15 minutes | Cook time: 5 to 6 minutes | Serves 4

◄ ½ pound (227 g) fresh string beans
◄ 2 eggs
◄ 4 teaspoons water
◄ ½ cup white flour
◄ ½ cup bread crumbs
◄ ¼ teaspoon salt

◄ ¼ teaspoon ground black pepper
◄ ¼ teaspoon dry mustard (optional)
◄ Oil for misting or cooking spray

1. Preheat the air fryer to 360ºF (182ºC). 2. Trim stem ends from string beans, wash, and pat dry. 3. In a shallow dish, beat eggs and water together until well blended. 4. Place flour in a second shallow dish. 5. In a third shallow dish, stir together the bread crumbs, salt, pepper, and dry mustard if using. 6. Dip each string bean in egg mixture, flour, egg mixture again, then bread crumbs. 7. When you finish coating all the string beans, open air fryer and place them in basket. 8. Cook for 3 minutes. 9. PAUSE and mist string beans with oil or cooking spray. 10. Cook for 2 to 3 more minutes or until string beans are crispy and nicely browned.

# Root Veggie Chips with Herb Salt

## Prep time: 10 minutes | Cook time: 8 minutes | Serves 2

◄ 1 parsnip, washed
◄ 1 small beet, washed
◄ 1 small turnip, washed
◄ ½ small sweet potato,
Herb Salt:
◄ ¼ teaspoon kosher salt
◄ 2 teaspoons finely chopped

washed
◄ 1 teaspoon olive oil
◄ Cooking spray

fresh parsley

1. Preheat the air fryer to 360ºF (182ºC). 2. Peel and thinly slice the parsnip, beet, turnip, and sweet potato, then place the vegetables in a large bowl, add the olive oil, and toss. 3. Spray the air fryer basket with cooking spray, then place the vegetables in the basket and air fry for 8 minutes, gently shaking the basket halfway through. 4. While the chips cook, make the herb salt in a small bowl by combining the kosher salt and parsley. 5. Remove the chips and place on a serving plate, then sprinkle the herb salt on top and allow to cool for 2 to 3 minutes before serving.

## Crispy Chili Chickpeas

### Prep time: 5 minutes | Cook time: 15 minutes | Serves 4

- 1 (15 ounces / 425 g) can cooked chickpeas, drained and rinsed
- 1 tablespoon olive oil
- ¼ teaspoon salt
- ⅛ teaspoon chili powder
- ⅛ teaspoon garlic powder
- ⅛ teaspoon paprika

1. Preheat the air fryer to 380°F(193°C). 2. In a medium bowl, toss all of the ingredients together until the chickpeas are well coated. 3. Pour the chickpeas into the air fryer and spread them out in a single layer. 4. Roast for 15 minutes, stirring once halfway through the cook time.

## Cinnamon-Apple Chips

### Prep time: 10 minutes | Cook time: 32 minutes | Serves 4

- Oil, for spraying
- 2 Red Delicious or Honeycrisp apples
- ¼ teaspoon ground cinnamon, divided

1. Line the air fryer basket with parchment and spray lightly with oil. 2. Trim the uneven ends off the apples. Using a mandoline on the thinnest setting or a sharp knife, cut the apples into very thin slices. Discard the cores. 3. Place half of the apple slices in a single layer in the prepared basket and sprinkle with half of the cinnamon. 4. Place a metal air fryer trivet on top of the apples to keep them from flying around while they are cooking. 5. Air fry at 300°F (149°C) for 16 minutes, flipping every 5 minutes to ensure even cooking. Repeat with the remaining apple slices and cinnamon. 6. Let cool to room temperature before serving. The chips will firm up as they cool.

## Eggplant Fries

### Prep time: 10 minutes | Cook time: 7 to 8 minutes per batch | Serves 4

- 1 medium eggplant
- 1 teaspoon ground coriander
- 1 teaspoon cumin
- 1 teaspoon garlic powder
- ½ teaspoon salt
- 1 cup crushed panko bread crumbs
- 1 large egg
- 2 tablespoons water
- Oil for misting or cooking spray

1. Peel and cut the eggplant into fat fries, ⅜- to ½-inch thick. 2. Preheat the air fryer to 390°F (199°C). 3. In a small cup, mix together the coriander, cumin, garlic, and salt. 4. Combine 1 teaspoon of the seasoning mix and panko crumbs in a shallow dish. 5. Place eggplant fries in a large bowl, sprinkle with remaining seasoning, and stir well to combine. 6. Beat eggs and water together and pour over eggplant fries. Stir to coat. 7. Remove eggplant from egg wash, shaking off excess, and roll in panko crumbs. 8. Spray with oil. 9. Place half of the fries in air fryer basket. You should have only a single layer, but it's fine if they overlap a little. 10. Cook for 5 minutes. Shake basket, mist lightly with oil, and cook 2 to 3 minutes longer, until browned and crispy. 11. Repeat step 10 to cook remaining eggplant.

## Vegetable Pot Stickers

### Prep time: 12 minutes | Cook time: 11 to 18 minutes | Makes 12 pot stickers

- 1 cup shredded red cabbage
- ¼ cup chopped button mushrooms
- ¼ cup grated carrot
- 2 tablespoons minced onion
- 2 garlic cloves, minced
- 2 teaspoons grated fresh ginger
- 12 gyoza/pot sticker wrappers
- 2½ teaspoons olive oil, divided

1. In a baking pan, combine the red cabbage, mushrooms, carrot, onion, garlic, and ginger. Add 1 tablespoon of water. Place in the air fryer and air fry at 370°F (188°C) for 3 to 6 minutes, until the vegetables are crisp-tender. Drain and set aside. 2. Working one at a time, place the pot sticker wrappers on a work surface. Top each wrapper with a scant 1 tablespoon of the filling. Fold half of the wrapper over the other half to form a half circle. Dab one edge with water and press both edges together. 3. To another pan, add 1¼ teaspoons of olive oil. Put half of the pot stickers, seam-side up, in the pan. Air fry for 5 minutes, or until the bottoms are light golden brown. Add 1 tablespoon of water and return the pan to the air fryer. 4. Air fry for 4 to 6 minutes more, or until hot. Repeat with the remaining pot stickers, remaining 1¼ teaspoons of oil, and another tablespoon of water. Serve immediately.

## Stuffed Figs with Goat Cheese and Honey

### Prep time: 5 minutes | Cook time: 10 minutes | Serves 4

- 8 fresh figs
- 2 ounces (57 g) goat cheese
- ¼ teaspoon ground cinnamon
- 1 tablespoon honey, plus more for serving
- 1 tablespoon olive oil

1. Preheat the air fryer to 360°F(182°C). 2. Cut the stem off of each fig. 3. Cut an X into the top of each fig, cutting halfway down the fig. Leave the base intact. 4. In a small bowl, mix together the goat cheese, cinnamon, and honey. 5. Spoon the goat cheese mixture into the cavity of each fig. 6. Place the figs in a single layer in the air fryer basket. Drizzle the olive oil over top of the figs and roast for 10 minutes. 7. Serve with an additional drizzle of honey.

## Sweet Bacon Tater Tots

### Prep time: 5 minutes | Cook time: 7 minutes | Serves 4

- ◄ 24 frozen tater tots
- ◄ 6 slices cooked bacon
- ◄ 2 tablespoons maple syrup
- ◄ 1 cup shredded Cheddar cheese

1. Preheat the air fryer to 400ºF (204ºC). 2. Put the tater tots in the air fryer basket. Air fry for 10 minutes, shaking the basket halfway through the cooking time. 3. Meanwhile, cut the bacon into 1-inch pieces. 4. Remove the tater tots from the air fryer basket and put into a baking pan. Top with the bacon and drizzle with the maple syrup. Air fry for 5 minutes, or until the tots and bacon are crisp. 5. Top with the cheese and air fry for 2 minutes, or until the cheese is melted. 6. Serve hot.

## Homemade Sweet Potato Chips

### Prep time: 5 minutes | Cook time: 15 minutes | Serves 2

- ◄ 1 large sweet potato, sliced thin
- ◄ ⅛ teaspoon salt
- ◄ 2 tablespoons olive oil

1. Preheat the air fryer to 380°F(193ºC). 2. In a small bowl, toss the sweet potatoes, salt, and olive oil together until the potatoes are well coated. 3. Put the sweet potato slices into the air fryer and spread them out in a single layer. 4. Fry for 10 minutes. Stir, then air fry for 3 to 5 minutes more, or until the chips reach the preferred level of crispiness.

## Parmesan French Fries

### Prep time: 10 minutes | Cook time: 25 minutes | Serves 2 to 3

- ◄ 2 to 3 large russet potatoes, peeled and cut into ½-inch sticks
- ◄ 2 teaspoons vegetable or canola oil
- ◄ ¾ cup grated Parmesan
- cheese
- ◄ ½ teaspoon salt
- ◄ Freshly ground black pepper, to taste
- ◄ 1 teaspoon fresh chopped parsley

1. Bring a large saucepan of salted water to a boil on the stovetop while you peel and cut the potatoes. Blanch the potatoes in the boiling salted water for 4 minutes while you preheat the air fryer to 400ºF (204ºC). Strain the potatoes and rinse them with cold water. Dry them well with a clean kitchen towel. 2. Toss the dried potato sticks gently with the oil and place them in the air fryer basket. Air fry for 25 minutes, shaking the basket a few times while the fries cook to help them brown evenly. 3. Combine the Parmesan cheese, salt and pepper. With 2 minutes left on the air fryer cooking time, sprinkle the fries with the Parmesan cheese mixture. Toss the fries to coat them evenly with the cheese mixture and continue to air fry for the final 2 minutes, until the cheese has melted and just starts to brown. Sprinkle the finished fries with chopped parsley, a little more grated Parmesan cheese if you like, and serve.

## Cheese Drops

### Prep time: 15 minutes | Cook time: 10 minutes per batch | Serves 8

- ◄ ¾ cup all-purpose flour
- ◄ ½ teaspoon kosher salt
- ◄ ¼ teaspoon cayenne pepper
- ◄ ¼ teaspoon smoked paprika
- ◄ ¼ teaspoon black pepper
- ◄ Dash garlic powder
- (optional)
- ◄ ¼ cup butter, softened
- ◄ 1 cup shredded sharp Cheddar cheese, at room temperature
- ◄ Olive oil spray

1. In a small bowl, combine the flour, salt, cayenne, paprika, pepper, and garlic powder, if using. 2. Using a food processor, cream the butter and cheese until smooth. Gently add the seasoned flour and process until the dough is well combined, smooth, and no longer sticky. (Or make the dough in a stand mixer fitted with the paddle attachment: Cream the butter and cheese on medium speed until smooth, then add the seasoned flour and beat at low speed until smooth.) 3. Divide the dough into 32 equal-size pieces. On a lightly floured surface, roll each piece into a small ball. 4. Spray the air fryer basket with oil spray. Arrange 16 cheese drops in the basket. Set the air fryer to 325ºF (163ºC) for 10 minutes, or until drops are just starting to brown. Transfer to a wire rack. Repeat with remaining dough, checking for doneness at 8 minutes. 5. Cool the cheese drops completely on the wire rack. Store in an airtight container until ready to serve, or up to 1 or 2 days.

## Cheese Wafers

### Prep time: 30 minutes | Cook time: 5 to 6 minutes per batch | Makes 4 dozen

- ◄ 4 ounces (113 g) sharp Cheddar cheese, grated
- ◄ ¼ cup butter
- ◄ ½ cup flour
- ◄ ¼ teaspoon salt
- ◄ ½ cup crisp rice cereal
- ◄ Oil for misting or cooking spray

1. Cream the butter and grated cheese together. You can do it by hand, but using a stand mixer is faster and easier. 2. Sift flour and salt together. Add it to the cheese mixture and mix until well blended. 3. Stir in cereal. 4. Place dough on wax paper and shape into a long roll about 1 inch in diameter. Wrap well with the wax paper and chill for at least 4 hours. 5. When ready to cook, preheat the air fryer to 360ºF (182ºC). 6. Cut cheese roll into ¼-inch slices. 7. Spray the air fryer basket with oil or cooking spray and place slices in a single layer, close but not touching. 8. Cook for 5 to 6 minutes or until golden brown. When done, place them on paper towels to cool. 9. Repeat previous step to cook remaining cheese bites.

## Corn Dog Muffins

**Prep time: 10 minutes | Cook time: 8 to 10 minutes per batch | Makes 8 muffins**

- ◄ 1¼ cups sliced kosher hotdogs (3 or 4, depending on size)
- ◄ ½ cup flour
- ◄ ½ cup yellow cornmeal
- ◄ 2 teaspoons baking powder
- ◄ ½ cup skim milk
- ◄ 1 egg
- ◄ 2 tablespoons canola oil
- ◄ 8 foil muffin cups, paper liners removed
- ◄ Cooking spray
- ◄ Mustard or your favorite dipping sauce

1. Slice each hotdog in half lengthwise, then cut in ¼-inch half-moon slices. Set aside. 2. Preheat the air fryer to 390ºF (199ºC). 3. In a large bowl, stir together flour, cornmeal, and baking powder. 4. In a small bowl, beat together the milk, egg, and oil until just blended. 5. Pour egg mixture into dry ingredients and stir with a spoon to mix well. 6. Stir in sliced hot dogs. 7. Spray the foil cups lightly with cooking spray. 8. Divide mixture evenly into muffin cups. 9. Place 4 muffin cups in the air fryer basket and cook for 5 minutes. 10. Reduce temperature to 360ºF (182ºC) and cook 3 to 5 minutes or until toothpick inserted in center of muffin comes out clean. 11. Repeat steps 9 and 10 to Air Fry remaining corn dog muffins. 12. Serve with mustard or other sauces for dipping.

## Roasted Pearl Onion Dip

**Prep time: 5 minutes | Cook time: 12 minutes | Serves 4**

- ◄ 2 cups peeled pearl onions
- ◄ 3 garlic cloves
- ◄ 3 tablespoons olive oil, divided
- ◄ ½ teaspoon salt
- ◄ 1 cup nonfat plain Greek yogurt
- ◄ 1 tablespoon lemon juice
- ◄ ¼ teaspoon black pepper
- ◄ ⅛ teaspoon red pepper flakes
- ◄ Pita chips, vegetables, or toasted bread for serving (optional)

1. Preheat the air fryer to 360ºF(182ºC). 2. In a large bowl, combine the pearl onions and garlic with 2 tablespoons of the olive oil until the onions are well coated. 3. Pour the garlic-and-onion mixture into the air fryer basket and roast for 12 minutes. 4. Transfer the garlic and onions to a food processor. Pulse the vegetables several times, until the onions are minced but still have some chunks. 5. In a large bowl, combine the garlic and onions and the remaining 1 tablespoon of olive oil, along with the salt, yogurt, lemon juice, black pepper, and red pepper flakes. 6. Cover and chill for 1 hour before serving with pita chips, vegetables, or toasted bread.

## Carrot Chips

**Prep time: 15 minutes | Cook time: 8 to 10 minutes | Serves 4**

- ◄ 1 tablespoon olive oil, plus more for greasing the basket
- ◄ 4 to 5 medium carrots,
- trimmed and thinly sliced
- ◄ 1 teaspoon seasoned salt

1. Preheat the air fryer to 390ºF (199ºC). Grease the air fryer basket with the olive oil. 2. Toss the carrot slices with 1 tablespoon of olive oil and salt in a medium bowl until thoroughly coated. 3. Arrange the carrot slices in the greased basket. You may need to work in batches to avoid overcrowding. 4. Air fry for 8 to 10 minutes until the carrot slices are crisp-tender. Shake the basket once during cooking. 5. Transfer the carrot slices to a bowl and repeat with the remaining carrots. 6. Allow to cool for 5 minutes and serve.

## Browned Ricotta with Capers and Lemon

**Prep time: 10 minutes | Cook time: 8 to 10 minutes | Serves 4 to 6**

- ◄ 1½ cups whole milk ricotta cheese
- ◄ 2 tablespoons extra-virgin olive oil
- ◄ 2 tablespoons capers, rinsed
- ◄ Zest of 1 lemon, plus more for garnish
- ◄ 1 teaspoon finely chopped
- fresh rosemary
- ◄ Pinch crushed red pepper flakes
- ◄ Salt and freshly ground black pepper, to taste
- ◄ 1 tablespoon grated Parmesan cheese

1. Preheat the air fryer to 380ºF (193ºC). 2. In a mixing bowl, stir together the ricotta cheese, olive oil, capers, lemon zest, rosemary, red pepper flakes, salt, and pepper until well combined. 3. Spread the mixture evenly in a baking dish and place it in the air fryer basket. 4. Air fry for 8 to 10 minutes until the top is nicely browned. 5. Remove from the basket and top with a sprinkle of grated Parmesan cheese. 6. Garnish with the lemon zest and serve warm.

# Chapter 9

## Fast and Easy Everyday Favorites

# Chapter 9 Fast and Easy Everyday Favorites

## Southwest Corn and Bell Pepper Roast

**Prep time: 10 minutes | Cook time: 10 minutes | Serves 4**

For the Corn:
- 1½ cups thawed frozen corn kernels
- 1 cup mixed diced bell peppers
- 1 jalapeño, diced
- 1 cup diced yellow onion
- ½ teaspoon ancho chile
- powder
- 1 tablespoon fresh lemon juice
- 1 teaspoon ground cumin
- ½ teaspoon kosher salt
- Cooking spray

For Serving:
- ¼ cup feta cheese
- ¼ cup chopped fresh cilantro
- 1 tablespoon fresh lemon juice

1. Preheat the air fryer to 375ºF (191ºC). Spritz the air fryer with cooking spray. 2. Combine the ingredients for the corn in a large bowl. Stir to mix well. 3. Pout the mixture into the air fryer. Air fry for 10 minutes or until the corn and bell peppers are soft. Shake the basket halfway through the cooking time. 4. Transfer them onto a large plate, then spread with feta cheese and cilantro. Drizzle with lemon juice and serve.

## Crunchy Fried Okra

**Prep time: 5 minutes | Cook time: 8 to 10 minutes | Serves 4**

- 1 cup self-rising yellow cornmeal
- 1 teaspoon Italian-style seasoning
- 1 teaspoon paprika
- 1 teaspoon salt
- ½ teaspoon freshly ground black pepper
- 2 large eggs, beaten
- 2 cups okra slices
- Cooking spray

1. Preheat the air fryer to 400ºF (204ºC). Line the air fryer basket with parchment paper. 2. In a shallow bowl, whisk the cornmeal, Italian-style seasoning, paprika, salt, and pepper until blended. Place the beaten eggs in a second shallow bowl. 3. Add the okra to the beaten egg and stir to coat. Add the egg and okra mixture to the cornmeal mixture and stir until coated. 4. Place the okra on the parchment and spritz it with oil. 5. Air fry for 4 minutes. Shake the basket, spritz the okra with oil, and air fry for 4 to 6 minutes more until lightly browned and crispy. 6. Serve immediately.

## Garlicky Knots with Parsley

**Prep time: 10 minutes | Cook time: 10 minutes | Makes 8 knots**

- 1 teaspoon dried parsley
- ¼ cup melted butter
- 2 teaspoons garlic powder
- 1 (11 ounces / 312 g) tube refrigerated French bread dough, cut into 8 slices

1. Preheat the air fryer to 350ºF (177ºC). 2. Combine the parsley, butter, and garlic powder in a bowl. Stir to mix well. 3. Place the French bread dough slices on a clean work surface, then roll each slice into a 6-inch long rope. Tie the ropes into knots and arrange them on a plate. Brush the knots with butter mixture. 4. Transfer the knots into the air fryer. You need to work in batches to avoid overcrowding. 5. Air fry for 5 minutes or until the knots are golden brown. Flip the knots halfway through the cooking time. 6. Serve immediately.

## Indian-Style Sweet Potato Fries

**Prep time: 5 minutes | Cook time: 8 minutes | Makes 20 fries**

Seasoning Mixture:
- ¾ teaspoon ground coriander
- ½ teaspoon garam masala
- ½ teaspoon garlic powder
- ½ teaspoon ground cumin
- ¼ teaspoon ground cayenne pepper

Fries:
- 2 large sweet potatoes, peeled
- 2 teaspoons olive oil

1. Preheat the air fryer to 400ºF (204ºC). 2. In a small bowl, combine the coriander, garam masala, garlic powder, cumin, and cayenne pepper. 3. Slice the sweet potatoes into ¼-inch-thick fries. 4. In a large bowl, toss the sliced sweet potatoes with the olive oil and the seasoning mixture. 5. Transfer the seasoned sweet potatoes to the air fryer basket and fry for 8 minutes, until crispy. 6. Serve warm.

## Easy Cinnamon Toast

### Prep time: 5 minutes | Cook time: 20 minutes | Serves 6

- 1½ teaspoons cinnamon
- 1½ teaspoons vanilla extract
- ½ cup sugar
- 2 teaspoons ground black
- pepper
- 2 tablespoons melted coconut oil
- 12 slices whole wheat bread

1. Preheat the air fryer to 400°F (204°C). 2. Combine all the ingredients, except for the bread, in a large bowl. Stir to mix well. 3. Dunk the bread in the bowl of mixture gently to coat and infuse well. Shake the excess off. 4. Arrange the bread slices in the preheated air fryer. Air fry for 5 minutes or until golden brown. Flip the bread halfway through. You may need to cook in batches to avoid overcrowding. 5. Remove the bread slices from the air fryer and slice to serve.

## Easy Devils on Horseback

### Prep time: 5 minutes | Cook time: 7 minutes | Serves 12

- 24 petite pitted prunes (4½ ounces / 128 g)
- ¼ cup crumbled blue cheese,
- divided
- 8 slices center-cut bacon, cut crosswise into thirds

1. Preheat the air fryer to 400°F (204°C). 2. Halve the prunes lengthwise, but don't cut them all the way through. Place ½ teaspoon of cheese in the center of each prune. Wrap a piece of bacon around each prune and secure the bacon with a toothpick. 3. Working in batches, arrange a single layer of the prunes in the air fryer basket. Air fry for about 7 minutes, flipping halfway, until the bacon is cooked through and crisp. 4. Let cool slightly and serve warm.

## Rosemary and Orange Roasted Chickpeas

### Prep time: 5 minutes | Cook time: 10 to 12 minutes | Makes 4 cups

- 4 cups cooked chickpeas
- 2 tablespoons vegetable oil
- 1 teaspoon kosher salt
- 1 teaspoon cumin
- 1 teaspoon paprika
- Zest of 1 orange
- 1 tablespoon chopped fresh rosemary

1. Preheat the air fryer to 400°F (204°C). 2. Make sure the chickpeas are completely dry prior to roasting. In a medium bowl, toss the chickpeas with oil, salt, cumin, and paprika. 3. Working in batches, spread the chickpeas in a single layer in the air fryer basket. Air fry for 10 to 12 minutes until crisp, shaking once halfway through. 4.

Return the warm chickpeas to the bowl and toss with the orange zest and rosemary. Allow to cool completely. 5. Serve.

## Beery and Crunchy Onion Rings

### Prep time: 10 minutes | Cook time: 16 minutes | Serves 2 to 4

- ⅔ cup all-purpose flour
- 1 teaspoon paprika
- ½ teaspoon baking soda
- 1 teaspoon salt
- ½ teaspoon freshly ground black pepper
- 1 egg, beaten
- ¾ cup beer
- 1½ cups breadcrumbs
- 1 tablespoons olive oil
- 1 large Vidalia onion, peeled and sliced into ½-inch rings
- Cooking spray

1. Preheat the air fryer to 360°F (182°C). Spritz the air fryer basket with cooking spray. 2. Combine the flour, paprika, baking soda, salt, and ground black pepper in a bowl. Stir to mix well. 3. Combine the egg and beer in a separate bowl. Stir to mix well. 4. Make a well in the center of the flour mixture, then pour the egg mixture in the well. Stir to mix everything well. 5. Pour the breadcrumbs and olive oil in a shallow plate. Stir to mix well. 6. Dredge the onion rings gently into the flour and egg mixture, then shake the excess off and put into the plate of breadcrumbs. Flip to coat the both sides well. 7. Arrange the onion rings in the preheated air fryer. Air fry in batches for 16 minutes or until golden brown and crunchy. Flip the rings and put the bottom rings to the top halfway through. 8. Serve immediately.

## Sweet Corn and Carrot Fritters

### Prep time: 10 minutes | Cook time: 8 to 11 minutes | Serves 4

- 1 medium-sized carrot, grated
- 1 yellow onion, finely chopped
- 4 ounces (113 g) canned sweet corn kernels, drained
- 1 teaspoon sea salt flakes
- 1 tablespoon chopped fresh cilantro
- 1 medium-sized egg, whisked
- 2 tablespoons plain milk
- 1 cup grated Parmesan cheese
- ¼ cup flour
- ⅓ teaspoon baking powder
- ⅓ teaspoon sugar
- Cooking spray

1. Preheat the air fryer to 350°F (177°C). 2. Place the grated carrot in a colander and press down to squeeze out any excess moisture. Dry it with a paper towel. 3. Combine the carrots with the remaining ingredients. 4. Mold 1 tablespoon of the mixture into a ball and press it down with your hand or a spoon to flatten it. Repeat until the rest of the mixture is used up. 5. Spritz the balls with cooking spray. 6. Arrange in the air fryer basket, taking care not to overlap any balls. Air Fry for 8 to 11 minutes, or until they're firm. 7. Serve warm.

# Cheesy Air Fryd Grits

## Prep time: 10 minutes | Cook time: 12 minutes | Serves 6

- ◀ ¾ cup hot water
- ◀ 2 (1 ounces / 28 g) packages instant grits
- ◀ 1 large egg, beaten
- ◀ 1 tablespoon butter, melted
- ◀ 2 cloves garlic, minced
- ◀ ½ to 1 teaspoon red pepper flakes
- ◀ 1 cup shredded Cheddar cheese or jalapeño Jack cheese

1. Preheat the air fryer to 400°F (204°C). 2. In a baking pan, combine the water, grits, egg, butter, garlic, and red pepper flakes. Stir until well combined. Stir in the shredded cheese. 3. Place the pan in the air fryer basket and air fry for 12 minutes, or until the grits have cooked through and a knife inserted near the center comes out clean. 4. Let stand for 5 minutes before serving.

# Air Fryd Cheese Sandwich

## Prep time: 5 minutes | Cook time: 8 minutes | Serves 2

- ◀ 2 tablespoons mayonnaise
- ◀ 4 thick slices sourdough bread
- ◀ 4 thick slices Brie cheese
- ◀ 8 slices hot capicola

1. Preheat the air fryer to 350°F (177°C). 2. Spread the mayonnaise on one side of each slice of bread. Place 2 slices of bread in the air fryer basket, mayonnaise-side down. 3. Place the slices of Brie and capicola on the bread and cover with the remaining two slices of bread, mayonnaise-side up. 4. Air Fry for 8 minutes, or until the cheese has melted. 5. Serve immediately.

# Honey Bartlett Pears with Lemony Ricotta

## Prep time: 10 minutes | Cook time: 8 minutes | Serves 4

- ◀ 2 large Bartlett pears, peeled, cut in half, cored
- ◀ 3 tablespoons melted butter
- ◀ ½ teaspoon ground ginger
- ◀ ¼ teaspoon ground cardamom
- ◀ 3 tablespoons brown sugar
- ◀ ½ cup whole-milk ricotta
- cheese
- ◀ 1 teaspoon pure lemon extract
- ◀ 1 teaspoon pure almond extract
- ◀ 1 tablespoon honey, plus additional for drizzling

1. Preheat the air fryer to 375°F (191°C). 2. Toss the pears with butter, ginger, cardamom, and sugar in a large bowl. Toss to coat well. 3. Arrange the pears in the preheated air fryer, cut side down.

Air fry for 5 minutes, then flip the pears and air fry for 3 more minutes or until the pears are soft and browned. 4. In the meantime, combine the remaining ingredients in a separate bowl. Whip for 1 minute with a hand mixer until the mixture is puffed. 5. Divide the mixture into four bowls, then put the pears over the mixture and drizzle with more honey to serve.

# Golden Salmon and Carrot Croquettes

## Prep time: 15 minutes | Cook time: 10 minutes | Serves 6

- ◀ 2 egg whites
- ◀ 1 cup almond flour
- ◀ 1 cup panko breadcrumbs
- ◀ 1 pound (454 g) chopped salmon fillet
- ◀ ⅔ cup grated carrots
- ◀ 2 tablespoons minced garlic cloves
- ◀ ½ cup chopped onion
- ◀ 2 tablespoons chopped chives
- ◀ Cooking spray

1. Preheat the air fryer to 350°F (177°C). Spritz the air fryer basket with cooking spray. 2. Whisk the egg whites in a bowl. Put the flour in a second bowl. Pour the breadcrumbs in a third bowl. Set aside. 3. Combine the salmon, carrots, garlic, onion, and chives in a large bowl. Stir to mix well. 4. Form the mixture into balls with your hands. Dredge the balls into the flour, then egg, and then breadcrumbs to coat well. 5. Arrange the salmon balls in the preheated air fryer and spritz with cooking spray. 6. Air fry for 10 minutes or until crispy and browned. Shake the basket halfway through. 7. Serve immediately.

# Air Fried Butternut Squash with Chopped Hazelnuts

## Prep time: 10 minutes | Cook time: 20 minutes | Makes 3 cups

- ◀ 2 tablespoons whole hazelnuts
- ◀ 3 cups butternut squash, peeled, deseeded, and cubed
- ◀ ¼ teaspoon kosher salt
- ◀ ¼ teaspoon freshly ground black pepper
- ◀ 2 teaspoons olive oil
- ◀ Cooking spray

1. Preheat the air fryer to 300°F (149°C). Spritz the air fryer basket with cooking spray. 2. Arrange the hazelnuts in the preheated air fryer. Air fry for 3 minutes or until soft. 3. Chopped the hazelnuts roughly and transfer to a small bowl. Set aside. 4. Set the air fryer temperature to 360°F (182°C). Spritz with cooking spray. 5. Put the butternut squash in a large bowl, then sprinkle with salt and pepper and drizzle with olive oil. Toss to coat well. 6. Transfer the squash in the air fryer. Air fry for 20 minutes or until the squash is soft. Shake the basket halfway through the frying time. 7. When the frying is complete, transfer the squash onto a plate and sprinkle with chopped hazelnuts before serving.

# Garlicky Zoodles

### Prep time: 10 minutes | Cook time: 10 minutes | Serves 4

- 2 large zucchini, peeled and spiralized
- 2 large yellow summer squash, peeled and spiralized
- 1 tablespoon olive oil, divided
- ½ teaspoon kosher salt
- 1 garlic clove, whole
- 2 tablespoons fresh basil, chopped
- Cooking spray

1. Preheat the air fryer to 360ºF (182ºC). Spritz the air fryer basket with cooking spray. 2. Combine the zucchini and summer squash with 1 teaspoon olive oil and salt in a large bowl. Toss to coat well. 3. Transfer the zucchini and summer squash in the preheated air fryer and add the garlic. 4. Air fry for 10 minutes or until tender and fragrant. Toss the spiralized zucchini and summer squash halfway through the cooking time. 5. Transfer the cooked zucchini and summer squash onto a plate and set aside. 6. Remove the garlic from the air fryer and allow to cool for a few minutes. Mince the garlic and combine with remaining olive oil in a small bowl. Stir to mix well. 7. Drizzle the spiralized zucchini and summer squash with garlic oil and sprinkle with basil. Toss to serve.

# Herb-Roasted Veggies

### Prep time: 10 minutes | Cook time: 14 to 18 minutes | Serves 4

- 1 red bell pepper, sliced
- 1 (8 ounces / 227 g) package sliced mushrooms
- 1 cup green beans, cut into 2-inch pieces
- ⅓ cup diced red onion
- 3 garlic cloves, sliced
- 1 teaspoon olive oil
- ½ teaspoon dried basil
- ½ teaspoon dried tarragon

1. Preheat the air fryer to 350ºF (177ºC). 2. In a medium bowl, mix the red bell pepper, mushrooms, green beans, red onion, and garlic. Drizzle with the olive oil. Toss to coat. 3. Add the herbs and toss again. 4. Place the vegetables in the air fryer basket. Roast for 14 to 18 minutes, or until tender. Serve immediately.

# Air Fryd Chorizo Scotch Eggs

### Prep time: 5 minutes | Cook time: 15 to 20 minutes | Makes 4 eggs

- 1 pound (454 g) Mexican chorizo or other seasoned sausage meat
- 4 soft-boiled eggs plus 1 raw egg
- 1 tablespoon water
- ½ cup all-purpose flour
- 1 cup panko bread crumbs
- Cooking spray

1. Divide the chorizo into 4 equal portions. Flatten each portion into a disc. Place a soft-boiled egg in the center of each disc. Wrap the chorizo around the egg, encasing it completely. Place the encased eggs on a plate and chill for at least 30 minutes. 2. Preheat the air fryer to 360ºF (182ºC). 3. Beat the raw egg with 1 tablespoon of water. Place the flour on a small plate and the panko on a second plate. Working with 1 egg at a time, roll the encased egg in the flour, then dip it in the egg mixture. Dredge the egg in the panko and place on a plate. Repeat with the remaining eggs. 4. Spray the eggs with oil and place in the air fryer basket. Air Fry for 10 minutes. Turn and Air Fry for an additional 5 to 10 minutes, or until browned and crisp on all sides. 5. Serve immediately.

# Lemony and Garlicky Asparagus

### Prep time: 5 minutes | Cook time: 10 minutes | Makes 10 spears

- 10 spears asparagus (about ½ pound / 227 g in total), snap the ends off
- 1 tablespoon lemon juice
- 2 teaspoons minced garlic
- ½ teaspoon salt
- ¼ teaspoon ground black pepper
- Cooking spray

1. Preheat the air fryer to 400ºF (204ºC). Line a parchment paper in the air fryer basket. 2. Put the asparagus spears in a large bowl. Drizzle with lemon juice and sprinkle with minced garlic, salt, and ground black pepper. Toss to coat well. 3. Transfer the asparagus in the preheated air fryer and spritz with cooking spray. Air fryer for 10 minutes or until wilted and soft. Flip the asparagus halfway through. 4. Serve immediately.

# Purple Potato Chips with Rosemary

### Prep time: 10 minutes | Cook time: 9 to 14 minutes | Serves 6

- 1 cup Greek yogurt
- 2 chipotle chiles, minced
- 2 tablespoons adobo sauce
- 1 teaspoon paprika
- 1 tablespoon lemon juice
- 10 purple fingerling potatoes
- 1 teaspoon olive oil
- 2 teaspoons minced fresh rosemary leaves
- ⅛ teaspoon cayenne pepper
- ¼ teaspoon coarse sea salt

1. Preheat the air fryer to 400ºF (204ºC). 2. In a medium bowl, combine the yogurt, minced chiles, adobo sauce, paprika, and lemon juice. Mix well and refrigerate. 3. Wash the potatoes and dry them with paper towels. Slice the potatoes lengthwise, as thinly as possible. You can use a mandoline, a vegetable peeler, or a very sharp knife. 4. Combine the potato slices in a medium bowl and drizzle with the olive oil; toss to coat. 5. Air fry the chips, in batches, in the air fryer basket, for 9 to 14 minutes. Use tongs to gently rearrange the chips halfway during cooking time. 6. Sprinkle the chips with the rosemary, cayenne pepper, and sea salt. Serve with the chipotle sauce for dipping.

## Simple Pea Delight

**Prep time: 5 minutes | Cook time: 15 minutes | Serves 2 to 4**

- 1 cup flour
- 1 teaspoon baking powder
- 3 eggs
- 1 cup coconut milk
- 1 cup cream cheese
- 3 tablespoons pea protein
- ½ cup chicken or turkey strips
- Pinch of sea salt
- 1 cup Mozzarella cheese

1. Preheat the air fryer to 390°F (199°C). 2. In a large bowl, mix all ingredients together using a large wooden spoon. 3. Spoon equal amounts of the mixture into muffin cups and Air Fry for 15 minutes. 4. Serve immediately.

## Peppery Brown Rice Fritters

**Prep time: 10 minutes | Cook time: 8 to 10 minutes | Serves 4**

- 1 (10 ounces / 284 g) bag frozen cooked brown rice, thawed
- 1 egg
- 3 tablespoons brown rice flour
- ⅓ cup finely grated carrots
- ⅓ cup minced red bell pepper
- 2 tablespoons minced fresh basil
- 3 tablespoons grated Parmesan cheese
- 2 teaspoons olive oil

1. Preheat the air fryer to 380°F (193°C). 2. In a small bowl, combine the thawed rice, egg, and flour and mix to blend. 3. Stir in the carrots, bell pepper, basil, and Parmesan cheese. 4. Form the mixture into 8 fritters and drizzle with the olive oil. 5. Put the fritters carefully into the air fryer basket. Air fry for 8 to 10 minutes, or until the fritters are golden brown and cooked through. 6. Serve immediately.

## Garlicky Air Fryd Cherry Tomatoes

**Prep time: 5 minutes | Cook time: 4 to 6 minutes | Serves 2**

- 2 cups cherry tomatoes
- 1 clove garlic, thinly sliced
- 1 teaspoon olive oil
- ⅛ teaspoon kosher salt
- 1 tablespoon freshly chopped basil, for topping
- Cooking spray

1. Preheat the air fryer to 360°F (182°C). Spritz the air fryer baking pan with cooking spray and set aside. 2. In a large bowl, toss together the cherry tomatoes, sliced garlic, olive oil, and kosher salt. Spread the mixture in an even layer in the prepared pan. 3. Air Fry in the preheated air fryer for 4 to 6 minutes, or until the tomatoes become soft and wilted. 4. Transfer to a bowl and rest for 5 minutes. Top with the chopped basil and serve warm.

## Parsnip Fries with Garlic-Yogurt Dip

**Prep time: 10 minutes | Cook time: 10 minutes | Serves 4**

- 3 medium parsnips, peeled, cut into sticks
- ¼ teaspoon kosher salt

Dip:
- ¼ cup plain Greek yogurt
- ⅛ teaspoon garlic powder
- 1 tablespoon sour cream
- 1 teaspoon olive oil
- 1 garlic clove, unpeeled
- Cooking spray

- ¼ teaspoon kosher salt
- Freshly ground black pepper, to taste

1. Preheat the air fryer to 360°F (182°C). Spritz the air fryer basket with cooking spray. 2. Put the parsnip sticks in a large bowl, then sprinkle with salt and drizzle with olive oil. 3. Transfer the parsnip into the preheated air fryer and add the garlic. 4. Air fry for 5 minutes, then remove the garlic from the air fryer and shake the basket. Air fry for 5 more minutes or until the parsnip sticks are crisp. 5. Meanwhile, peel the garlic and crush it. Combine the crushed garlic with the ingredients for the dip. Stir to mix well. 6. When the frying is complete, remove the parsnip fries from the air fryer and serve with the dipping sauce.

## Classic Poutine

**Prep time: 15 minutes | Cook time: 25 minutes | Serves 2**

- 2 russet potatoes, scrubbed and cut into ½-inch sticks
- 2 teaspoons vegetable oil
- 2 tablespoons butter
- ¼ onion, minced
- ¼ teaspoon dried thyme
- 1 clove garlic, smashed
- 3 tablespoons all-purpose
- flour
- 1 teaspoon tomato paste
- 1½ cups beef stock
- 2 teaspoons Worcestershire sauce
- Salt and freshly ground black pepper, to taste
- ⅔ cup chopped string cheese

1. Bring a pot of water to a boil, then put in the potato sticks and blanch for 4 minutes. 2. Preheat the air fryer to 400°F (204°C). 3. Drain the potato sticks and rinse under running cold water, then pat dry with paper towels. 4. Transfer the sticks in a large bowl and drizzle with vegetable oil. Toss to coat well. 5. Place the potato sticks in the preheated air fryer. Air fry for 25 minutes or until the sticks are golden brown. Shake the basket at least three times during the frying. 6. Meanwhile, make the gravy: Heat the butter in a saucepan over medium heat until melted. 7. Add the onion, thyme, and garlic and sauté for 5 minutes or until the onion is translucent. 8. Add the flour and sauté for an additional 2 minutes. Pour in the tomato paste and beef stock and cook for 1 more minute or until lightly thickened. 9. Drizzle the gravy with Worcestershire sauce and sprinkle with salt and ground black pepper. Reduce the heat to low to keep the gravy warm until ready to serve. 10. Transfer the fried potato sticks onto a plate, then sprinkle with salt and ground black pepper. Scatter with string cheese and pour the gravy over. Serve warm.

# Chapter 10

## Family Favorites

# Chapter 10 Family Favorites

## Scallops with Green Vegetables

**Prep time: 15 minutes | Cook time: 8 to 11 minutes | Serves 4**

- ◄ 1 cup green beans
- ◄ 1 cup frozen peas
- ◄ 1 cup frozen chopped broccoli
- ◄ 2 teaspoons olive oil
- ◄ ½ teaspoon dried basil
- ◄ ½ teaspoon dried oregano
- ◄ 12 ounces (340 g) sea scallops

1. In a large bowl, toss the green beans, peas, and broccoli with the olive oil. Place in the air fryer basket. Air fry at 400ºF (204ºC) for 4 to 6 minutes, or until the vegetables are crisp-tender. 2. Remove the vegetables from the air fryer basket and sprinkle with the herbs. Set aside. 3. In the air fryer basket, put the scallops and air fry for 4 to 5 minutes, or until the scallops are firm and reach an internal temperature of just 145ºF (63ºC) on a meat thermometer. 4. Toss scallops with the vegetables and serve immediately.

## Beignets

**Prep time: 30 minutes | Cook time: 6 minutes | Makes 9 beignets**

- ◄ Oil, for greasing and spraying
- ◄ 3 cups all-purpose flour, plus more for dusting
- ◄ 1½ teaspoons salt
- ◄ 1 (2¼ teaspoons) envelope active dry yeast
- ◄ 1 cup milk
- ◄ 2 tablespoons packed light brown sugar
- ◄ 1 tablespoon unsalted butter
- ◄ 1 large egg
- ◄ 1 cup confectioners' sugar

1. Oil a large bowl. 2. In a small bowl, mix together the flour, salt, and yeast. Set aside. 3. Pour the milk into a glass measuring cup and microwave in 1-minute intervals until it boils. 4. In a large bowl, mix together the brown sugar and butter. Pour in the hot milk and whisk until the sugar has dissolved. Let cool to room temperature. 5. Whisk the egg into the cooled milk mixture and fold in the flour mixture until a dough forms. 6. On a lightly floured work surface, knead the dough for 3 to 5 minutes. 7. Place the dough in the oiled bowl and cover with a clean kitchen towel. Let rise in a warm place for about 1 hour, or until doubled in size. 8. Roll the dough out on a lightly floured work surface until it's about ¼ inch thick. Cut the dough into 3-inch squares and place them on a lightly floured baking sheet. Cover loosely with a kitchen towel and let rise again until doubled in size, about 30 minutes. 9. Line the air fryer basket with parchment and spray lightly with oil. 10.

Place the dough squares in the prepared basket and spray lightly with oil. You may need to work in batches, depending on the size of your air fryer. 11. Air fry at 390ºF (199ºC) for 3 minutes, flip, spray with oil, and cook for another 3 minutes, until crispy. 12. Dust with the confectioners' sugar before serving.

## Coconut Chicken Tenders

**Prep time: 10 minutes | Cook time: 12 minutes | Serves 4**

- ◄ Oil, for spraying
- ◄ 2 large eggs
- ◄ ¼ cup milk
- ◄ 1 tablespoon hot sauce
- ◄ 1½ cups sweetened flaked coconut
- ◄ ¾ cup panko bread crumbs
- ◄ 1 teaspoon salt
- ◄ ½ teaspoon freshly ground black pepper
- ◄ 1 pound (454 g) chicken tenders

1. Line the air fryer basket with parchment and spray lightly with oil. 2. In a small bowl, whisk together the eggs, milk, and hot sauce. 3. In a shallow dish, mix together the coconut, bread crumbs, salt, and black pepper. 4. Coat the chicken in the egg mix, then dredge in the coconut mixture until evenly coated. 5. Place the chicken in the prepared basket and spray liberally with oil. 6. Air fry at 400ºF (204ºC) for 6 minutes, flip, spray with more oil, and cook for another 6 minutes, or until the internal temperature reaches 165ºF (74ºC).

## Steak and Vegetable Kebabs

**Prep time: 15 minutes | Cook time: 5 to 7 minutes | Serves 4**

- ◄ 2 tablespoons balsamic vinegar
- ◄ 2 teaspoons olive oil
- ◄ ½ teaspoon dried marjoram
- ◄ ⅛ teaspoon freshly ground black pepper
- ◄ ¾ pound (340 g) round steak, cut into 1-inch pieces
- ◄ 1 red bell pepper, sliced
- ◄ 16 button mushrooms
- ◄ 1 cup cherry tomatoes

1. In a medium bowl, stir together the balsamic vinegar, olive oil, marjoram, and black pepper. 2. Add the steak and stir to coat. Let stand for 10 minutes at room temperature. 3. Alternating items, thread the beef, red bell pepper, mushrooms, and tomatoes onto 8 bamboo or metal skewers that fit in the air fryer. 4. Air fry at 390ºF (199ºC) for 5 to 7 minutes, or until the beef is browned and reaches at least 145ºF (63ºC) on a meat thermometer. Serve immediately.

## Cheesy Roasted Sweet Potatoes

**Prep time: 7 minutes | Cook time: 18 to 23 minutes | Serves 4**

◄ 2 large sweet potatoes, peeled and sliced
◄ 1 teaspoon olive oil
◄ 1 tablespoon white balsamic
◄ vinegar
◄ 1 teaspoon dried thyme
◄ ¼ cup grated Parmesan cheese

1. In a large bowl, drizzle the sweet potato slices with the olive oil and toss. 2. Sprinkle with the balsamic vinegar and thyme and toss again. 3. Sprinkle the potatoes with the Parmesan cheese and toss to coat. 4. Roast the slices, in batches, in the air fryer basket at 400°F (204°C) for 18 to 23 minutes, tossing the sweet potato slices in the basket once during cooking, until tender. 5. Repeat with the remaining sweet potato slices. Serve immediately.

## Fish and Vegetable Tacos

**Prep time: 15 minutes | Cook time: 9 to 12 minutes | Serves 4**

◄ 1 pound (454 g) white fish fillets, such as sole or cod
◄ 2 teaspoons olive oil
◄ 3 tablespoons freshly squeezed lemon juice, divided
◄ 1½ cups chopped red
◄ cabbage
◄ 1 large carrot, grated
◄ ½ cup low-sodium salsa
◄ ⅓ cup low-fat Greek yogurt
◄ 4 soft low-sodium whole-wheat tortillas

1. Brush the fish with the olive oil and sprinkle with 1 tablespoon of lemon juice. Air fry in the air fryer basket at 390°F (199°C) for 9 to 12 minutes, or until the fish just flakes when tested with a fork. 2. Meanwhile, in a medium bowl, stir together the remaining 2 tablespoons of lemon juice, the red cabbage, carrot, salsa, and yogurt. 3. When the fish is cooked, remove it from the air fryer basket and break it up into large pieces. 4. Offer the fish, tortillas, and the cabbage mixture, and let each person assemble a taco.

## Avocado and Egg Burrito

**Prep time: 10 minutes | Cook time: 3 to 5 minutes | Serves 4**

◄ 2 hard-boiled egg whites, chopped
◄ 1 hard-boiled egg, chopped
◄ 1 avocado, peeled, pitted, and chopped
◄ 1 red bell pepper, chopped
◄ 3 tablespoons low-sodium salsa, plus additional for
◄ serving (optional)
◄ 1 (1.2 ounces / 34 g) slice low-sodium, low-fat American cheese, torn into pieces
◄ 4 low-sodium whole-wheat flour tortillas

1. In a medium bowl, thoroughly mix the egg whites, egg, avocado, red bell pepper, salsa, and cheese. 2. Place the tortillas on a work surface and evenly divide the filling among them. Fold in the edges and roll up. Secure the burritos with toothpicks if necessary. 3. Put the burritos in the air fryer basket. Air fry at 390°F (199°C) for 3 to 5 minutes, or until the burritos are light golden brown and crisp. Serve with more salsa (if using).

## Steak Tips and Potatoes

**Prep time: 10 minutes | Cook time: 20 minutes | Serves 4**

◄ Oil, for spraying
◄ 8 ounces (227 g) baby gold potatoes, cut in half
◄ ½ teaspoon salt
◄ 1 pound (454 g) steak, cut into ½-inch pieces
◄ 1 teaspoon Worcestershire sauce
◄ 1 teaspoon granulated garlic
◄ ½ teaspoon salt
◄ ½ teaspoon freshly ground black pepper

1. Line the air fryer basket with parchment and spray lightly with oil. 2. In a microwave-safe bowl, combine the potatoes and salt, then pour in about ½ inch of water. Microwave for 7 minutes, or until the potatoes are nearly tender. Drain. 3. In a large bowl, gently mix together the steak, potatoes, Worcestershire sauce, garlic, salt, and black pepper. Spread the mixture in an even layer in the prepared basket. 4. Air fry at 400°F (204°C) for 12 to 17 minutes, stirring after 5 to 6 minutes. The cooking time will depend on the thickness of the meat and preferred doneness.

## Pork Burgers with Red Cabbage Salad

**Prep time: 20 minutes | Cook time: 7 to 9 minutes | Serves 4**

◄ ½ cup Greek yogurt
◄ 2 tablespoons low-sodium mustard, divided
◄ 1 tablespoon lemon juice
◄ ¼ cup sliced red cabbage
◄ ¼ cup grated carrots
◄ 1 pound (454 g) lean ground pork
◄ ½ teaspoon paprika
◄ 1 cup mixed baby lettuce greens
◄ 2 small tomatoes, sliced
◄ 8 small low-sodium whole-wheat sandwich buns, cut in half

1. In a small bowl, combine the yogurt, 1 tablespoon mustard, lemon juice, cabbage, and carrots; mix and refrigerate. 2. In a medium bowl, combine the pork, remaining 1 tablespoon mustard, and paprika. Form into 8 small patties. 3. Put the sliders into the air fryer basket. Air fry at 400°F (204°C) for 7 to 9 minutes, or until the sliders register 165°F (74°C) as tested with a meat thermometer. 4. Assemble the burgers by placing some of the lettuce greens on a bun bottom. Top with a tomato slice, the burgers, and the cabbage mixture. Add the bun top and serve immediately.

# Churro Bites

**Prep time: 5 minutes | Cook time: 6 minutes | Makes 36 bites**

◄ Oil, for spraying
◄ 1 (17¼ ounces / 489 g) package frozen puffed pastry, thawed
◄ 1 cup granulated sugar
◄ 1 tablespoon ground cinnamon
◄ ½ cup confectioners' sugar
◄ 1 tablespoon milk

1. Preheat the air fryer to 400°F (204°C). Line the air fryer basket with parchment and spray lightly with oil. 2. Unfold the puff pastry onto a clean work surface. Using a sharp knife, cut the dough into 36 bite-size pieces. 3. Place the dough pieces in one layer in the prepared basket, taking care not to let the pieces touch or overlap. 4. Cook for 3 minutes, flip, and cook for another 3 minutes, or until puffed and golden. 5. In a small bowl, mix together the granulated sugar and cinnamon. 6. In another small bowl, whisk together the confectioners' sugar and milk. 7. Dredge the bites in the cinnamon-sugar mixture until evenly coated. 8. Serve with the icing on the side for dipping.

# Fried Green Tomatoes

**Prep time: 15 minutes | Cook time: 6 to 8 minutes | Serves 4**

◄ 4 medium green tomatoes
◄ ⅓ cup all-purpose flour
◄ 2 egg whites
◄ ¼ cup almond milk
◄ 1 cup ground almonds
◄ ½ cup panko bread crumbs
◄ 2 teaspoons olive oil
◄ 1 teaspoon paprika
◄ 1 clove garlic, minced

1. Rinse the tomatoes and pat dry. Cut the tomatoes into ½-inch slices, discarding the thinner ends. 2. Put the flour on a plate. In a shallow bowl, beat the egg whites with the almond milk until frothy. And on another plate, combine the almonds, bread crumbs, olive oil, paprika, and garlic and mix well. 3. Dip the tomato slices into the flour, then into the egg white mixture, then into the almond mixture to coat. 4. Place four of the coated tomato slices in the air fryer basket. Air fry at 400°F (204°C) for 6 to 8 minutes or until the tomato coating is crisp and golden brown. Repeat with remaining tomato slices and serve immediately.

# Elephant Ears

**Prep time: 5 minutes | Cook time: 5 minutes | Serves 8**

◄ Oil, for spraying
◄ 1 (8 ounces / 227 g) can buttermilk biscuits
◄ 3 tablespoons sugar
◄ 1 tablespoon ground cinnamon
◄ 3 tablespoons unsalted butter, melted

◄ 8 scoops vanilla ice cream    (optional)

1. Line the air fryer basket with parchment and spray lightly with oil. 2. Separate the dough. Using a rolling pin, roll out the biscuits into 6- to 8-inch circles. 3. Place the dough circles in the prepared basket and spray liberally with oil. You may need to work in batches, depending on the size of your air fryer. 4. Air fry at 350°F (177°C) for 5 minutes, or until lightly browned. 5. In a small bowl, mix together the sugar and cinnamon. 6. Brush the elephant ears with the melted butter and sprinkle with the cinnamon-sugar mixture. 7. Top each serving with a scoop of ice cream (if using).

# Old Bay Tilapia

**Prep time: 15 minutes | Cook time: 6 minutes | Serves 4**

◄ Oil, for spraying
◄ 1 cup panko bread crumbs
◄ 2 tablespoons Old Bay seasoning
◄ 2 teaspoons granulated garlic
◄ 1 teaspoon onion powder
◄ ½ teaspoon salt
◄ ¼ teaspoon freshly ground black pepper
◄ 1 large egg
◄ 4 tilapia fillets

1. Preheat the air fryer to 400°F (204°C). Line the air fryer basket with parchment and spray lightly with oil. 2. In a shallow bowl, mix together the bread crumbs, Old Bay, garlic, onion powder, salt, and black pepper. 3. In a small bowl, whisk the egg. 4. Coat the tilapia in the egg, then dredge in the bread crumb mixture until completely coated. 5. Place the tilapia in the prepared basket. You may need to work in batches, depending on the size of your air fryer. Spray lightly with oil. 6. Cook for 4 to 6 minutes, depending on the thickness of the fillets, until the internal temperature reaches 145°F (63°C). Serve immediately.

# Cajun Shrimp

**Prep time: 15 minutes | Cook time: 9 minutes | Serves 4**

◄ Oil, for spraying
◄ 1 pound (454 g) jumbo raw shrimp, peeled and deveined
◄ 1 tablespoon Cajun seasoning
◄ 6 ounces (170 g) cooked kielbasa, cut into thick slices
◄ ½ medium zucchini, cut into ¼-inch-thick slices
◄ ½ medium yellow squash, cut into ¼-inch-thick slices
◄ 1 green bell pepper, seeded and cut into 1-inch pieces
◄ 2 tablespoons olive oil
◄ ½ teaspoon salt

1. Preheat the air fryer to 400°F (204°C). Line the air fryer basket with parchment and spray lightly with oil. 2. In a large bowl, toss together the shrimp and Cajun seasoning. Add the kielbasa, zucchini, squash, bell pepper, olive oil, and salt and mix well. 3. Transfer the mixture to the prepared basket, taking care not to overcrowd. You may need to work in batches, depending on the size of your air fryer. 4. Cook for 9 minutes, shaking and stirring every 3 minutes. Serve immediately.

# Pecan Rolls

## Prep time: 20 minutes | Cook time: 20 to 24 minutes | Makes 12 rolls

- ◄ 2 cups all-purpose flour, plus more for dusting
- ◄ 2 tablespoons granulated sugar, plus ¼ cup, divided
- ◄ 1 teaspoon salt
- ◄ 3 tablespoons butter, at room temperature
- ◄ ¾ cup milk, whole or 2%
- ◄ ¼ cup packed light brown sugar
- ◄ ½ cup chopped pecans, toasted
- ◄ 1 to 2 tablespoons oil
- ◄ ¼ cup confectioners' sugar (optional)

1. In a large bowl, whisk the flour, 2 tablespoons granulated sugar, and salt until blended. Stir in the butter and milk briefly until a sticky dough forms. 2. In a small bowl, stir together the brown sugar and remaining ¼ cup of granulated sugar. 3. Place a piece of parchment paper on a work surface and dust it with flour. Roll the dough on the prepared surface to ¼ inch thickness. 4. Spread the sugar mixture over the dough. Sprinkle the pecans on top. Roll up the dough jelly roll-style, pinching the ends to seal. Cut the dough into 12 rolls. 5. Preheat the air fryer to 320°F (160°C). 6. Line the air fryer basket with parchment paper and spritz the parchment with oil. Place 6 rolls on the prepared parchment. 7. Air Fry for 5 minutes. Flip the rolls and Air Fry for 5 to 7 minutes more until lightly browned. Repeat with the remaining rolls. 8. Sprinkle with confectioners' sugar (if using).

# Apple Pie Egg Rolls

## Prep time: 10 minutes | Cook time: 8 minutes | Makes 6 rolls

- ◄ Oil, for spraying
- ◄ 1 (21 ounces / 595 g) can apple pie filling
- ◄ 1 tablespoon all-purpose flour
- ◄ ½ teaspoon lemon juice
- ◄ ¼ teaspoon ground nutmeg
- ◄ ¼ teaspoon ground cinnamon
- ◄ 6 egg roll wrappers

1. Preheat the air fryer to 400°F (204°C). Line the air fryer basket with parchment and spray lightly with oil. 2. In a medium bowl, mix together the pie filling, flour, lemon juice, nutmeg, and cinnamon. 3. Lay out the egg roll wrappers on a work surface and spoon a dollop of pie filling in the center of each. 4. Fill a small bowl with water. Dip your finger in the water and, working one at a time, moisten the edges of the wrappers. Fold the wrapper like an envelope: First fold one corner into the center. Fold each side corner in, and then fold over the remaining corner, making sure each corner overlaps a bit and the moistened edges stay closed. Use additional water and your fingers to seal any open edges. 5. Place the rolls in the prepared basket and spray liberally with oil. You may need to work

in batches, depending on the size of your air fryer. 6. Cook for 4 minutes, flip, spray with oil, and cook for another 4 minutes, or until crispy and golden brown. Serve immediately.

# Meatball Subs

## Prep time: 15 minutes | Cook time: 19 minutes | Serves 6

- ◄ Oil, for spraying
- ◄ 1 pound (454 g) 85% lean ground beef
- ◄ ½ cup Italian bread crumbs
- ◄ 1 tablespoon dried minced onion
- ◄ 1 tablespoon minced garlic
- ◄ 1 large egg
- ◄ 1 teaspoon salt
- ◄ 1 teaspoon freshly ground black pepper
- ◄ 6 hoagie rolls
- ◄ 1 (18 ounces / 510 g) jar marinara sauce
- ◄ 1½ cups shredded Mozzarella cheese

1. Line the air fryer basket with parchment and spray lightly with oil. 2. In a large bowl, mix together the ground beef, bread crumbs, onion, garlic, egg, salt, and black pepper. Roll the mixture into 18 meatballs. 3. Place the meatballs in the prepared basket. 4. Air fry at 390°F (199°C) for 15 minutes. 5. Place 3 meatballs in each hoagie roll. Top with marinara and Mozzarella cheese. 6. Place the loaded rolls in the air fryer and cook for 3 to 4 minutes, or until the cheese is melted. You may need to work in batches, depending on the size of your air fryer. Serve immediately.

# Meringue Cookies

## Prep time: 15 minutes | Cook time: 1 hour 30 minutes | Makes 20 cookies

- ◄ Oil, for spraying
- ◄ 4 large egg whites
- ◄ 1 cup sugar
- ◄ Pinch cream of tartar

1. Preheat the air fryer to 140°F (60°C). Line the air fryer basket with parchment and spray lightly with oil. 2. In a small heatproof bowl, whisk together the egg whites and sugar. Fill a small saucepan halfway with water, place it over medium heat, and bring to a light simmer. Place the bowl with the egg whites on the saucepan, making sure the bottom of the bowl does not touch the water. Whisk the mixture until the sugar is dissolved. 3. Transfer the mixture to a large bowl and add the cream of tartar. Using an electric mixer, beat the mixture on high until it is glossy and stiff peaks form. Transfer the mixture to a piping bag or a zip-top plastic bag with a corner cut off. 4. Pipe rounds into the prepared basket. You may need to work in batches, depending on the size of your air fryer. 5. Cook for 1 hour 30 minutes. 6. Turn off the air fryer and let the meringues cool completely inside. The residual heat will continue to dry them out.

# Phyllo Vegetable Triangles

## Prep time: 15 minutes | Cook time: 6 to 11 minutes | Serves 6

◄ 3 tablespoons minced onion
◄ 2 garlic cloves, minced
◄ 2 tablespoons grated carrot
◄ 1 teaspoon olive oil

◄ 3 tablespoons frozen baby peas, thawed
◄ 2 tablespoons nonfat cream cheese, at room temperature
◄ 6 sheets frozen phyllo dough, thawed
◄ Olive oil spray, for coating the dough

1. In a baking pan, combine the onion, garlic, carrot, and olive oil. Air fry at 390ºF (199ºC) for 2 to 4 minutes, or until the vegetables are crisp-tender. Transfer to a bowl. 2. Stir in the peas and cream cheese to the vegetable mixture. Let cool while you prepare the dough. 3. Lay one sheet of phyllo on a work surface and lightly spray with olive oil spray. Top with another sheet of phyllo. Repeat with the remaining 4 phyllo sheets; you'll have 3 stacks with 2 layers each. Cut each stack lengthwise into 4 strips (12 strips total). 4. Place a scant 2 teaspoons of the filling near the bottom of each strip. Bring one corner up over the filling to make a triangle; continue folding the triangles over, as you would fold a flag. Seal the edge with a bit of water. Repeat with the remaining strips and filling. 5. Air fry the triangles, in 2 batches, for 4 to 7 minutes, or until golden brown. Serve.

# Pork Stuffing Meatballs

## Prep time: 10 minutes | Cook time: 12 minutes | Makes 35 meatballs

◄ Oil, for spraying
◄ 1½ pounds (680 g) ground pork
◄ 1 cup bread crumbs
◄ ½ cup milk
◄ ¼ cup minced onion
◄ 1 large egg

◄ 1 tablespoon dried rosemary
◄ 1 tablespoon dried thyme
◄ 1 teaspoon salt
◄ 1 teaspoon freshly ground black pepper
◄ 1 teaspoon finely chopped fresh parsley

1. Line the air fryer basket with parchment and spray lightly with oil. 2. In a large bowl, mix together the ground pork, bread crumbs, milk, onion, egg, rosemary, thyme, salt, black pepper, and parsley. 3. Roll about 2 tablespoons of the mixture into a ball. Repeat with the rest of the mixture. You should have 30 to 35 meatballs. 4. Place the meatballs in the prepared basket in a single layer, leaving space between each one. You may need to work in batches, depending on the size of your air fryer. 5. Air fry at 390ºF (199ºC) for 10 to 12 minutes, flipping after 5 minutes, or until golden brown and the internal temperature reaches 160ºF (71ºC).

# Appendix Air Fryer Cooking Chart

## Air Fryer Cooking Chart

### Beef

| Item | Temp (°F) | Time (mins) | Item | Temp (°F) | Time (mins) |
|------|-----------|-------------|------|-----------|-------------|
| Beef Eye Round Roast (4 lbs.) | 400 °F | 45 to 55 | Meatballs (1-inch) | 370 °F | 7 |
| Burger Patty (4 oz.) | 370 °F | 16 to 20 | Meatballs (3-inch) | 380 °F | 10 |
| Filet Mignon (8 oz.) | 400 °F | 18 | Ribeye, bone-in (1-inch, 8 oz) | 400 °F | 10 to 15 |
| Flank Steak (1.5 lbs.) | 400 °F | 12 | Sirloin steaks (1-inch, 12 oz) | 400 °F | 9 to 14 |
| Flank Steak (2 lbs.) | 400 °F | 20 to 28 | | | |

### Chicken

| Item | Temp (°F) | Time (mins) | Item | Temp (°F) | Time (mins) |
|------|-----------|-------------|------|-----------|-------------|
| Breasts, bone in (1 ¼ lb.) | 370 °F | 25 | Legs, bone-in (1 ¾ lb.) | 380 °F | 30 |
| Breasts, boneless (4 oz) | 380 °F | 12 | Thighs, boneless (1 ½ lb.) | 380 °F | 18 to 20 |
| Drumsticks (2 ½ lb.) | 370 °F | 20 | Wings (2 lb.) | 400 °F | 12 |
| Game Hen (halved 2 lb.) | 390 °F | 20 | Whole Chicken | 360 °F | 75 |
| Thighs, bone-in (2 lb.) | 380 °F | 22 | Tenders | 360 °F | 8 to 10 |

### Pork & Lamb

| Item | Temp (°F) | Time (mins) | Item | Temp (°F) | Time (mins) |
|------|-----------|-------------|------|-----------|-------------|
| Bacon (regular) | 400 °F | 5 to 7 | Pork Tenderloin | 370 °F | 15 |
| Bacon (thick cut) | 400 °F | 6 to 10 | Sausages | 380 °F | 15 |
| Pork Loin (2 lb.) | 360 °F | 55 | Lamb Loin Chops (1-inch thick) | 400 °F | 8 to 12 |
| Pork Chops, bone in (1-inch, 6.5 oz) | 400 °F | 12 | Rack of Lamb (1.5 – 2 lb.) | 380 °F | 22 |

### Fish & Seafood

| Item | Temp (°F) | Time (mins) | Item | Temp (°F) | Time (mins) |
|------|-----------|-------------|------|-----------|-------------|
| Calamari (8 oz) | 400 °F | 4 | Tuna Steak | 400 °F | 7 to 10 |
| Fish Fillet (1-inch, 8 oz) | 400 °F | 10 | Scallops | 400 °F | 5 to 7 |
| Salmon, fillet (6 oz) | 380 °F | 12 | Shrimp | 400 °F | 5 |
| Swordfish steak | 400 °F | 10 | | | |

# Air Fryer Cooking Chart

| Vegetables | | | | | |
| --- | --- | --- | --- | --- | --- |
| INGREDIENT | AMOUNT | PREPARATION | OIL | TEMP | COOK TIME |
| Asparagus | 2 bunches | Cut in half, trim stems | 2 Tbsp | 420°F | 12-15 mins |
| Beets | 1½ lbs | Peel, cut in ½-inch cubes | 1Tbsp | 390°F | 28-30 mins |
| Bell peppers (for roasting) | 4 peppers | Cut in quarters, remove seeds | 1Tbsp | 400°F | 15-20 mins |
| Broccoli | 1 large head | Cut in 1-2-inch florets | 1Tbsp | 400°F | 15-20 mins |
| Brussels sprouts | 1lb | Cut in half, remove stems | 1Tbsp | 425°F | 15-20 mins |
| Carrots | 1lb | Peel, cut in ¼-inch rounds | 1 Tbsp | 425°F | 10-15 mins |
| Cauliflower | 1 head | Cut in 1-2-inch florets | 2 Tbsp | 400°F | 20-22 mins |
| Corn on the cob | 7 ears | Whole ears, remove husks | 1 Tbps | 400°F | 14-17 mins |
| Green beans | 1 bag (12 oz) | Trim | 1 Tbps | 420°F | 18-20 mins |
| Kale (for chips) | 4 oz | Tear into pieces, remove stems | None | 325°F | 5-8 mins |
| Mushrooms | 16 oz | Rinse, slice thinly | 1 Tbps | 390°F | 25-30 mins |
| Potatoes, russet | 1½ lbs | Cut in 1-inch wedges | 1 Tbps | 390°F | 25-30 mins |
| Potatoes, russet | 1lb | Hand-cut fries, soak 30 mins in cold water, then pat dry | ½ -3 Tbps | 400°F | 25-28 mins |
| Potatoes, sweet | 1lb | Hand-cut fries, soak 30 mins in cold water, then pat dry | 1 Tbps | 400°F | 25-28 mins |
| Zucchini | 1lb | Cut in eighths lengthwise, then cut in half | 1 Tbps | 400°F | 15-20 mins |

Made in the USA
Las Vegas, NV
30 September 2024